W9-AOG-614

❀

CONTEMPORARY
SPANISH-AMERICAN FICTION

❀

CONTEMPORARY
SPANISH-AMERICAN
FICTION

✳

JEFFERSON REA SPELL

✳

BIBLO and TANNEN
NEW YORK
1968

Printed in U.S.A. by
NOBLE OFFSET PRINTERS, INC.
NEW YORK 3, N. Y.

This volume is dedicated

to the

INSTITUTE OF LATIN-AMERICAN STUDIES

of the University of Texas

❁

PREFACE

❁

THE PURPOSE of this work is to introduce to English readers ten of the most important Spanish-American writers—nine novelists and one short-story writer—whose principal or entire work has been published since the outbreak of the first World War, and thereby to make possible a better understanding of the Spanish-speaking peoples in the western hemisphere. It is not a collection of secondhand comments, but is based on a personal knowledge of the countries and life discussed and on more than twenty years' teaching of Spanish and Latin-American literature.

In the selection of the ten authors, quality of work has been the sole criterion; yet it happens that they are fairly representative geographically of Spanish America as a whole. Their order of appearance in the volume is based on the date their first or most important work appeared and bears no relation whatever to their comparative merit as writers. In the case of the more prolific authors, fictional works have been, as a rule, classified by groups according to subject matter, style, geographical background, or some other common characteristic, and each novel has then been discussed in proportion to its value and interest. The translations from Spanish of all passages quoted are my own. The full title and publication date of each work are given in the appended bibliography, which also indicates those which have been translated into English.

The opportunity to know personally the contemporary novelists of Ecuador was afforded me by a grant in 1941 from the Institute of Latin-American Studies of the University of Texas, to which I wish to express my thanks. I am also deeply indebted to Professor Clyde W. Wilkinson of the University of Illinois and to Dr. R. H. Williams of the University of Texas for careful reading of the manuscript and many helpful suggestions and criticisms.

J. R. Spell

Austin, Texas
September 15, 1943

CONTENTS

❀

CONTEMPORARY
SPANISH-AMERICAN FICTION

❀

CHAPTER I ❊

FICTION IN SPANISH AMERICA
BEFORE 1914

❊

A SURVEY OF Spanish-American fiction at the close of the
first decade of the twentieth century would have
brought to light few works whose charm or literary interest
had been sufficiently great to arouse comment, inspire translations, or even induce reading beyond the confines of the
country which gave them birth. Such had not been the case
with poetry, some of which had been accorded high merit, or
with other prose forms. Chronicles dating from the Spanish
conquest had laid claim to terse, stirring language, realistic
powers of description, and certain novelistic elements; the
essay, too, had received original treatment which presaged
the possibilities of the short story. But neither in volume nor
in character had the novel acquired much claim to distinction.
Lately, however, it had begun to show evidence of the general social discontent that was then beginning to stir certain
classes to action. For Spanish America, after spending two
decades in shaking off the Spanish yoke, had devoted almost
half of the nineteenth century to civil strife and disorder in
the process of trying to adjust itself to a new form of government; finally those in control and their satellites imposed a
semi-colonial rule under which Spanish officials were replaced
by local administrators, but the lives of the great majority

3

moved on in the century-old ruts. As in the colonial period, a wide gap separated the two great social groups—the rich and the poor; the rulers and the ruled. Of the unbridged social and economic chasm, few poets or essayists had told. And the novelist was just beginning to realize the great new literary province that awaited him.

Not only had reference to many social problems not been introduced into polite literary circles but great geographical areas had never been given literary treatment. It was not that such regions were unexplored or undescribed, but that existing accounts had little of literary flavor to commend them. Travelers had seen with their eyes but had failed to catch the spirit of what they saw. Thus there remained many regions of Spanish America awaiting an interpreter.

The absence of much original or distinctive fiction in the Spanish-speaking countries of America was not attributable to a lack of attempts to create fiction or to an ignorance of the main literary currents which had determined fictional trends in Europe and the United States. For Spanish-American writers, too, had been fully aware of the successive movements of Romanticism, Realism, and Modernism. But the nineteenth century was for Spanish-American fiction a period of absorption and experimentation; it remained for the twentieth to become one of worthy self-expression.

Landmarks as evidence of progress were by no means lacking. As early as 1816—three years before Washington Irving opened new vistas to English readers with his *Sketch Book*— the first piece of fiction written in the Spanish language in America which fully deserves the term of novel, *El Periquillo Sarniento* (*The Scaly Parakeet*), was published in Mexico City. Its author was José Joaquín Fernández de Lizardi, who had earlier become known for his cutting political articles. It was only because governmental authorities forced him to abandon that field that he took cover in fiction and produced three novels: the one just mentioned and *Don Catrín de la Fachenda* —both largely picaresque in flavor—and *La Quixotita y su*

Prima (*Little Miss Quixote and Her Cousin*), a fictionalized educational treatise. The theme common to these novels was the need of a new type of education in Mexico; the ideas Lizardi drew from Rousseau and his followers in France and Spain, for by this time French thought, early a vitalizing force in Spain, was exerting its influence also in her colonies, particularly in the political and educational fields. Only one of these novels has lived, and that largely because Lizardi succeeded in transferring to his pages the spirit of the Mexican capital in the closing years of the colonial period. Here we see the few very rich and the many miserably poor; the Spaniards untrained to a profession but disdaining manual labor; the corrupt government officials; the ignorant and avaricious clergy; the charlatan doctors; and the endless array of beggars skilled in trickery. In contact with all the dregs of society was the *pícaro* Periquillo, Spanish in type but Mexican in flavor. With this work a new link was forged in the chain of picaresque literature, for both the background and the characters were essentially American. Here, too, was realism but not yet art, for Lizardi was more the moralist than the novelist.

From France also came the inspiration which led other writers to attempt the creation of national literature through the use of local background and legend, for many of the elements of Romanticism which had as yet made little impress in Spain were filtering into her colonies. Evidence of their absorption in Mexico was the first romantic poem written in the Spanish language, "En el teocalle de Cholula" ("On the Cholula Pyramid"), the work of the gifted Cuban José María Heredia, who gave further impetus to the romantic trend during his residence in Mexico through his translations of Byron and articles on Rousseau and Chateaubriand. The first traces of Romanticism in Spanish-American fiction appeared, also in Mexico, in the tales and novelettes of Rodríguez Galván and J. J. Pesado. But if Romanticism was slow in making its appearance in fictional garb, it compensated for that tardiness by lingering as a force in Spanish-American literature long after its spirit was largely spent in Europe. In general its vogue in Spanish America paralleled the period of rank civil disorder in which the early efforts at self-government were being made.

Another influence in the production of Spanish-American prose literature was the *costumbrista* sketch, an essay on manners or customs somewhat in the manner of Washington Irving, which reached the height of popularity in Spain in the early thirties through the work of Mesonero Romanos and Larra, and soon was widely imitated abroad. Admitting that he wished to do for Mexico City what Mesonero had done for Madrid, Guillermo Prieto in 1840 began to publish sketches dealing with local manners and customs. In Colombia, "Emiro Kastos" (Juan de Dios Restrepo); in Chile, "Jotabeche" (J. J. Vallejo); in Cuba, "Jeremías Docaransa" (José María Cárdenas); and in Venezuela, Daniel Mendoza soon devoted themselves to portraying the native scene.

Paralleling in point of time the short tales and the *costumbrista* sketches, longer fictional works of a romantic nature made their appearance serially, but seldom completely, in short-lived literary periodicals of the late thirties; and this type continued to dominate the field for more than three decades. In Cuba, Villaverde's celebrated novel, *Cecilia Valdés*, appeared in part in *La Siempreviva;* the first novel in Colombia, *María Dolores* by J. J. Ortiz, in *El Condor;* in Mexico, Payno's *El Fistol del Diablo* (*The Devil's Scarf Pin*) and Justo Sierra's *Un Año en el Hospital de San Lázaro* (*A Year in Saint Lazarus Hospital*) were partially printed respectively in *El Museo Mexicano*, 1843-45, and the *Registro Yucateco*, 1845-46; and in Chile, Sarmiento published his masterpiece, *Facundo*, in *El Progreso* in 1845. Other outstanding romantic novels appeared later: José Marmol's *Amalia*, in part in 1851 in Montevideo and in complete form four years later in Buenos Aires; Jorge Isaacs' *María*, whose many imitators greatly prolonged the romantic era in South American fiction, in 1867; and, finally, J. L. de Mera's *Cumandá* in 1871.

The element in these novels that gave them interest was

neither their loose and rambling plots nor their overly sentimental characters, but their definitely authentic background—
probably the result of the *costumbrista* vogue. Each novel was
thereby definitely linked to the land which gave it birth.
Cecilia Valdés presents a great variety of types and customs
peculiar to Cuba in the thirties of the past century; and *El
Fistol del Diablo*, many distinctive of Mexico in the same era;
Facundo is permeated with the spirit of the Argentine pampas
and the gauchos that live there; and *Amalia* survives not for
the romantic love story but for its detailed presentation of
many aspects of social life in Buenos Aires during the dictatorship of Rosas. Even in *María*, which is charged with more
genuine feeling than any other romantic novel written in
Spanish America, one of the greatest charms lies in the mar-
velous descriptions of the fertile Cauca Valley, of the tor-
tuous Magdalena River, and of the majestic Andes. By this
time it was clear that Spanish America could furnish an adequate background for fiction.

The presence of such realistic elements in the best romantic
novels could not long compensate for their main defects—
fantastic plots and exaggerated characters. With the early
sixties an attempt to remedy both showed itself in certain
countries in an increased realism, a more faithful presentation
of life, traceable to the influence of contemporary French novelists, particularly Balzac. One of the first writers to make his
plots more plausible, his characters more human, and his portrayal of the society about him more vivid was the Chilean
Blest Gana. Discarding completely the screen that Romanticism had drawn over personal, environmental, and social ugliness, he produced some ten novels of a decidedly realistic
character, of which *La Aritmética de Amor* (*The Arithmetic
of Love*), 1860, was the first. In his second, *Martín Rivas*
(1862), the theme of the struggle of a representative of the
middle class against the old aristocracy enters Spanish-American literature. Realism, but of a type colored by the idealism
of Fernán Caballero rather than of Balzac, also characterized

the work of the Mexican Ignacio Altamirano, whose novel *Clemencia* appeared first in the periodical *El Renacimiento*, 1869.

The title of this periodical well described certain aspects of the period upon which Spanish America as a whole was then entering. Peace in general was maintained by force; wealth was increasing rapidly; foreign capital and immigration were being encouraged; large cities were beginning to dot the map; means of communication improved; and efforts to establish public education were being made. But the material progress achieved benefited only a relatively small class. Actually, the wealth was concentrated in the hands of a few, and though democratic forms were maintained, the legislative bodies were controlled by the small minority. Corruption, political and otherwise, was rife, and the increase in general enlightenment was slight. There was little social justice, and the doors of opportunity were still tightly closed to the masses.

This period also gave rise to a new aristocracy made up largely of the families of certain persons who had achieved power by the sword or by political chicanery. This group now had the means and the leisure to seek the culture they did not inherit. Their eyes were directed to Europe, especially France, as had been those of the old colonial families. Leaving their immense estates in the rural districts to the supervision of *mayordomos,* they built fine homes in the capitals, but resided much of the time abroad. They attempted to encourage and even to create music, art, and literature in the spirit of Europe; but they disdained completely the people, the country, and the atmosphere in which they were bred. America served them only to provide liberally for a comfortable life elsewhere. Others who had risen to power, uncultivated and disdainful of everything cultural, lived as great land barons on their estates, where the labor was performed by natives under practically the feudal system of colonial days. Equally despotic were men of like nature who controlled the life of the small towns.

In these conditions novelists found ample material which lent itself to the realistic treatment then in vogue, and certain aspects of life in the two largest and most rapidly-growing cities were sordid enough to deserve the naturalistic treatment of Zola. The depravity of Buenos Aires, during these hectic years in which its wealth increased many fold, is depicted in a series of novels of that type—*La gran Aldea* (*The Big Village*), 1884, by Lucio López; *Sin Rumbo* (*Uncharted Course*) and *En la Sangre* (*In the Blood*), 1887, by Eugenio Cambacèrés; and *La Bolsa* (*The Stock Exchange*), 1890, a portrayal of the manipulations of the stock exchange, by Julián Martel—while prostitution and degenerate life in Mexico City furnished Federico Gamboa material for *Suprema Ley* (*Supreme Law*), 1896, and *Santa*, 1903.

Another group of writers, influenced probably by the regional novelists of Spain, turned for their material to the rural districts and the small towns. In *Peonía*, 1890, Romero García tells of conditions which he saw, with by no means rose-colored glasses, on a country estate in Venezuela. Various localities in three states of Mexico were also realistically exploited: Oaxaca by Emilio Rabasa in *La Bola* (*The Ball*) and *La gran Ciencia* (*The Great Science*), 1888; Jalisco by López Portillo in *La Parcela* (*A Parcel of Land*), 1898; and Vera Cruz by Rafael Delgado in *La Calandria* (*The Lark*), 1891, *Angelina*, 1895, and *Los Parientes ricos* (*The Rich Relations*), 1903.

Such value as these novels have lies much less in their depiction of manners and customs than in the interest of their writers in social reforms. Like Galdós in Spain, these men not only satirized the foibles of the society about them, but they pleaded for social justice, enlightenment, and honesty in politics. Novels motivated by such a thesis include *Aves sin Nido* (*Birds Without Nest*), 1889, by Clorinda Matto de Turner, which reveals injustices to the Indians on the part of the landowning classes of Peru; *Frutos de mi Tierra* (*Fruits of My Land*), 1896, and many others by Tomás Carrasquilla, in which he lays bare the weaknesses of his fellow townsmen of Medellín (Colombia); Eduardo Pardo's *Todo un Pueblo* (*The Whole Town*), 1899, which satirizes the political corruption in Venezuela; Orrego Luco's *Casa grande* (*Ancestral Mansion*), 1908, which portrays the decadence of the old aristocracy in Chile; and, finally, *El Casamiento de Laucha* (*Laucha's Marriage*), 1906, and *Historias de Pago chico*, 1908, by the Argentine Roberto Payró, the most gifted storyteller of them all, who had much to say, particularly in the latter book, about both personal and political dishonesty in Argentina.

Completely hostile to the didactic, reformatory purpose of the realistic novel and to nineteenth-century literature in general were a group of writers—the so-called Modernists—who, after the publication of Rubén Darío's *Azul* (*Azure*), 1886, came to occupy the center of the literary stage. Inspired by the ideals of the Parnassians and the Symbolists of France, this group sought, first of all, beauty in expression itself, however vague the meaning, and attained its end to some extent by a new emphasis on the effects of sound and color. Self-centered and individualistic, these writers gave voice to their own personal feelings; and, out of tune with the world about them, they often created for themselves one purely artificial. While the greatest Modernists were poets, many Spanish-American prose writers were members of the group. One of the earliest to come thoroughly under the spell of Modernism was the Venezuelan Manuel Díaz Rodríguez, whose first short stories, *Cuentos de Color* (*Tales in Color*), are entirely without plot, but their lyrical and varied nuances enchant the poetically-minded. The same style characterizes his novels *Sangre patricia* (*Patrician Blood*), 1901, and *Idolos rotos* (*Broken Idols*), 1902, in both of which the protagonist is one of those typical neo-romantic products of the age—an aristocratic, gifted, half-mad individual who, completely out of tune with his native environment, seeks the more congenial atmosphere of Paris.

Much in the same vein, but more concerned with the actual political problems that confronted Venezuela, where a ruth-

less dictator still held despotic sway, are the *Cuentos americanos* (*American Tales*), 1904, of Blanco Fombona; but in his
later novels, *El hombre de Hierro* (*The Man of Iron*) and
El hombre de Oro (*The Man of Gold*), he became infinitely
more realistic. Outstanding, too, for their poetical charm are
the novels of the Uruguayan Carlos Reyles—*Beba*, 1894, and
La Raza de Caín (*The Race of Cain*), 1900. Although gifted
as an artificer in language and equalled by few in his ability
to inject both feeling and color into his scenes, Reyles showed
greatest skill as a novelist in his analysis of character, whether
of an humble *gaucho* on an *estancia* or a member of the Paris-
loving aristocracy of Uruguay. With their wider interests and
vision, Blanco Fombona and Reyles came to be regarded not
merely as stylists but rather as novelists of considerable importance. By the end of the first decade of the new century
it was clear that the influence of Modernism on Spanish-
American fiction was on the wane, but its traces were to
linger in the works of many later writers.

Even the fiction writers of the early years of the twentieth
century whose style was most influenced by the Modernists
realized that Spanish America faced many serious problems.
They saw that the opportunities of the masses to enjoy the
good things of the world were limited. Around them they saw
wretched workers huddled together, in villages on the great
estates, in mining camps in the mountains, and, as industriali-
zation increased, in factories in the cities. They saw the low
status of the Indian and the negro; the economic and social
problems confronting those of mixed racial strains; and the
many obstacles which faced the youth without means or influence. Already those enjoying the advantages of education
were learning of organizations of workers and the power they
might thereby wield; they were learning of countries where
every child had some educational opportunities, and where
men had a chance to own their own homes and the lands they
cultivated. But the majority of those entrenched in power in
Spanish America were opposed to the dissemination of such

ideas, and would not listen to those who voiced them. Nor did they heed as the sullen undercurrent of dissatisfaction grew ever stronger, nor realize, when revolution flared in Mexico in 1910, that the age wherein dictators could flourish with security, land barons hold immense untaxed estates with impunity, and masters legally work their laborers long hours at starvation wages, was in process of passing.

From the outbreak of that revolution the contemporary period of Spanish-American literature may be said to date, although the publication of the most distinctive work of a novelist of the contemporary group coincided with the outbreak of the first World War. In the decades which have since passed, Spanish-American novelists have published many distinctive works—so many that it would be impossible to discuss them all in a volume such as this. For that reason it has seemed best to present, as representative of them, the ten most important writers and their works, as one means of interpreting the Spanish-American mind and the Spanish-American world to a non-Spanish-reading public. The ten selected, solely on the basis of the intrinsic worth of their novels, include Manuel Gálvez and Ricardo Güiraldes of Argentina; Horacio Quiroga of Uruguay; Mariano Azuela of Mexico; Carlos Loveira of Cuba; Eduardo Barrios of Chile; José Eustacio Rivera of Colombia; Rómulo Gallegos of Venezuela; Jorge Icaza of Ecuador; and Ciro Alegría of Peru.

These ten writers in their eighty-odd novels or collections of short stories have spread upon their pages life in Spanish America as they conceive it; and it is through their eyes that we shall survey it. Such a presentation should have much interest for the English-reading public, for in this twentieth century the thought and actions of the countries here portrayed, extending from the Rio Grande to Patagonia, can no longer be disregarded. Some of these ten writers have attained their spiritual and intellectual majority, assumed their responsibility before the world, and set seriously about the tasks they see ahead.

It can hardly be hoped that the calm, peaceful atmosphere of the best type of American home will prevail in their novels any more than in those of the United States; or that the man content with his rôle in life and playing it to the best of his ability will frequently figure here. Nor can we reasonably expect a preponderance of scenes of beauty rather than ugliness; of portraits of noble rather than weak or cruel beings; or stories blessed with happy endings rather than crowned by defeat. For the novelist will select his materials with reference to his objective, and neither subject nor type of treatment may win our approval, even if the excellence of the craftsmanship is recognized.

While the order in which these writers are taken up is chronological in so far as either the first or the most outstanding work of each is concerned, proceeding from *La Maestra normal* (*The Normal-School Teacher*) of Gálvez in 1914 to *El Mundo es Ancho y Ajeno* (*Broad and Alien is the World*) of Alegría in 1941, the ten authors are nevertheless classifiable in distinct groups by the general character of their works. The first group to be presented are the novelists of great sweep in point of time—those whose canvasses cover long periods of history—Gálvez, Azuela, and Loveira. Barrios stands as the lone representative of the analysts of individual psychology. Painters of distinctive background form another group; here there are four—Quiroga with sketches of northern Argentina; Rivera with the *selvas* of Colombia; Güiraldes, as an interpreter of the *gaucho* on the Argentine pampas; and Gallegos with both the llanos and *selvas* of Venezuela. In the last group are two novelists, Icaza and Alegría, who concern themselves primarily with the sociological problems of their respective countries, Ecuador and Peru, which are in many features similar.

The work of four of the ten writers has been completed; Rivera, Loveira, Güiraldes, and Quiroga are dead. Of the six alive today, Eduardo Barrios has published no fiction in twenty years; but the others are still writing and their future work will be welcomed with interest by many. Among them, it is hoped, will be those who read these pages. For Spanish America is today in truth the land of the future, and from the many countries and islands of America whose people speak the Spanish language must come others who will carry on the work of the ten who figure here. It should also be realized at the outset that these writers, unlike those of the United States, have not cultivated literature as a means of subsistence. Each has regarded his literary efforts as a means of benefiting his country. This application of their talent, their ability to analyze the life about them and to transfer its essence to the printed page, has been a service which has brought as reward little money, but instead the appreciation of the most understanding of their countrymen, of Spanish Americans in general, and—in the case of the best of them—of discerning critics the world over.

CHAPTER II

CITY LIFE IN
THE ARGENTINE AS SEEN BY
MANUEL GALVEZ

❧

I N THE last decades of the nineteenth century certain Argentine writers, applying the technique of the French naturalistic novelists to their own conditions, began to portray life, particularly urban, as it actually appeared to them; and to concern themselves with certain social ills that had grown out of the steady flow of European immigration into their country and the consequent growth and greatly increased wealth of the city of Buenos Aires. The pioneer was Eugenio Cambacèrés, whose four novels—*Pot-pourri*, *Música sentimental* (*Sentimental Music*), *Sin Rumbo*, and *En la Sangre*—published during the eighties, aroused much discussion by their treatment of subjects hitherto taboo. Both Lucio López in *La gran Aldea* (1884) and Carlos Ocantos in *León Saldívar*, 1888, tell of worldly maidens who prefer money to love, and García Merou in the truly Zolaesque *Ley social* (*Social Law*), 1885, deals with promiscuity among the rich and socially élite.

In the present century one of the most notable as well as the most prolific of Spanish-American novelists, the Argentine Manuel Gálvez, has maintained most successfully the traditions of the naturalistic school in a series of canvases which give a good insight into the life of his country. For this task he had excellent preparation. Born on July 18, 1882, in Paraná, the capital of Entre-Ríos, of one of its foremost families, he received his primary education from the Jesuits in Santa Fé and his secondary in their college in Buenos Aires. After entering the law school of the University of Buenos Aires at sixteen, he was graduated in 1904, offering as his thesis *La Trata de Blancas* (*The White-Slave Trade*)—a study of prostitution in the city of Buenos Aires, a theme of which he was later to make extensive use in many of his novels.

During these six years law by no means absorbed his entire attention; he devoted himself seriously to music; besides learning English and French, he read widely in the Golden Age literature of Spain; he wrote a few articles which were published in a newspaper of Santa Fé; and most noteworthy of all, he established in 1903 a monthly literary review, *Ideas*, which existed until 1905. Associated with him were several young men who have since made their mark in Argentine letters. At this period in his life, Gálvez took an active part in the Bohemian life of the struggling literati of Buenos Aires and reached the conclusion that Catholicism was an inefficient agency in the promotion of social justice. Among the wide and varied influences which left their impress on his spiritual development were modernistic poetry, the plays of Ibsen, and the idealistic views of Tolstoy.

The eight-year period beginning in 1905, when young Gálvez extended his horizon by visiting Europe, was one in which he attempted to find himself. Although the study of art claimed much of his attention while abroad, he made important literary acquaintances, among them Valle-Inclán in Madrid and Rubén Darío in Paris. On his return to Buenos Aires in 1906 he was appointed to an inspectorship of secondary schools, a position he still holds. Its duties took him to all the distant corners of his native Argentina, and thus provided him with first-hand knowledge which he was later to put to use in fiction.

Although Gálvez is known today primarily as a novelist, his earliest literary efforts were in verse—*El Enigma interior* (*The*

Inner Enigma), 1907, and *El Sendero de Humildad* (*The Path of Humility*), 1909. The first is in the manner of Bécquer —lyric and signally introspective; the poet reveals his melancholy, his grief, and his unrealized ambitions; and if he sings of nature, his predilection is the autumnal season, with its bare trees, its frosts, and withered leaves. But in *El Sendero de Humildad*, Gálvez has abandoned introspection for objectivity, and a marked change has taken place in his mood and point of view. He has become acquainted with Argentina itself, and the Argentina that inspired him was not tropical Misiones or frozen Patagonia, but the semi-arid plains, the pampas, not unlike Castile in Spain, whose somberness has appealed to Azorín, Antonio Machado, and other writers of the present century. "I tried," he said of the second volume, "to reproduce the sensations that the Argentine landscape produced in me, and primarily to evoke the atmosphere of those provincial towns where . . . there still exists the old national spirit, the feeling of the lands of one's fathers, the spiritual depth of the race, and that ingenious languid and romantic character peculiar to the old Argentine towns." Representative of this collection is "Aldea triste" ("*Sad Village*"), which pictures in an impressionistic manner a village on a hot, sunless afternoon— the oppressive heat, the leaden skies, the low grassy hills in the distance, the slow-flowing water in the irrigation ditches, the deserted streets, the creaking of passing oxcarts, and the thick clouds of dust raised by a coach as it went on its way. In this slight volume Gálvez idealizes the past and confesses his return to the faith of his ancestors.

In his first volume of prose, *El Diario de Gabriel Quiroga* (*The Diary of Gabriel Quiroga*), 1910, he has not only returned to Catholicism but shows a decided antipathy to Protestantism, which had been suggested as a means of salvation for Latin America. Catholicism, he feels, is in the very marrow of the people of Latin America and the introduction of Protestantism would result only in their complete denaturalization. The full extent of the heritage of Latin America from Spain, he says, he comprehended only after his travels in that country; not till then did he realize that the Argentines had not ceased, in spite of immigration and other influences, to be Spaniards. This point he emphasizes in *El Solar de la Raza* (*The Cradle of the Race*), written a few years later. "Within the vast Spanish soul is contained the Argentine soul, with as much reason as the Castilian and Andalusian. We are Spaniards because we speak Spanish just as the Spaniards were Latins because they spoke Latin." While he believes that Spaniards and Argentines are basically the same, he admits the differences between them, just as between the Galicians and Andalusians, and points out certain reasons for their existence:

> The Indian exists in nearly all the people in the interior and in many of those on the coast. The revolutions in the provinces and the brutal acts which young men of rich families commit in the capital, especially in the carnival season, when howling like Pampa Indians they attack peaceful folk in their raids, reveal the Indian in certain civilized Argentines, and the same thing occurs in regard to the mulatto. There are respectable, cultured, and punctilious people in whom the influence of white blood has blotted out the remote mulatto grandfather, and yet in such and such a moment of their lives these people commit an act that is unworthy of them. It is the mulatto that reappears.

With a passion for everything truly representative of Argentina, he attempts in this book to fathom the psychology of its people and concludes that of the two contending political forces in the first half of the nineteenth century—the federals and unitarians, who represented respectively barbarism and European culture—the federals were more genuinely Argentine; that of all the literature produced in the country, only a small amount—certain works of Sarmiento and the epics *Fausto* and *Martín Fierro*—was truly indigenous; and that the Argentine spirit was to be encountered in the provinces rather than in Buenos Aires.

At the same time Gálvez was planning a novel which would have a provincial city as its background, and in order to master the technique of novel writing he read extensively the French novelists, especially Flaubert and Zola, as well as Galdós, with whom he has much in common. In 1910 he married Delfina Bunge, also a writer of note, and the two went to Europe. During their stay there (1910-11) he wrote *El Solar de la Raza*. In its foreword he reaffirms the conscious spiritual affinity of himself and a few other Argentine intellectuals with the so-called generation of 1898 of Spain:

> The small group that we form performs a mission similar to that of the generation of thinkers that appeared in Spain after the national disaster. Spain, through Ganivet, Macías Picavea, Costa, Unamuno, and others, took stock of herself and became profoundly acquainted with herself. Also my country, through her young writers, is observing herself, and I think that she has begun to get acquainted with herself.
>
> Ours is a valiant struggle. We have to fight bravely—in books, in daily newspapers, in university lecture-rooms, in short, everywhere—against those deadening interests that a materialistic conception of life has created among us. We have to preach madly the love of country, our landscapes, our writers, our great men; we have to awaken a realization of the idealism and the originality of our past; and we have to show how these qualities, which we possessed in our romantic and poor past, can save our living country today, without any detriment to it in its present material greatness.

He goes on to tell his purpose in writing a book dealing with the inner life, the soul, of Spain, which, although hidden to the average traveler, had aroused in him deep emotions, and his reasons for feeling himself, an Argentine, capable of doing so:

> Since I am a believer in our admirable Latin race, and especially in the Spanish stock to which we belong, my

preference could not be other than for Spain. Spanish influence is necessary for us; for, far from denaturalizing us,
like certain exotic influences, it helps to strengthen our
own American and Argentine nature.

In his interpretation of the spiritual urge that motivated the
generation of '98, Gálvez shares their enthusiasm for what they
regard as typically Spanish—the desolate and barren landscape
of Castile, the artless, rude verse of such poets as Berceo, and the
impressionistic paintings of the long-unappreciated El Greco,
who disregarded conventional concepts of beauty and technical perfection in favor of an idea or purpose.

Gálvez's interest, during these early years, in art, in the
provincial cities, in the literature, and also in the sociological
conditions of Argentina is amply reflected in a series of articles that appeared principally in the literary periodicals *Noso-
tros* (Buenos Aires) and ·*L'Amérique Latine* (Paris), some
thirty-two of which were revised and republished under the
title of *La Vida múltiple (Arte y Literatura: 1910-1916)*.
(*Complex Life [Art and Literature: 1910-1916])*. Outstanding among the twelve that treat of art is one on El Greco, for
whom Gálvez had earlier conceived a profound admiration.
Others pass judgment on exhibitions of paintings, both individual and collective, held in Buenos Aires between 1912 and
1914. The provincial cities he interprets include La Rioja,
which was to be the scene of his first novel; Córdoba—the
background of another—which appeared to him essentially
Castilian in both its landscape and the prevailing spirit of its
peoples; and Santa Fé, in which he had spent a part of his
childhood. In regard to Argentine literature, particularly that
of the nineteenth century, he expresses a preference for only
the unaffected: the vigorous but unpolished prose of Miguel
Cané; the *Mémoires* of General José María Paz, of which he
later probably made use; and above all the epic poem *Martín
Fierro*. Informative are his comments on the new era in Argentine letters, which he regards as beginning in 1909, and re-

markably accurate are his judgments in regard to the literary productions of his own contemporaries and literary coterie: Payró's *El Casamiento de Laucha*, Larreta's *La Gloria de don Ramiro* (*The Glory of Don Ramiro*), the dramas of Florencio Sánchez, the short stories of Horacio Quiroga, the essays of Ricardo Rojas, and the verse of Arturo Capdevila. Of an entirely different nature, *La Inseguridad de la Vida obrera* (*The Insecurity of the Workingman*), 1913, an exposé of living conditions among the laboring classes of Argentina—is evidence of his interest in the proletariat of Buenos Aires, whose cause he was to espouse in more than one of his novels. And it is on his novels, the first of which, *La Maestra normal*, appeared in 1914, that his literary reputation rests.

Into the writings of these went the preparation of thirty years of broad education, extensive travel, almost a decade of professional experience which had made him familiar with his country and its problems, a profound religious conviction, and an aroused interest in the life of the masses based on firsthand knowledge of their living conditions. In addition, he had tried his hand at poetry and essay and, as has been stated, had studied intensively the technique of French and Spanish novelists. The results of all this preparatory training, of his observation, and his personal interests were to find a place in his novels.

Simple in plot, *La Maestra normal* is none the less engaging and emotive, and its two principal characters, Solís and Raselda, are human beings, not admirable, but interesting. They are brought together in La Rioja, a small provincial city in the semi-arid region of northwestern Argentina. Solís, physically impaired by loose living in Buenos Aires, where he had been an employee of the government for several years, decided on La Rioja for the sake of his health; and through influence secured, as a livelihood, a position as a grade teacher in a normal school there. A blasé, well educated member of the Bohemian literary circles of the metropolitan capital, he anticipated on his arrival in La Rioja no great pleasure from his stay in that out-of-the-way place. Raselda, too, the first grade teacher, had only recently arrived from the nearby town Nonogasta. Young, beautiful, and voluptuous, she attracted the attention of Solís, and in turn fell hopelessly in love with him. Like Solís, she was of illegitimate birth. She was not, however, a stranger in La Rioja, for she had a grandmother there, with whom she was to live, and eight years previously she had graduated from the normal school. Of a sweet and gentle temperament, impressionable, given to day-dreaming and the reading of romantic novels, versed in native songs, and proficient as a dancer of the tango and the zamba, she had never been more than a mediocre student. During the last two years in school she had a love affair and studied barely enough to graduate. Then followed eight long years of boredom and of hopeless waiting in Nonogasta, at the end of which time she secured through an uncle's influence the position in La Rioja. The love that Solís awakened in her heightened her natural proclivity to pleasant reveries. In the classroom she was from the very beginning a hopeless failure, for the realization of her incompetence and the fear of a brutal but efficient supervisor made her forgetful, self-conscious, and ill-at-ease. Then, too, a gossipy woman, envious of her position, began to spread abroad unsavory stories about her and Solís. Although there was nothing between the two at the time, certain intimacies that followed inflamed Raselda more than ever. And Solís desired her, too, when he was in her presence; but, more apathetic in nature and more timid, he let some time go by before he finally, through the help of Plácida, the abortionist and go-between of the town, gained admittance to Raselda's room at night and effected his conquest. Dejected at times but on the whole supremely happy, for she thought Solís would keep his promise to marry her, Raselda was insatiable in her love. Solís, on the other hand, sated, began to tire of her and had to feign an infatuation that did not exist. As time went on matters became more involved. Solís had an altercation with the director, who had prevented his securing a much better position in another school; and Raselda had to ask for a leave in order to care for her sick grandmother. When vacation came, Solís left for Buenos Aires to counteract the influence of the director. Raselda in the meanwhile realized that she was pregnant and was persuaded by Plácida to let her effect an abortion, from which she would have died had not Dr. Nilamón Arroyo, a sincere friend, come to her rescue. The shock of Raselda's shame killed her grandmother, and the girl lost her position in the school, although she could have retained it had she submitted to the desires of one of the inspectors who came to investigate both her case and the revolt of most of the teachers against the director. When Solís was transferred to Salta, Raselda was happy, for she thought he would take her with him. It is at this point that the full extent of the despicability, the inconstancy, the timidity of Solís in facing a responsibility, is felt, for, although pained by Raselda's plight, he refused to marry her. Five years later, according to the epilogue in which Gálvez disposes of most of the characters, Raselda, having lost still another position on account of her past, and still unmarried, was teaching in a small Andean village, while Solís was in the last stages of alcoholism and tuberculosis in Buenos Aires.

But the main interest of *La Maestra normal* is less in the simple story of seduction than in the setting, the provincial town of La Rioja and its people. From the very first chapters the spirit of the place is sensed: the aridity, the irregularity, and the barrenness of the region in which the town lies; the intense languor-producing atmosphere permeated with the odor of orange blossoms; the crumbling buildings and the neglected streets; the general appearance of lassitude on the part of the population itself; and their remoteness from contemporary currents of thought. Not a very promising setting for a novel it might be argued; yet, in that sleepy city to which Solís and Raselda had come to play their parts, they came into contact with individuals who are interesting for their ideas, customs, sentiments, and attitude toward life.

The descriptions of these people, of many different types and from every social level, are short but very effective. Doña Críspula, at whose house Solís went to board, was a fat, short woman in the fifties; her stomach protruded; her face was like a full moon, and her cheeks shone like polished billiard balls; her double chin, surmounted by a mole with long hairs, shook like gelatine; but she was pleasant, talked incessantly, and laughed loudly at the slightest provocation. The furniture of her small sitting-room consisted of chairs lined against the walls; an old piano with yellow, broken keys; and a small table on which rested an album for photographs, crowned by a vase. On the walls were three old faded lithographs and a daguerreotype of Doña Críspula herself at the time of her marriage. As a stranger in La Rioja was always a matter of great concern, scarcely had Solís been installed before the girls who knew of it took occasion to pass the house in order to get a peek at him, while the more fortunate friends of Doña Críspula's daughter elected at once to call.

At Doña Críspula's house, Solís heard much lore about La Rioja and all of the local gossip, but discussion of a more intellectual nature was provided by a group to which a fellow boarder, Pérez, a stuttering musician, presented him. It met at a pharmacy shop and consisted of the dyspeptic, self-centered, anticlerical worshipper of Kant and of pedagogical theories, Albarenque, director of the normal school; the coarse and vulgar but charitable Catholic, Nilamón Arroyo, physician and teacher of chemistry; the town's practical joker, the young, clownish Palmarín, who did not know a word of French when appointed to teach that language; and Sánchez Masculino, teacher of civics and, until ruined by drink, one of the best lawyers in La Rioja, but ruled over at home by his wife, from whom he escaped temporarily on trips to Buenos Aires; and of Sofanor Molina, a petty office-holder whose entire life was wrapped up in politics. The first time that Solís met with them educational practice and theory happened to be the topic of conversation. Palmarín initiated it by rebuking Albarenque for extending his authority to the private life of his teachers and students, and so heated did the argument become that Nilamón had to quiet them. But he, too, although in a more dignified manner, took up the cudgel against normal-school ideas, in the dominance of which he saw "the subjugation of university to primary education, the death of higher studies, the disappearance of that cultural aristocracy that was called humanism." Disapproving the idea of increasing the number of schools in order to extend education to all classes, which he thought would tend to general mediocrity, Nilamón advocated the education of a selected and talented few; he ridiculed such pet theories of the normal schools as sex-education and co-education; and affirmed that the normal-school graduates were lacking entirely in culture, that educational psychology on which so much time was spent was a pseudo rather than a true science, and that the normal school was hostile to both home and church.

Bored in time with this circle, Solís began to frequent the "confitería" of one of the hotels—a sort of social hall, with a bar and billiard tables—the general meeting place of the male population.

The patrons, seated in groups of three or four at tables covered with glasses and flies, killed time by looking at each other. Here the papers from Buenos Aires were eagerly received and read, and politics, the invariable topic of interest, was discussed. Among the notable habitués were Sofanor Molina, who enjoyed an enviable reputation as the teller of risqué stories; Miguel Araujo, a liberal in politics and an effective orator; and the governor of the province himself, drowsy looking and slow of speech, who came wearing high boots and a Panama hat.

From the "confitería" Solís extended his visits to other levels of the town's society. An invitation to a dance at the home of Gamaliel Frutos, a man of means, enabled him to know the highest social circle in La Rioja. Outside of the house that night some of the poorer class had gathered to watch the dancing. "They were heavy people; they moved about slowly, and some rested their lazy bodies, like sacks, against others. From their bodies emanated a filthy odor. When a guest arrived they withdrew humbly." Inside, the women were seated around the four walls of the sitting-room, while the piano was hammered incessantly. There were only three or four young marriageable men; the older ones were sitting about in groups, telling jokes or discussing politics. A recent visitor in the town had also been invited, a certain Quiroga, a passionate admirer of Argentine provincial life, an advocate of everything native to the region, with whom Solís had already had long discussions concerning its literature and music. Solís danced with Gamaliel's sister Lolita, a vivacious girl educated in Buenos Aires, who let him understand that she would consider him as a husband and at the same time ridiculed Raselda mercilessly; and Quiroga flirted with Lucia—of French parentage, married in La Rioja but from Buenos Aires, and bored to death. The women of the town, she told him, "were sedentary and lazy. They spent the time doing nothing, sunk down in their hammock-like chairs. They were like Turks, like Arabs."

The lowest social class lived in miserable huts on the outskirts of the town; here Indian blood rather than European predominated. Accompanied by some very colorful street musicians, Araujo took Solís to several houses in this district to amuse themselves at dancing. At the first house there lived three girls and their old mother. Solís was impressed not only by their phlegmatic nature, but by the indifference of the mother toward Araujo, whose obvious purpose was to seduce one of the girls. But Araujo explained that such families, more or less respectable, had no regard for certain aspects of morality, and that among them an unmarried girl did not lose her reputation just because she had a child. Then after a call at another house, far, far more indecent, Solís and his cicerone returned to the city with their musicians to serenade more respectable girls. If the people on the outskirts of the city were indigenous, even more so was the very striking feast of the

"Niño Alcalde" with its procession to the accompaniment of fatalistic music and the subsequent orgies—that was held every year by the Indians of the region to celebrate their conversion to Christianity.

In the repleteness of its setting, *La Maestra normal* stands unequaled by any of Gálvez's subsequent novels, or, in fact, by any other novel in Spanish-American fiction; and in its technique the author is a worthy disciple of his master, Flaubert. In like manner so seemingly honest and impartial is he in the depiction of La Rioja and its people as to imply a secret contempt for provincial towns and their inhabitants. He attempts also to explain why people of towns like this attach great importance to trivial incidents, such as the rebellion of the teachers of the normal school against the director and their efforts to dislodge him; why they meddled in the personal affairs of others; and why once a man and a girl were seen talking together, some immediately set to work to spy upon them and to connect them in some illicit love affair. Gálvez finally attributes these propensities to the "frightful monotony of provincial life, which had its influence even on the morality of the people, making them cowardly and envious."

More limited in scope, *La Sombra del Convento* (*The Shadow of the Convent*), 1917, likewise has as its setting a provincial city—Córdoba, a cultural center whose buildings give it a colonial atmosphere. The university was established there in the seventeenth century by the Jesuits, who continued to exercise a dominating influence in all aspects of life. Not until the beginning of the twentieth century did Córdoba begin to awaken from her lethargy. Wealth was increasing and the city expanded. New buildings, both public and private, were erected. With material progress came a quickening of the spirit that fostered opposition to the proud and domineering clergy, as unchanged as in Spain in the sixteenth century. Within the church itself, some members favored a more liberal attitude toward modern tendencies; outside of it entirely, agnostics and Freemasons were its sworn enemy. The interpretation of the attitudes of these groups as they began to clash is the chief interest of the author of *La Sombra del Convento*. Various parts of the city and religious processions and demonstrations during Holy Week pass before our eyes as in a series of slides. The pervading atmosphere of austerity and gloom is effectively conveyed through emphasis upon the grayness of the Cordovan landscape and the old buildings, which seem to symbolize the sentiments of those who stubbornly resisted all liberalizing tendencies.

It was to this city in 1906 that José Alberto Flores, a descendant of a distinguished Cordovan family, then a man of thirty, returned after an absence of ten years in Europe. He had been educated by the Jesuits and had studied law for three years in the University of Córdoba, but he was not in sympathy with its teachings. For "that University, which was almost colonial, still kept the spirit of the cloisters that its founder had given it; it signified no change in ideas for José Alberto; the teachers and students were all, or almost all, good believers; the texts were indisputably orthodox." Bored with existence, José had sought distraction in the dissolute life about him —the only diversion, Gálvez comments, of a provincial city. Finally, he became so involved in gambling debts that a rupture with his father was imminent. After he attempted suicide as a way out of his difficulty, his father sent him to Europe. Although he traveled much while there, he lived mostly in Paris where he interested himself in art and literature, but continued his profligate habits.

On his return to Córdoba, he was a disillusioned man, not indifferent to the aesthetic element in the Catholic service but as hostile as ever to the reactionary ideas and attitudes prevalent in his native city. Since both his parents were dead, he lived in the ancient ancestral home with an aged aunt, of whom he was very fond. There he spent most of his time, going out only at night, and then avoiding places where he might meet relatives or acquaintances. On one of these nightly excursions he was impelled by a sudden religious impulse to enter the cathedral; there he saw a cousin and former sweetheart, Teresa Belderrain. The old love flamed up anew in both, even while José realized that her father would object to him.

Of one of the most distinguished families of Córdoba, austere and cold by nature, Ignacio Belderrain was a professor of law in the University, a militant and intolerant Catholic, and a stern father. He had resigned as a member of congress when that body passed a law permitting civil marriage, and had never again gone to Buenos Aires; he distrusted even its liberal Catholics; he allowed only a Catholic newspaper in his house; and he had disowned a son whose ideas were not in conformity with his own. One of Teresa's sisters persuaded her father to admit José Alberto to their house, on the ground that he had returned to his religion, as they had seen him in church. Belderrain received him coldly, and his eldest son, Ignacio, a judge thoroughly in accord with his father's principles, took the occasion to admonish him either to change his ideas or to leave Córdoba.

Just when a reconciliation between José Alberto and the Belderrains seemed possible, the judge delivered the commencement address at the University. In discussing the speech later with some acquaintances, José Alberto characterized it as intolerant and fanatical, and added that Ignacio and others of his stripe were medieval in their attitude toward religion; that the Catholics of Europe held no such prejudices; and that it was folly to close the University to modern thought. These remarks soon came to the ears of the elder Belderrain, who promptly closed the doors of his house to his nephew and sent Teresa to a convent. Possessed by an insane rage, José Alberto wandered about the city, at one time vilifying the Church, at another lamenting that he was an unbeliever. Associating himself with an anti-Church group—all agnostics, Freemasons, or worshipers of such writers as Darwin—he published a most vindictive article against the Jesuits. His old aunt fell critically ill when apprised of what her nephew had done; but through her influence and that of her confessor, the lovable and practical-minded Father Rincón, as well as through an innate desire on his part to return to his religion, José Alberto repented and made his confession during Holy Week. Father Rincón also interceded in his behalf with Belderrain, who finally pardoned him and recalled Teresa from the convent. Shortly after the marriage of the two, Belderrain fell ill and died, and Gálvez ends the novel in his favorite way—with a magnificent funeral.

Belderrain is the master creation of the novel; he, at least, has character and personality. José Alberto, although well conceived, fails to excite admiration. He is a weak type not unusual in Spanish-American fiction: the young man who, after years of loose and profligate living in Paris, returns to his native land embittered and out of sympathy with his environment. One might question the motive that inspired his conversion. Did not love for Teresa outweigh any genuine desire to return to his religion? Had Belderrain known his real sentiments—for José Alberto remained as liberal in views as ever—he would not have admitted him to his house. Teresa herself is a colorless character. Her mother, who in her ignorance insists that the San José of one church has more power than that of another, is an amusing type, very ably presented. Excellent, too, are the portraits of the leaders of the extreme radical group.

The plot of the novel is less than mediocre. Lacking entirely, too, are the emotive qualities of *La Maestra normal*. Teresa passively bows to the will of her father. José Alberto's acts are impetuous and childish, and his dilemma—whether to acknowledge religion and perhaps win Teresa, or to ally himself with the enemies of the Church and certainly lose her—fails to arouse sympathy. The little miracle, too—the sudden change for the better in José's old aunt after he, unknown to her, made his confession—seems out of place in a realistic novel.

As Gálvez has insisted that his opinions are not necessarily in accord with those of his characters, perhaps he voices none

in *La Sombra del Convento*, which reads like a Galdós novel
with religious intolerance for its theme until the extreme liberal
group is characterized; then one feels that the author prefers
the intolerant Catholics to the unbelievers. Liberal, indeed, is
his own attitude if he is in accord with José Alberto in saying:

> In my opinion there is nothing so sad, so terribly sad, as
> believing in nothing. I am not speaking of Catholic belief.
> Whether we are theosophists, protestants, spiritualists, or
> simply deists, let us at least believe in Divinity, in the soul,
> in the life to come. I look upon the spiritualists as my
> brothers and I love them. I, a Catholic, have with the
> theosophist a great common ground: the belief in Divin-
> ity, in a life to come, and in the soul; fundamentally we
> are united. Consequently, I do not comprehend why the
> Church should condemn so violently those brothers of
> ours with whom we have so many things in common. My
> enemies, our enemies, are the materialists; those that deny
> God....

El Mal metafísico (*Idealism—An Ill*), which was published
in 1916, between *La Maestra normal* and *La sombra del Convento*, is the first of a series of Gálvez's novels that have
Buenos Aires as their setting. It and three others—*Nacha
Regules, Historia de Arrabal* (*A Den of Vice*), and *El
Cántico espiritual* (*Hymn to the Spiritual*)—interpret certain
aspects of life in the capital during the first decade of the
twentieth century. The central figures of the four, while differing from each other in most respects, are alike in being
impractical, idealistic people who, with one exception, go
down to defeat in the struggle against their untoward surroundings.

In *El Mal metafísico* this figure is Carlos Riga, who went
from a provincial town to Buenos Aires to study law. But instead of devoting himself to it, he became interested in literature; and in time his modernistic verse won a certain amount
of recognition. Unable to cope with the practical side of life,
he became the butt of the jokes in the sorry student boarding

house, a victim of the "metaphysical ill," which one of his friends defined as "the disease of creating, dreaming, and contemplating." Carlos and other young literati undertook to establish a periodical, "La Idea moderna," as a medium for their productions. One of the founders was Eduardo Iturbide, son of a rich physician, a skeptic and an admirer of Renan and Anatole France. Work on the review led to Riga's visiting in Eduardo's home, where he fell in love with Lita, his friend's sister, who was also interested in literature. She had just persuaded him to return to the study of law when a students' strike closed the doors of the institution. Her parents, who regarded the penniless Riga as a most undesirable suitor, determined to send their daughter to Europe; and Riga, heartbroken, said farewell to her on the boat. The grief over losing the only one in whom he had found spiritual companionship alternated in his mind with resentment against a society that denied him love because he lacked money. The analysis of the emotional crisis that this unhappy love affair caused is the most stirring feature of the book.

Four years later Riga was an habitual drunkard, working now and then on various newspapers. His devotion to his art was as strong as ever, but he was unable to make a living with either his verses or his plays. He renewed his association with Eduardo at whose house, presided over by a mistress brought from France, a Bohemian literary clique gathered. Riga mended his ways and was for a time happy, for his friends enabled him to publish a volume of his verse. For a short time he lived with a certain Heloísa, who would gladly have supported him; but she disgusted him, and he left her. Another fit of despondence, brought on by seeing Lita's photograph, led him to desert his friends. When a veritable human derelict, the victim of neurasthenia and tuberculosis, he met Nacha Regules, a daughter of the woman who had kept the boarding house in which he lived as a student. A prostitute, but kind by nature, Nacha took him in and cared for him for three years; then penniless, she deserted him to return to her old calling.

Again friends rescued him and sent him to a sanitorium, but scarcely was he restored to health when he saw Lita and learned that she was about to be married. Unable to endure that blow, he again took to drink, and died a few days later in a drunken stupor.

Riga is not a tragic figure although he arouses a certain type of pity. From the opening pages of the book to the end he is a fixed character: an over-sensitive being, pure in thought and action, exceptionally endowed mentally, devoted to his art, and uncompromising in his attitude toward his materialistic surroundings. Had the novelist made him go down in defeat, the victim of his materialistic surroundings, and meet death from starvation, for instance, rather than prostitute his art, he would have been tragically a greater character. Fate in closing the law school seemed to contribute to his downfall, but his ultimate undoing was his disappointment in love, which aroused in him no struggle but led him to become a drunken sot. Among the minor characters—and the book literally swarms with them—there are a few with Riga's idealism, but the greater part forgot their Tolstoy and Kropotkin and adapted themselves to their surroundings, becoming finally, in a purely materialistic way, successful individuals. In comparison with *La Maestra normal*, this novel has very little physical description of places and people; but it is rich in accounts of student and university life, in opinions of Argentine literature and the stage, in interpretations of the attitudes of the rich, and in the ideas and sentiments of the socialists, anarchists, authors, and journalists who held their meetings in the Café Brasileña.

Nacha Regules, a minor character in *El Mal metafísico*, assumes the principal rôle in the novel that bears her name (1919). She became the mistress of Eduardo Iturbide's younger brother, the vicious Arnedo. One night, in a cafe in Buenos Aires, when Arnedo was abusing her for failing to enter into the hilarity of the group of ruffians with them, a certain Fernando Monsalvat, attracted by her pensive mien, intervened in her behalf. The dispute that followed, happily for Monsalvat, did not end in violence.

Monsalvat, at that time a young man of thirty-two, was an illegimate son, but his father had given him a good education. After early success in legal practice, he had entered the consular service, in which he spent eight years in Europe. The story opens only six months after his return to the Foreign Office in Buenos Aires. While he was admitted to some of the best homes in the capital, the stigma of his birth prevented him from being considered a desirable husband in the upper circles.

Lately Monsalvat had undergone a change in his attitude toward life. Shortly before he befriended Nacha, he had seen some soldiers brutally disperse a parade of socialists, and his resentment against capitalism was aroused. He began to despise the complacent rich and to rebuke himself for having lived a life of pleasure and ease. Desiring to do something for the downtrodden, he mortgaged a piece of property in order to so improve it as to provide some of the comforts of life for its poor tenants. He resolved to visit his mother, a common, ordinary woman, and to find his sister, who had been lured from home by Arnedo Iturbide; but too late, for both soon died. He went to see Nacha, who told him the story of her life. At various times, she emphasized, she had attempted to lead a decent life, but fate seemed to have destined her to be a bad woman.

It was about this time that Riga died. Moved greatly by his death, for he had been the greatest influence for good in her life, Nacha determined again to mend her ways; but before she could form a plan, Arnedo cast her off. Her determination lasted only as long as her money—a few months; then to live, she had to resort again to prostitution. Although she purposely avoided Monsalvat, she remembered him tenderly and often spoke of him to the other girls, who twitted her with having fallen in love with a man she had only seen twice. Monsalvat, after a search through numberless houses of prostitution,

found her eventually and asked her to marry him; but she refused, for she was unwilling to bring him to her level. His
love, too, for her was quite spiritual, a type incomprehensible
to her. Life was going badly with him; his radical ideas had
estranged him from influential friends; the mortgaged property was lost; and sickness came. Then Nacha went to care
for him, supporting herself by working in a store; but a few
months later Arnedo, out of pure spite, abducted her, and
again she was a prostitute. When Monsalvat once more made
the rounds of the brothels in an effort to find her, she had
returned, after her mother's death, to live with her sister in the
old home. She was about to marry an honorable country fellow when she and Monsalvat, now an invalid and almost blind,
met. Feeling that he needed her more, she married him instead,
and the two went on keeping the old boarding house for
students.

While *Nacha Regules* was the most favorably received of
all of Gálvez's novels, it is far from being his best. In it are
various elements that contribute to making it what is generally
termed a popular book: its idealism, its naturalistic vein, and
its propaganda. Its main characters are not ordinary human
beings. In the extent to which his idealism carries him, Monsalvat is monomaniacal. Nacha, the plaything of fate, noble
and generous in spite of her contradictory conduct, is the
romantic type of the fallen woman who is regenerated through
love. Arnedo is of one stripe, an outright villain. The story
itself, with its violent incidents piled one upon the other in
rapid succession, is melodramatic. On the other hand, the setting is full of naturalistic details, such as conditions in houses
of prostitution and the life and ideas of the desperately poor
in tenement houses. Injected are a number of case histories of
prostitutes, which Gálvez probably borrowed from his doc-
toral thesis. The book voices also a sweeping condemnation
of vice and other social evils. When Nacha was working in a
store she made only thirty pesos a month, on which it was
impossible for her to live decently. "It was necessary for that

poor girl, a daughter of the Argentine Republic, to suffer in order that the English shareholders, the millionaires of London, might receive magnificent dividends." And a keeper of a house of prostitution enumerates some of the causes of that evil:

> In the twenty years that I have been in this business I have never misled any woman. . . . You say it's an illicit trade. But it is licit to be the owner of a big department store, "The City of Paris," where they pay the women employees so little that they are forced to go wrong. . . . I don't exploit anybody, strictly speaking, as they do in those stores. I'm no accomplice to crime in the same way as the shareholders of those huge establishments. Look here: we women don't lead other women astray. The men do that, the rich ones, the owners of tenement houses and of factories.

Even more naturalistic than *Nacha Regules* is *Historia de Arrabal* (1923), to which the term feuilletonistic fittingly applies. The action takes place in one of the worst districts of Buenos Aires and centers about Rosalinda Corrales, a beautiful young woman with a natural tendency toward uprightness. She was susceptible, however, to the evil influence of her stepbrother, nicknamed El Chino, one of the most vicious criminals of that capital. On account of her connection with him, Rosalinda gave up hope of marrying Daniel Forti, an intelligent young Italian workman who loved her. For the three years that El Chino was serving a prison sentence, Rosalinda was free of him; but when he was discharged he took her away from her home and kept her virtually a prisoner. Then he put her to work in a packing plant, took her earnings, and treated her brutally; later, he forced her to sell herself and to rob and to steal. When she had reached the lowest stage of degradation, she again met Daniel Forti, who still loved her. The two went to live together, but El Chino found her and, through the hypnotic power he exercised, forced her to stab Daniel to death. Again she became a tool for evil in El

Chino's hands. So ends the story, by no means an impossible one, for without doubt such characters do exist in actual life. But the author seeks to interest and shock primarily through violent crimes and harrowing incidents, and in this respect the novel is cheap and sensational.

In *El Cántico espiritual* (1923) Gálvez turns to more cultured folk. Mauricio Sandoval is an idealist. Of an aristocratic family of Buenos Aires, he, like Carlos Riga, abandoned law, which his father had insisted he study, to devote himself to painting and sculpture. He married, when still very young, Genoveva Santangelo, whose father, Ludovico, became his teacher. Under the tutelage of father and daughter, for Genoveva was an artist herself, Mauricio produced work excellent in technique, but conservative. His first exhibition secured for him a stipend from the Argentine government to study in Europe. An earlier rift, which developed when Mauricio became absorbed in the modernistic tendencies in art, widened in Paris and eventually separated them. Sandoval soon found other friends, among them a beautiful and accomplished married woman, Susana de Olózoga, whose husband, totally uncultured and interested only in the frivolous side of Parisian life, gave her entire freedom. Drawn to her intellectually—for she contributed both inspiration and sympathy with his ideals —Mauricio attempted a conquest, but she "was one of those women for whom physical love has a certain horror, that accept a flirtation and intimacies, but surrender themselves to the man they love only after a long struggle." In time Mauricio became less sensual and more capable of sensibility, a better man and a greater artist. He came to the realization that spiritual love did exist and that it was "the essence of the world," "the supreme harmonizer." He even came to believe that their relationship would be sullied by physical love. Their child, he insisted, would be the flowering of art, including the renaissance of sculpture, and the contribution of greater beauty to the world. He maintained this attitude even after they returned to Buenos Aires; and, on one occasion when she would have yielded, he pushed her aside, for suddenly an idea for a new piece of sculpture, which he would call "El Cántico espiritual," flashed through his mind.

The story of *El Cántico espiritual* is unusual but within the realm of plausibility, and its plot is better unified and more direct than many Gálvez created. For, although it does give an insight into the life of the rich Argentines, both in Buenos Aires and Paris, and the ideology of artists, it unfolds with much less of such detail. Its unpopularity, for it has neither been reprinted nor translated into a foreign language, may be traceable both to his choice of a theme which appeals more to speculation than to emotion—that Platonic love is possible—and to his failure to present a genuine example of such love. Mauricio is perplexing. He accepts the Platonic relation at first from necessity and talks ethereally about it. Later, when he might have changed their relationship and is even tempted to yield to physical pleasure, he refuses because Platonic love has proved such a valuable asset to his art. But Palacio Valdés's *La Alegría del Capitán Ribot* (*The Joy of Captain Ribot*), to which *El Cántico espiritual* is comparable, is more convincing and artistic.

If *El Cántico espiritual* is of interest as a psychological study, even more so are *Miércoles Santo* (*Holy Wednesday*), 1930, and *La Noche Toca a su Fin* (*The End of Night Draws Near*), 1935, which belong in a category of their own. In them the element of interest lies neither in the action of the story nor in its setting, but in the struggle that goes on within the tortured soul of the two protagonists, and in the charm of the style of the portrayal. While the two men are totally different in other respects, their main concern—religion—is the same. In *Miércoles Santo* it is the mind of a priest, Father Solanas, that is bared for some eighteen hours—from 12 o'clock at night, when he was called to a fashionable district of Buenos Aires to administer the last rites to a dying man, to the end of the following day, a Holy Wednesday. Although pious and austere and reputedly great as a confessor, Father Solanas suf-

fered at times the calls of the flesh, and for this he was wont
to flagellate himself as were the saints of old. His curse was
that in his youth, just before ordination, he had been tempted
by a girl whom he had never been able to forget.

Father Solanas began that Holy Wednesday ill at ease and
perplexed. Certain incidents of the previous night had recalled
the girl to his mind. He heard the confessions in turn of the
many sinners that came, for the most part adulterers. Just
before noon a doubter came to confess, but suddenly disappeared, leaving Solanas more bewildered than ever and convinced that he had seen the Devil. In vain his fellow priests, at
the noonday meal, tried to convince him that the Devil no
longer appeared on earth. In the afternoon, as he heard further confessions, there came among the sinners the girl who
had tempted him; without knowing who he was, she confessed
that she loved him still. As Solanas was leaving at the end of
the day he saw again, either in his imagination or actually,
the doubter he had taken for the Devil; under Solanas' fixed
gaze, the figure assumed the guise of a huge bat. The strain
proved too great for the priest's overwrought nerves; he
fell to the ground lifeless.

The supernatural does not enter to such an extent in *La
Noche toca a su Fin*. Autobiographic in form, with comments
interspersed by the supposed editor, the book purports to be
the confessions of Claudio Vidamor, who was born in Córdoba in 1892. His father, a Freemason and such an enemy of
the Church as not to permit his son to be baptized, died while
Claudio was still young. His Catholic mother was unable to
influence the boy, who led a roguish and sinful life. Forced to
leave Córdoba after her death, he went to Buenos Aires, where
he won a reputation for his journalistic vituperations against
the Church and, free of all moral restraint, lived the life of a
libertine and seducer. In 1934 when a Eucharistic Congress
was being held in Buenos Aires, he ridiculed that assembly,
although his mistress Justina attended the meetings and was
touched by the divine fervor that possessed the city. One

evening while the Congress was still in progress, he and some unregenerate friends went to a café to mock the religious demonstrations; but while there they heard by radio a sermon that proved so touching that his friends repented and received the sacrament. Although Claudio made sport of them at first, he, too, finally yielded, and was baptized. The rest of the night he spent in writing his confessions, which form the main content of the book. When dawn came, it was for him not only another day but a spiritual rebirth, as the title signifies.

Gálvez's style on the whole is simple, clear, direct, and unadorned, but in both these books he is seeking a more elevated medium of expression. The tone of *La Noche Toca a su Fin* is persuasive and its prose flows easily and melodiously. *Miércoles Santo* is still more lyrical; its vocabulary is highly poetic; and it abounds in tropes that are new and striking. In the opening paragraph the poetic tone that characterizes the entire book is struck:

> The piercing tone of the doorbell penetrated the shadows which were gathering in the darkened house. Father Eudosio Solanas heard a second ring; and in his eyes he felt the pressure of the light which the sound had given rise to in the vestibule. He turned on his electric light; the shadows about him recoiled with a leap into the corners. Doors and footsteps were heard; and on the glass three successive knocks. The servant, who was also the sexton, came in clad in wide-striped blue pajamas. Solanas sat up in bed. The crisp voice of the Galician announced: "Confession for a dying man in Belgrano."

Gálvez's remaining novels—*La Tragedia de un Hombre fuerte* (*The Tragedy of a Superior Man*), 1922, *La Pampa y su Pasión* (*The Pampa and Its Craze*), 1926, *Cautiverio* (*In Captivity*), 1935, and *Hombres en Soledad* (*Lonely Men*), 1938,—and a short story, *Una Mujer muy moderna* (*A Very Modern Woman*), 1927, mirror in the main certain changes in attitude, especially on the part of the women of the élite, that took place in Buenos Aires during the second and third decades. Gálvez himself offers an explanation of the conditions which brought them about:

The European war enriched the Argentines. Superficial, without any imperative norms of duty in those years, they seemed to have no other occupation than enjoying material pleasures. Dance halls sprang up throughout the capital. Women, who in the second decade had begun to change their attitude toward men, came later almost to the point of wantonness in their search of thrills. The moving pictures, pornographic periodicals, and obscene books corrupted the young.

The first novel in which Gálvez treats this new era, *La Tragedia de un Hombre fuerte,* is rather long, and its plot is both slender and trite. It recounts the high points of interest for four years in the life of Victor Urgel, a successful and dynamic individual who had come to Buenos Aires as a congressman from a provincial city. He was married to Asunción Belderrain, who figures as a character in *La Sombra del Convento;* but as they had drifted apart, he decided to seek love outside his home. During the four years a like number of women—two married and two single—figured intimately in his life. They were superior and intelligent women, and charming, too, each in her own particular way. But Urgel's hopes of finding a lasting love were blasted, through his own indifference in the first three cases, and in the other, by the woman's decision that her love for him was not genuine. The tragedy of his life seems to have been his inability to requite love or to inspire it in one who might have awakened a lasting passion in him. While Urgel arouses no pity, he is by no means an entirely romantic and frothy character; he does give way at times to introspection, but he is, primarily, a man of action in spite of a family inheritance and an early environment—that of a provincial town—that normally would have made him otherwise.

But the genuine worth of the book lies not in the charac-

terization of Urgel or in the story of his quest for love, but in
the candid account it gives of a people whose ideas in regard
to social law and custom had just undergone certain drastic
changes. On all sides in Buenos Aires Urgel observed "the
conflict between the static and dynamic spirit." The greatest
change was in the attitude of women, who, while men devoted
themselves to business, flocked to the universities and normal
schools, devoted themselves to journalism and to literature,
and filled the lecture halls. "Formerly they read nothing, but
now hundreds of women reading books and periodicals were
to be seen on the trains and streetcars."

The greatest changes, however, were in matters of dress
and in the relations between men and women. Particularly in
women's clothes, the stiffness and rigidity of the earlier styles
contrasted violently with the looseness and natural elegance of
the modern. Women had lost, too, their timidity toward men.
Formerly, "they were very circumspect; they sat at a good
distance from men; they took care that their skirts covered
down to their ankles; and decorum forbade their crossing
their legs." Ten or fifteen years earlier they had danced as if
they were afraid to touch each other, but now "light couldn't
be seen" between a couple. Parents had lost all control over
their daughters.

Now they governed themselves. They were free in
fact, if not in outward appearance. They were modifying
also sexual relationship. Many sought a sweetheart openly.
With men they established a relationship that is peculiar
to the United States, that is, a relationship that does not
lead to a formal engagement. They kissed their sweethearts openly, a thing that was condemned up to a few
years ago. The more daring went out with their men
friends to distant road-houses, and many of them had a
lover.

The *garconniére*, or bachelor's quarters, to which men invited women, had become an established institution in Buenos
Aires. The same spirit of license had seized married women,

many of whom yielded to forbidden love, and hundreds
sought divorce in Montevideo, "risking, for love, the anathema
of social condemnation." Although of a prominent and aristocratic family, the young married woman, Lucy, with whom
Urgel had an affair, stated openly to him her convictions in
regard to such matters:

> I tolerate no imposition, no law. I consult only myself.
> I detest social conventions, lies, hypocrisy, and the norms
> to which the world wishes to subject us unhappy women.
> I accept authority from nobody, not even from my par-
> ents. I have as much a right to be free as anybody.

The breaking down of moral restraint in the next novel of
this group, *La Pampa y su Pasión*, is only incidental to the
main issue, which is the part that their favorite sport—horse-
racing [1]—plays in the life of the people of Buenos Aires. In

[1] "Luna de Miel" ("Honeymoon"), one of Gálvez's short stories in
a collection with the same title, tells of a honeymoon that came near
to ending tragically when the man, who is of interest because of his
uniquely prosaic character, neglects his sensitive and romantic bride
to follow his only passion, horse racing.
The seven remaining stories in the collection are: "El Hombre
feliz" ("Happy Man"), also singular for one of its characters, an
innocent, good-natured and credulous doctor who insisted on marrying a woman with an unsavory past, in spite of the advice of his friends;
"Historia de un Momento espiritual" ("The Story of a Spiritual Moment"), which relates the boredom of a sensitive musician in a provincial town where he was to give a concert, until he met three congenial young women, with each of whom he fell equally in love; "El
terrible Efecto de una Causa pequeña" ("The Terrible Effect of a
Minor Incident"), an amusing account of a horrible dream occasioned
by having eaten too heavily; "La Casa colonial" ("The Colonial
House"), a hair-raising story of a haunted house in Córdoba; "Los
Ciudadanos de Payostá" ("Citizens of Payostá"), which exemplifies,
at the time of a revolutionary change in government, the pusillanimity
of the leading citizens of a small town, who, in the face of having
expressed great indignation over the arrest of one of their number, let
him be executed without protest after each realized what the consequences might be to himself; "La Dicha" ("Happiness"), an excellent
piece of dialogue in which a wife successfully defends her good-for-
nothing husband against members of her family that had assembled

regard to various phases of that pastime—the general passion of the people for the recreation, the love for and interest in race horses and their care, the popularity of successful jockeys and of owners of winning horses, the betting on the races, the underhanded tricks employed to weaken a horse and make him lose a race—the book is a veritable mine of information. Into this background, the main concern of the author, there is woven a loose, disjointed story with many ramifications, which in its lack of unity in structure defies every canon of good storytelling.

The principal character is Fermín Contreras, one of the most popular jockeys in Buenos Aires, whose wife, Albertina, a handsome but dissatisfied woman, socially his superior, had married him solely as a means of support. The owner of the horse that Fermín had made famous was Federico Wilkinson, socially prominent and well-to-do but a dissolute idler. As Albertina had grown tired of Fermín, who was ill-favored physically, she engaged in an affair with Wilkinson, who was unwilling, however, to take her as his mistress, for he had recently become interested in María Jesús Ortiz, an upright and strait-laced girl of a prominent family. On account of her he had broken with his paramour of some years—the handsome, highly-sexed, self-willed, revengeful Indiana Reyes, also of the landed aristocracy. Incensed over the rupture, Indiana set about harassing him. She contrived the ruination of his horse; she won immense sums from him through betting; she attempted, although in vain, to turn Fermín against him by revealing his relations with Albertina; and eventually she caused him to lose the woman he really loved, María de Jesús. Of the characters, the best developed and the only admirable one is Fermín, who, in his indecision, his lack of

---

to express their indignation against him; and "La santa Criatura" ("Blessed Woman"), a sympathetic treatment of a young girl who was deceived by her lover but later became a teacher in Buenos Aires. After the death of her own child, she was irresistibly drawn to one of the children in her class; he proved to be a nephew of the man who had wronged her.

will power, and his resignation, exemplifies the weak, defeated creature for which Gálvez has a predilection. Largely responsible for his undoing, Albertina typifies the restless woman of the day, ready to sacrifice her home and honor for a life of excitement and freedom.

The short story "Una Mujer muy moderna" (1927)[2] relates a single incident in the life of a young modern married woman in Buenos Aires, Quica by name, who "smoked, danced in close embrace with her partner, conversed over the telephone with her men friends, dressed to let her physical charms be seen, read obscene books, had very advanced ideas in regard to morality, knew indecent stories and liked to tell them, scorned religion, and flirted scandalously." Irked one day by her rich but humdrum and even-tempered husband, she left him, much to the consternation of her parents, although they, too, were imbued with modern licentiousness. But the story ends happily, for at the end of the day Quica returned to her husband.

[2] This story is the first in a collection of the same name which contains also an amusing account of an irresponsible individual who failed to arrive at a banquet that was given in his honor, "El Banquete platónico" ("A Platonic Banquet"); a clever story of the outwitting of a Jewish money-lender by a slick-tongued character, "Un buen Negocio" ("A Good Deal"); and an incident probably of Gálvez's own childhood concerning some guests not to his mother's liking he invited to her house, "Pequeña Sinfonía en blanco y negro" ("A Little Symphony in Black and White"); the confession of a young widow to her father when she is about to be married again that she had hated her deceased husband, who was false to her and worthless, and that she had made a great show of mourning for him in order to make herself more attractive to men, "La Viuda inconsolable" ("The Disconsolate Widow"); an interesting account of a trip by train between two towns, and of a stop-over at the junction, where the author attended a funeral and met, among other unusual individuals, a young anarchist who was living there in disguise, "De Santiago a Catamarca" ("From Santiago to Catamarca"); and a fanciful tale of the dire misfortunes that befell an idealistic and over-honest writer of popular plays when he attempted to find the owner of a hundred pesos he had found in a taxi, "La Tragedia de un Hombre honrado" ("The Tragedy of an Honest Man").

A more serious problem of marital relations is presented in *Cautiverio*. The principal characters are Juan Larrandy, a devout Catholic judge, and his wife María Elena, frivolous but very attractive to men, who had won her husband through a pretense of piety. When the story opens they had been married six years; in the last three she had had as many as five lovers. While she did not wish to leave her well-to-do husband, he, suspicious of her fidelity, finally—but much against his will, for she had a great attraction for him—sent her back to her own poor and morally contemptible family. Missing her accustomed comforts, María Elena began to long for her husband's home and money. Sexually he, too, missed her, for his religion prevented him from seeking pleasure with other women. Finally, through Juan's confessor, a reconciliation was effected. Although María Elena exacted a promise from Juan to let her use rouge, to dance, to go to picture shows, and to read the books she pleased, she confessed her sins to a priest and sincerely determined to lead an honest life. But after a week of exemplary conduct, she became bored and returned to her gay parties and infidelities. She and Juan grew so far apart again that he would have divorced her except for the advice of his confessor. On the other hand, she admired him so greatly for his uprightness that she shot one of her lovers who sent a woman to Juan's house to tempt him. The incident, which led to a nervous collapse, proved the turning point in her life. She confessed her adulteries to Juan, and he, through his position, shielded her from the police. This time her repentance proved more enduring. For ten years later—we have the author's word for it—she was a happy mother, a faithful wife, and a devoted Catholic.

Although *Cautiverio* has not enjoyed the popularity that other Gálvez novels have, it is, from a technical standpoint, one of his best. The background—the circle of idle and vicious rich in which María Elena moved, and her own family with whom she lived while separated from Juan—is briefly but effectively sketched. The story itself is told directly and without digressions, and is characterized by a singleness of tone and purpose. While the plight of the two chief characters moves the reader but slightly, their psychology is well analyzed.

On the other hand, *Hombres en Soledad*, 1938, which contains material enough for three or four novels, is a completely formless book. As a gory canvas of upper-class society in Buenos Aires during the first years of the third decade of the present century, it is, however, invaluable. The novel is made up largely of a succession of scenes, more or less related, in which figure some forty characters, whose ideas are revealed to a greater extent through dialogue than in any of Gálvez's other novels.

Typical of the scenes that fill the book is a cinematographic representation, in which there is abundant conversation, of a reception by the rich clubman Ezequiel Toledo, long renowned in Buenos Aires for his philandering, to welcome home from Europe his son Bebe, a superficial, pleasure-loving youth. Of the two daughters in the Toledo family, Flavia was married to Albano Loira, a rich lawyer, ambitious and conservative, while Andrea was wedded to another lawyer, Gervasio Claraval, who was unhappy and cynical, for he was interested in literature rather than in law, and besides poverty had prevented the realization of the dream of his life, to live in Paris. Flavia was typical of the socially prominent and well-to-do young married woman of Buenos Aires.

> She was pretty and elegant, and she had a passion for golf, dancing, cocktails and flirting. She enjoyed complete liberty, which she employed to carry on her flirtations and to amuse herself; she smoked in public, danced immoderately, and attended all the lectures on philosophy and literature by the learned foreigners who visited Buenos Aires, although she understood very little of what they talked about.

Rather than an orderly novel, *Hombres en Soledad* is a mosaic of illicit love affairs, seductions, marital unrest, and frustrated hopes. The most dissatisfied of all was Claraval, the central figure, who was continually dreaming of Paris. Typical of the restless woman were his two friends, Brígida, who was related to the Toledos, and Dalila Mayr. Both had lived a gay life in Paris; both were separated from their husbands; and both enjoyed love freely with whomsoever they chose. It was to Brígida that Claraval turned, in his loneliness, after his wife left him to return to her paternal home.

In addition to the eighteen works of fiction ending with *Hombres en Soledad*, Gálvez treats in novelistic style in five volumes the two most fascinating and colorful periods in Argentine history—the era of Rosas and the war with Paraguay. Of the two novels that compose the first series, *El Gaucho de "Los Cerrillos"* (*The Gaucho of "Los Cerrillos" Ranch*) and *El General Quiroga*, based respectively on the events of the years 1828-29 and 1830-37, the first is, as a novel, superior and the only one of the historical group in which there is a well-developed fictional plot to which the historical element is subservient.

The story concerns two distinguished and well-to-do families of Buenos Aires, the Hinojosas and the Montellanos. Formerly friends, they became allied with opposing political factions—the Montellanos with the Unitarians; the Hinojosas with the Federalists, who were then in power. The enmity of the two factions led to brawls in public places; as the result of one in which he wounded slightly José Rafael Hinojosa, Juliancito Montellano was jailed, but soon released. Another Hinojosa son, Tomás, was at the same time very much in love with Remedios, a daughter of the Montellanos. When the Unitarians came into power, Julián became the chief of police in Buenos Aires; vindictive by nature, he tried to arrest José Rafael, but killed him in the attempt. When his death brought on also that of his mother, Tomás, who was employed at "Los Cerrillos," the estate of the dictator Rosas, renounced the idea of marrying Remedios. When the Federalists returned to power, the Hinojosas were again in the ascendancy while the

Montellanos were in danger of their lives and lost their wealth. Remedios and her mother went to live as dependents with Federalist relatives, while Juliancito committed suicide.

The second novel of this series, *El General Quiroga*, would have gained much artistically if Gálvez had focused his attention on that famous *caudillo*, the henchman of Rosas; instead the book consists of a series of historically accurate panoramic scenes of social and political conditions, chiefly in Buenos Aires, from 1830 to 1837. It begins with the arrival there of Facundo Quiroga, traces the campaigns in which he brought the provinces under the Federalist yoke, pictures the pandemonium in the capital from 1833 to 1834, and concludes with an account of his assassination the next year, and the execution, two years later when Rosas was firmly established in power, of his murderers—although Rosas himself probably had a hand in the assassination.

The fictional element in the novel is slight; without any well-developed plot, it traces the lives, during those years, of a number of people. Only these threads, which are woven into the history of the period, give a certain human interest to otherwise dry facts. One of these, rather pointless as a story, is a passing love affair of Quiroga, while he was in Buenos Aires, with Eldemira Mendoza, a beautiful middle-class widow who had been the paramour of several men, but who now became insanely infatuated with him. Of more interest is the very ordinary, middle-class Lanzas family—Don Eleuterio, his wife Zenovia, six sons and four daughters. Politically, they represented various shades, and nearly all of the male members had served in either the campaigns against the Unitarians or in Rosas' expedition against the Indians. Illustrative of the frontier conditions in Argentina at the time is the story of Juan, one of the Lanzas sons, and his wife, who had earlier been carried away by the Indians; after being rescued, she slipped away and returned to the Indian chief by whom she had children. Don Eleuterio, Zenovia, and at least two of their sons were fanatical partisans of Rosas; another son, Régulo, followed the lead of his wife's family in hating the *caudillo*. Unlike most of his own relatives, he showed great sympathy for his sister, Encarnación, who ran off with the man of her choice, only to be deserted in Montevideo. Two of the Lanzas daughters were married, one to a Frenchman who was looked upon with considerable distrust at the time on account of Rosas' difficulties with France, and the other to a Unitarian. Not only did they suffer indignities and tongue lashings from their own mother but also fear of mobs that from time to time attacked their homes at night.

The characters, largely cruel and vindictive, in the *Escenas de la Época de Rosas* (*Scenes from the Days of Rosas*), whether historical or fictitious, are on the whole impressive, convincing, and not exaggerated; the motive that actuates most of them is the hatred born of civil strife. In his treatment of them, Gálvez is quite impartial, showing sympathy and understanding for both factions. The historical characters are fairly represented. Although Rosas as an actual character enters the story very little, he dominates it so completely that one feels the almost supernatural influence he exerted over his followers. Of all the historical figures, the novelist's imagination enters most into the characterization of Lavalle—in actual life an able man, generally the tool of the Unitarians, at times generous, yet impulsive and arrogant; but in the novel he appears as a genuine patriot, a man of noble sentiments who condemned a political opponent to death only after a great struggle between his duty and humanitarian instincts.

While Gálvez's re-creation of Buenos Aires of the 1830's in these two novels is chiefly from the point of view of civil strife, he did not neglect the purely social. In *El General Quiroga* life is depicted in the home of the middle-class Lanzas, in that of the wealthy family into which Régulo has married, and in Eldemira's establishment, where gentlemen came to gamble and amuse themselves; and in *El Gaucho* is a very interesting chapter that details the life of women in well-to-do families. Here we learn how they occupied themselves with making their own clothes—sitting meanwhile in oriental fashion on the floor; what refreshments they served when callers came; what pieces they played on the piano; how they amused themselves at window shopping, at card playing, and at dancing.

Following the same loose pattern as *El General Quiroga*, the *Escenas de la Guerra del Paraguay (Scenes from the Paraguayan War)*, which includes three volumes—*Los Caminos de la Muerte (The Paths of Death)*, *Humaitá* and *Jornadas de Agonía (Agony-fraught Marches)*—traces in broad outline the history of the Paraguayan War, which began in 1865, when the Paraguayan dictator Solano López, angered because Argentina refused him permission to cross her territory to attack Brazil and Uruguay with whom he was at war, seized two Argentine gunboats near Corrientes and occupied that city. Argentina then entered the war, and the three countries pledged themselves not to make peace until López was overthrown. That was accomplished only after five years of hard fighting, in which Paraguay lost five-sixths of her population. *Los Caminos de la Muerte* covers the events of the first seven months of the war, including the march northward of the allied forces and the retreat of López from Argentina; *Humaitá* recounts the hardships of the allied march through the jungles and swamps into Paraguay, battles, the cholera epidemic, and finally the capture of the Paraguayan fort Humaitá; and *Jornadas de Agonía* pictures the capture of Asunción and the pursuit of López, who continued to murder and torture his people until his death at the hands of Brazilian soldiers in 1870. In his discussions of the characteristics of the various nationalities that took part in the war, Gálvez shows absolute impartiality: he praises the Paraguayans for their bravery, discipline, and patriotism; and he represents the Brazilians as culturally superior.

Taking part in this vast drama are some dozen and a half historical figures, whose characterization accords in general with history. The most important are President Mitre and

Solano López. The one appears, deservedly, as a brave, honorable gentleman, a great statesman and general. López was proud and cruel; in battle he was brave; in warfare he was crafty; and he possessed in a rare degree the ability to attract men, to read their minds and to bend them to his will. Not until the third volume, in which he is in flight, is he seen spending hours before an image in some church, heeding no one except Madame Lynch, his mistress; driving his people, even his own relatives, ruthlessly before him; and torturing inhumanly anyone he suspected of disloyalty.

Interwoven with the main plot—the sketch of the Paraguayan War—are many fictional episodes, which are concerned, in the main, with members of certain families—in *Los Caminos de la Muerte*, with the wealthy, aristocratic Guevara family of Buenos Aires and the Taboada family of Corrientes, well-to-do but not their social equals. Antonio Guevara, a young idealist, joined the Argentine army at the outbreak of the war, but just before leaving married Dorila Carvajal. Intense were his longings for his virgin bride during that overland march to Corrientes. Although acting as Mitre's secretary, he returned to his company when the fighting began, and just as he was about to be united with his wife, who had come up the river with her parents, he was killed in battle. Quite a different type of man was the uncultured, waspy, sexually promiscuous Jerónimo Del Cerro, an army officer married to Antonio's cultured sister, Florinda. Del Cerro, after being wounded at Corrientes, remained in the home of Rudecindo Taboada, an Argentine partisan, and while there attempted to seduce Rudecindo's wife, who, fascinated by him but fearing for her honor, aided him in escaping from the town. After long wanderings Del Cerro came upon Rudecindo, to whom he boasted falsely of his Corrientes conquest. Convinced that the woman in question was his wife, Rudecindo returned home and stabbed her to death; Del Cerro was killed in a battle in Paraguay. The paths of the Guevaras and the Taboadas crossed again when the Guevaras reached Corrientes and secured quarters in the Taboada home. Pedro Guevara, a physician, also in Mitre's army, fell in love with Paulina Taboada, Rudecindo's sister; but she, on account of his relationship with Del Cerro, refused to listen.

In *Humaitá*, there is, among other fictional episodes, one of Evaristo Sauce, an Argentine officer, who became infatuated with a popular Brazilian widow and lost his life through a jealous rival; and, in the third volume another that reveals the anxiety with which Damasceno Fragoso sought his wife Joaninha, who was unable to escape to Brazil from Asunción when the war began. Running through both novels are threads connected with the lives of members of the Yánez Cienfuegos, a large Paraguayan family of Asunción. The father, having expressed his belief that Paraguay would lose the war, was put to death by López. His wife and two daughters lived in poverty and disgrace but with enough spirit left to hate that tyrant. Another daughter, Ramona, was, with her husband, a Paraguayan army officer, a rabid adherent of López. Of the four sons, Gerardo—who out of hatred for López joined the allies and thereby brought more indignities and persecutions on the family—was eventually killed by his brother Justo, one of the most daring of López's soldiers; Eusebio, a Paraguayan soldier although he hated López personally, became later secretary to Padre Maíz, who tortured and put to death hundreds that López suspected of treason; and Domingo became a Paraguayan soldier at thirteen.

But what distinguishes the *Escenas de la Guerra del Paraguay* is the wealth of material that makes the work a living document of the social life of the period, not only in the allied army, whose amusements and diversions receive as much attention as their military campaigns, but in Buenos Aires, in Corrientes, and in Asunción. In the opening chapter of the first part, Buenos Aires of 1865—with its 50,000 inhabitants, its first streetcars, its theaters, especially the famous Colón at which Italian opera was then being given; with its first important periodical, *La Revista de Buenos Aires*, and that now

well-known daily, *La Nación*—is seen, in spite of the lingering
of certain customs of Spanish and Moorish origin, in spite of
the vogue of romantic literature already out of fashion in other
parts of the world, as a palpitating organism just entering
upon a new stage of growth.

The description of the provincial town Corrientes is one
of the finest bits of writing that Gálvez has done:

> Like a lazy, dreamy Creole woman, Corrientes, a small
> city, at the time, of ten thousand inhabitants, whiled away
> the hours gazing upon the magnificent serenity of the
> Paraná River. It had nothing better in which to occupy
> its time. There were no industries save those of a house-
> hold nature; no business except on a small scale; and no
> intellectual life except that of its primary school, of its
> drowsy convent, and of its meager weekly newspaper.
> Surrounded by magnificent orange groves, gathered up
> under its palm trees, lying in its Paraguayan hammocks,
> Corrientes vegetated in its indolence. During the morning
> there was scarcely any life at all. Then, after a long
> siesta, it came to life late in the afternoon. Its unpaved
> streets were as calm as the desert. At the doors of the
> houses, horses stood saddled. Men in poncho and balloon-
> like trousers, some with their long hair tied with ribbons,
> others with a handkerchief around their necks, went by
> on horseback. The women of the town also rode horse-
> back, decked out in their shawls like bandits' wives, their
> heads tied up with red or yellow hempen cloths, and al-
> ways in the corners of their mouths the stub of a thick
> cigarette rolled up in corn husk. Upperclass people
> scarcely ever went out-of-doors. The old women went
> to church, to attend the masses or "novenas"; the girls
> went to the plaza and the men went to their clubs or
> political gatherings. At night, sweet and aromatic but
> miserably lighted by oil-burning street lamps fastened to
> twisted posts of quebracho wood, Corrientes sighed and
> gazed out upon the serene and starry heavens. Families
> would gather under the eaves of their houses. They drank
> "mate," and the men and the old women smoked corn-

husk-wrapped cigarettes. Sometimes, diffused on the calm air and accompanied by the melancholy guitar, could be heard songs in the Guaraní tongue.

Excellent, too, are the descriptions of the market place and its activity, of the homes and the life within them, and the interpretation of the Guaraní population of Corrientes, which on account of blood ties favored in general Paraguay rather than Argentina.

In *Humaitá* he pictures the Paraguayan capital, Asunción— a typical provincial city with its public buildings and low, squatty houses showing the familiar Spanish red tile roofs and barred windows, grouped around the principal square. Like Corrientes, it is tropical, noisy with the cry of parrots; but its population is not predominantly Guaraní, but Spanish, descendants of colonists from Extremadura and Andalusia. Before the war, Asunción was a lazy, silent, sleepy place, where one killed time smoking, sleeping, and drinking "mate"; where the occupation of the women consisted of weaving and making sweetmeats; where the diversions were gossiping, band concerts, dances; where the monotony of existence was broken only when some stranger arrived from down the river and the people began to wonder what his business was.

In these descriptions and analyses of life of Corrientes and Asunción—written in the late twenties—Gálvez reverts to the provincial cities which had first interested him so keenly and served him as such excellent literary material. It was probably his continued interest in them that led him to his first fictionalized biography—*Vida de Fray Mamerto Esquiú* (*The Life of Fray Mamerto Esquiú*), 1933. Of Fray Mamerto, who suffered no passions of the flesh, in whom there were absent so many of the weaknesses of human nature, who was most austere, almost saintly, it might seem indeed difficult for a novelist to write an interesting biography, but Gálvez accomplished it. The charm of the book is largely the result of a judicious selection of facts and skillful interweaving of background, characterization, and narrative.

Mamerto was born in 1826 of poor but devout parents near Catamarca, in a semi-desert region of bare Andean peaks in the northwestern part of Argentina. But ungrateful soil often produces resolute men, and such was Mamerto, not only in piety but in zeal for learning. At ten he entered the Franciscan order as a novitiate—at the same time that the famous *caudillo* Facundo Quiroga was passing through Catamarca, comments Gálvez. In 1841 he took the final vows and three years later began to teach. Ordained a priest in 1848, he became so favorably known as an orator that he was chosen to deliver, in 1853, the sermon sanctioning the constitution that followed the fall of Rosas—a sermon that made him known throughout the country. During the next eight years of civil strife Fray Mamerto took an active part in both religious and civil affairs. Early in 1862 he was sent to Bolivia, where he remained for ten years—eight of them in Sucre, the Chuquisaca of colonial days, a famous center of culture. There he taught theology in the old seminary, preached, and published a religious periodical. So widely and favorably known had he become that in 1871, during the presidency of Sarmiento, he was offered, but declined, the archbishopric of Buenos Aires; then, as if fearful his resignation might not be accepted, he left Sucre. Traveling by mule across the mountians and second class on the ocean, he preached in Guayaquil, Lima, and other places, returning finally in 1875, after an absence of thirteen years, to his native Catamarca.

The following year he set out for Europe and spent some six months in the Holy City itself, but it was not entirely a happy experience, for ill health had already begun to undermine his constitution. In 1879 he was back in Catamarca, and the next year was consecrated bishop of Córdoba in the Cathedral of Buenos Aires.

A striking picture Gálvez draws of Córdoba at the time Fray Mamerto went there. The clergy had great influence, but it was a clergy "in the Spanish style," one that lived apart from the people, proud, dominating, and uncharitable. Fray

Mamerto, beloved for his sincerity, piety, charity, and mani-
fest disinterestedness, presents a striking contrast to the ecclesiastics he came among. He lived in that uncongenial
atmosphere only until 1884, but his death was genuinely and
widely regretted.

The second biography (1939) that Gálvez produced was
the life of Hipólito Yrigoyen, the man of mystery, twice
president of Argentina. In the lives of these two men Gálvez
exalted there are certain parallels. The mothers of both were
Argentine, while their fathers were Spanish—Mamerto's
a Galician peasant, Hipólito's a Basque laborer, unable to read
and write. In spite of their humble origin, both rose in their
respective fields to high positions. Yrigoyen, as pictured by
Gálvez, was a most singular individual, both psychologically
and in the political influence he commanded. And in some
four hundred pages, Gálvez, as a novelist, attempts to analyze
his character, and, as a historian, to place him in his proper
historical background. The result is that this biography not
only affords an example of Gálvez in his best moments of
character analysis, but is also an animated account of politics
and social conditions in the Argentine from the Rosas period
to 1932. Yet it lacks in general the directness of style that
characterizes the life of Fray Mamerto, and would have benefited by considerable pruning and revision.

The first of its three parts sketches the life of Yrigoyen from
his birth in 1852 in Buenos Aires to his election to the presidency of the republic in 1916. As a prelude is an account of
his mother's family, the Aléns, people of some property but
not of the highest social circles, and their connection with
Rosas. Hipólito's grandfather, a Rosas official, was executed
after the dictator's fall, and the rest of the family lived indoors
as much as possible to avoid attention.

Hipólito received much of his education in the *Colegio de
la América del Sur,* where his uncle, Leandro Alén, a teacher
of marked ability, encouraged him to continue his education,
and later directed his political bent. As a young man, Hipólito

was employed as a copyist in a law office, as a government clerk during Sarmiento's administration, and as a police captain. At this time he began the study of law and became a member of the legislature of the state of Buenos Aires. In 1882 he was appointed to a position in the *Escuela Normal de Maestras.*

Shortly before this he had become interested in the philosophy of Krause, which left an indelible imprint upon him. The influence this philosophy exerted in Spain is analyzed by Gálvez as throwing light on the probable source of Yrigoyen's later political creed:

> The philosophy of Krause appeared in Spain about 1850, having been introduced there from Germany by Julién Sanz del Río. Ten years later it was disseminated in almost all of the universities. It had no small part in the revolution of '68 and in the establishment of the Republic in '72. Its influence lasted until the end of the century. Among its followers were such eminent men as Emilio Castelar, Nicolás Salmerón, and Francisco Pi y Margall, who occupied the presidency of the Republic and were writers and philosophers; Gumersindo de Azcárate and Francisco Giner de los Ríos, teachers of teachers and publicists of exceptional merit; and Don Francisco Canalejas, president of the cabinet of ministers. All were austere and respectable.... They were democrats, they believed in the panacea of free suffrage, and all their lives they went about grave, reserved, and dressed in black.

During the latter part of the eighties Yrigoyen lived austerely on his country estate, analyzing himself and meditating on the wave of corruption, materialism, sensuality, and indifference that had swept over the country. Equally austere was his life in Buenos Aires, where he lived with his Uncle Leandro. His room was Spartan-like in its simplicity, a veritable monk's cell. He went to bed early and got up at dawn; he spent the day in his room reading; he never attended the theater, the clubs, or entertainments of any nature; nor did he drink, smoke, or take coffee. Even in his conversation with Leandro's political friends, he was taciturn.

His active participation in politics dates from 1870 when he joined the "Unión Cívica," a radical party his uncle Leandro had organized to combat the absolutist reactionary government then in control. Soon he became its leader. A sentence from a manifesto he wrote that year—"We overturn a government in order to remove men from positions and replace them with others; we overturn the government in order to return it to the people so that they may reconstruct it in accordance with the national will"—is, according to Gálvez, the essence of its writer's political creed. In the revolutions of 1890, 1893, and 1905 the radicals accomplished little; and, except for Yrigoyen's indomitable energy, the party would probably have ceased to exist. A law passed in 1912 which provided for secret ballot and compulsory voting of all adult males made it at last possible for the radical candidate for the presidency in 1916, Yrigoyen, then aged 64, to be overwhelmingly elected.

At the opening of the second general division of the work Gálvez pauses to describe the man physically and to sum up his mental and moral characteristics:

> In a country of men without fixed principles, he lived according to a few principles. Here where we all change, he never changed. Here where almost all of us are materialists, he was an idealist and a mystic. In the midst of millions of individuals that are indifferent, he had faith and feeling. He renounced the pleasures of this life when all about him were only pleasure seekers or those who desired to be so. He was the only Argentine that never spoke ill of anyone, that never used dirty or obscene language. He was the only one that never looked toward Europe. The opposition between Yrigoyen and those about him was the same as that between an austere man from the country and a luxury-loving city dweller, the same as that between the solitude of the country and the vanities of the city.

Obstinate, taciturn, subjective, lacking in action and in a practical knowledge of life, he was essentially an introvert of the most pronounced type.

In Yrigoyen's first administration, the underprivileged were favored; they received nearly all of the governmental positions, and many laws were enacted in their behalf. But the positions were not intended as sinecures, and the president visited the various offices to see that the work was done. During the World War he insisted on the rights of his country as a neutral nation, but refused to be drawn into the conflict, in spite of sharp criticism from those that favored the allies and demonstrations when Argentine ships were sunk by Germany. Although he was hated by the aristocratic rich who had hitherto enjoyed special privileges, not even his enemies questioned his integrity or honor. A radical in politics, he was not a radical in all that this word generally connotes. While not a practicing Catholic, he believed in God and in the immortality of the soul; and he opposed a divorce law which many hoped to see enacted while he was president. In 1928, when old and childish, he was again elected to the presidency, but became the tool of those about him; and so general was the discontent that a popular uprising in 1932 forced him to resign, and his death soon followed.

As to the place that Yrigoyen will ultimately hold, Gálvez predicts:

> The people, radical or not, will give him a large place in their hearts, a place that they have given to no man of this country, perhaps one that they have not given even to the Independence heroes. For the radicals he will be a symbol and a motto.... The conservatives, the distinguished class, will look upon him with less hatred.... The nationalists ... will regard him for some years as their enemy; but other nationalists will comprehend that if anyone did a work that was essentially nationalistic it was Hipólito Yrigoyen.... His name will always be revered by those of us who believe that the spirit ought to

take precedence over material values, and who hope to see the country free of the foreign clutches that have snatched from it its moral and economic independence.

In addition to these biographical works, Gálvez has written defenses of his own novelistic art and three volumes of essays of an ideological nature—*El Espíritu de Aristocracia*... (*The Spirit of Aristocracy*), 1924, *Este Pueblo necesita*... (*This Nation Needs*...), and *La Argentina en nuestros Libros* (*Argentina in Our Books*), 1934. He also tried his hand at play writing—*Nacha Regules* was presented on the stage in 1924 and *El Hombre de los Ojos azules* (*The Blue-eyed Man*), four years later.

But his seventeen novels and two volumes of short stories, presenting a variety of carefully studied backgrounds, interesting and human characters, some well integrated plots, and an easy style of writing, have given him a high place in contemporary Spanish-American literature. The range of the background he employs is wide. In point of time, he covers the period from 1830 to 1930; in geographical area, a large part of Argentina; and he utilizes thoroughly and realistically the political, social, cultural, and religious history of his country as no other Argentine writer has done. All this he sees and describes impersonally, as would an historian viewing the scene in retrospect, usually at a considerable distance. There is wide divergence, too, in the social levels of the characters he presents, for they range from one extreme to the other. His preference is for men rather than women, although he presents many women; and consistently in the purely fictional works he selects as protagonists weak characters who yield to love, disappointment, social or religious pressure. In his biographies and historical novels, in contrast, noble characters predominate. In his treatment of character psychological analysis enters, but there is little character development; the type is as first presented when the tale is ended. In this respect his work fails to arouse the maximum of interest.

In his technique Gálvez is the product of nineteenth-century models and far more conservative than most of his Spanish-American contemporaries. On some of his plots, especially that of *La Maestra normal*, he expends great care; but others show the influence of a more modern group, for they tend toward formlessness. All are simple in structure and more like the Spanish than the French models Gálvez studied. On the whole his workmanship is superior to his inventive ability.

While the impersonal attitude which Gálvez consistently assumes in his fictional work tends to lessen its emotional appeal, he is unable to absent himself completely from any of the pictures he paints. In the most forceful—*La Maestra normal*—he identifies himself closely with the background, both in point of time and place, and his personal knowledge of and feeling for the region is persistently felt. Here is landscape painting at its best. Personal acquaintance with the individual has a marked influence on his portrait painting, too; Yrigoyen, who stands out most prominently on his canvas, he knew personally both as man and president. It was Gálvez's intention not to betray his own attitudes and preferences, but had he been freer in permitting his feelings expression, the personal note would have given a stronger emotional tone to his work as a whole.

In contrast to some of the writers whose works we shall review, Gálvez devotes far more attention to society than to landscape as a background. In his novels of Buenos Aires—even those in which the psychological element predominates—there is almost no description of the city; instead the emphasis is laid on social groups of various levels, which receive detailed treatment. Aside from his strong historical bent, Gálvez is a sociologist who employs his knowledge of society as a basis for his fiction. Even while he presents an individual, it is the group which that individual represents that is the author's real interest. And the plight of the group he lays bare through a typical individual.

In his work as a whole there is ample evidence that his purpose in writing as set forth clearly in *El Solar de la Raza* continues to actuate him. In all his works one feels his love of his native country; in several his deep sympathy for the provincial city. In the five historical novels and the two biographies is his continued realization of the importance of the "idealism and originality of the past," which alone, he believes, can save his country "without detriment to its material greatness." His portrayal of "the deadening interests that a materialistic conception of life has created" is intended to lead his people back to the calmer, traditional way of life through which Argentina became a great nation. He holds up to admiration some of its great men; some of their great deeds. He seeks to arouse his countrymen to an appreciation of their inheritance; to halt their hasty progress along ill-chosen ways. He tries to turn their attention to the scene about them so that they may eradicate the ugliness.

Gálvez, though not unconcerned with his country's ills, many of which are strikingly pointed out in the great body of his work, is not such a poor novelist as to let the bigotry and static life of the provinces, the materialism and immorality of Buenos Aires, the general lack of a truly religious spirit, of idealism, of patriotism, and of self-discipline overshadow his art. For, in general, these defects are not the main issue in his novels but are incidental and subordinate to the story. Neither does his artistic sense permit him, except indirectly, to suggest solutions or remedies for these conditions. For these he reserves that volume of essays, *Este Pueblo necesita...*, in which he states precisely and logically what he believes his country needs. For Gálvez is not only a good novelist but a truly patriotic citizen.

CHAPTER III

MARIANO AZUELA, PORTRAYER OF
THE MEXICAN REVOLUTION

❀

I F SPANISH AMERICA were divided into four geographical zones based on the prevailing cultural characteristics, it would be the most southern and the most northern that would show the greatest agreement in general. Among the common literary characteristics of Argentina and Mexico are the predominance of novelists, an emphasis on larger forms, and a more serious style. For this reason the Mexican novelist of greatest scope may well take his place beside Gálvez in the galaxy of Spanish-American writers.

Conditions in Mexico in the last decades of the nineteenth century, however, offered some marked contrasts to those in Argentina. The latter had few Indians to offer a serious problem. Its accessibility to Europe and the facilities of communication took the Argentine élite to Europe and brought the European immigrant in numbers to Argentina. As a result, the population of that republic became largely white, and the early interest of Sarmiento in education had raised the standard of literacy above that of any other country of Spanish America. In Mexico, on the other hand, the Indians in large numbers remained almost as serfs on the lands they had earlier worked in a communistic fashion. Much less progress had been made there in the education of the masses, for only a poor beginning of a system of public education had been attempted. As in Argentina there had been a great increase in wealth, a rapid growth of the cities, and considerable cultural advance made between 1870 and the close of the first decade of the twentieth century, but between state and church there was greater enmity; between labor and capital, greater gulfs; and between the social classes, wider differences than in the southern republic.

The revolution that Francisco Madero set on foot in Mexico in 1910 loosed a force that ultimately brought about the complete disruption of the scheme of life that had prevailed there for more than three decades under the government of Porfirio Díaz, who rose to power through military prowess. In time, especially after the assassination of Madero, class hatred came to be the ruling spirit. Throughout the length and breadth of the land, the underprivileged, oppressed and crassly ignorant peasants, rose spontaneously against their wealthy and powerful masters. Moved by idealism and sympathy with the masses, a few men of education and vision attached themselves to revolutionary chieftains in one capacity or another, such as advisers or secretaries. Those of this type who possessed artistic temperaments were impelled, either while the struggle was in progress or later, to interpret the masses in general—for the most part of Indian blood—and particularly to justify the temper that had impelled them to rebel against the conditions under which they lived. While the most aesthetic interpretation of the spirit that moved the indigenous population is to be found in painting, that decade of revolution had a most stimulating effect on Mexican literature and contributed some of its most distinguishing characteristics.

It is prose in a wide variety of forms—history, biography, autobiography, personal memoirs, and fiction[1]—rather than

[1] Among the personal memoirs, *El Aguila y la Serpiente* (*The Eagle and the Serpent*), 1928, ranks high not only for its literary excellence but for its subject matter, especially the characterization of Pancho Villa, whom Luis Guzmán, the author, served as secretary. On the

poetry that embodies the expression and influence of the revolution. But of all the writers inspired by that great social upheaval, the one of greatest scope in point of time is Mariano Azuela, whose successive works cover a period comparable to that of the memoirs of José Vasconcelos. His novels, conceived generally in the heat of conflict before the ultimate outcome is known, have an added interest because each presents the conditions that prevailed at the moment it was written. Those of the first decade of the century, in their portrayal of existing social and political conditions, foreshadow the revolution; those of the second decade, written while fighting was in progress, afford an intimate insight into the psychology of various types affected one way or the other by it; and those of the third and fourth decades, written after the establishment of the new political order, present political and social problems which are its outgrowth.

Of the many writers who have taken the Revolution as their theme, Azuela is the oldest; and his life has been rich in experience and observation. He was born in Lagos de Moreno, in the state of Jalisco, in 1873, of middle-class parents, the

---

same revolutionary leader, Guzmán has recently published an extensive four-volume work, *Las Memorias de Pancho Villa* (*The Memoirs of Pancho Villa*), 1938-40. The most outstanding autobiography today in Spanish-American literature is *Ulises Criollo* (*The Creole Ulysses*), 1936, together with its sequels *La Tormenta* (*The Storm*), *El Desastre* (*The Disaster*), in 1938, and *El Proconsulado* (*The Proconsulate*), 1939, in which José Vasconcelos, while telling with charm and emotion the story of his eventful life, paints a fascinating picture of Mexico from the nineties of the past century to the present day. In pure fiction, Rafael F. Muñoz depicts in short stories, *El feroz Cabecilla* (*The Ferocious Chieftain*), 1928, the pillaging and murdering that was one aspect of the revolution; in longer works, López y Fuentes presents various problems confronting Mexico today, including in *El Indio* (*The Indian*), 1935, that of the indigenous population; and in seven novels, of which *Apuntes de un Lugareño* (*Jottings of A Villager*), 1932, is the first—all of them delightful reading for their intimately personal note and their lyric and rhythmic charm—Rubén Romero, who is himself ever the central figure, touches freely on his connection in his native state, Michoacán, with the revolution.

owners of a small hacienda near that town; and his youth and early manhood were spent in the heyday of the Díaz régime. He received, in spite of the modest circumstances of his parents, a good education, first in Lagos, and later in Guadalajara, where in 1899 he was graduated in medicine; but it is clear, from the tone of his early works, that he himself felt the humbleness of his position in comparison with that of others more favored financially and socially. Guadalajara was a city second only in culture to the national capital, and it was there that Azuela's interest in literature was awakened, that he read extensively and became especially interested in French nineteenth-century fiction, and wrote his first published work —seven short sketches that appeared under the pen name "Beleño" in various issues of *Gil Blas Cómico* (Mexico City) during 1896. Nor did his interest in literature cease after he became a practicing physician, in 1899, in his native Lagos. During the first decade of the new century he published five short stories[2] and three novels—*María Luisa*, 1907, *Los Fracasados* (*The Disillusioned*), 1908, and *Mala Yerba* (*Bad Blood*), 1909.

From these early works it is evident that Azuela was from the outset a friend of the proletarian classes. Further evidence that he was a partisan of the Revolution was his appointment in 1911, after the ascendancy of Madero, as mayor of Lagos, a position he resigned after a few months on account of the political intrigues of Díaz partisans. In the same year he published *Andrés Pérez, Maderista* (*Andrés Pérez, a Madero Partisan*), which treats of certain aspects of the early stages of the Revolution; and the following year another novel, *Sin Amor* (*Without Love*), which makes little reference to contem-

---

[2] "De mi tierra" ("Of My Homeland"), in *El Imparcial*, Mexico, June, 1903; "Víctimas de la Opulencia" ("Victims of Wealth") in *El Defensor del Pueblo*, Lagos, October, 1904; "Lo que se Esfuma" ("In Passing"), in *Ocios Literarios*, Mexico, 1907; "En Derrota" ("In Flight"), in *Kalendas*, Revista mensual de Lagos, 1908; and "Avichuelos negros" ("Black Vultures"), in *Ocios Literarios*, Mexico, 1909.

porary events. In the dramatic period of the Revolution that followed the assassination of Madero in 1913, during which the government was controlled by the former Díaz adherents under the leadership of Huerta until the popular uprising forced him to flee the country, Azuela does not seem to have taken an active part. His activity is more evident in the events that followed—in the struggle for supremacy between the two military chieftains Carranza and Villa. In 1914 it seemed that Villa was destined to become the master of the country, and while *Villistas* were in power in Jalisco, Azuela was state director of public education. Then, early in 1915, when the situation grew more tense, Azuela joined, in the capacity of a surgeon, a band of *Villistas* under the leadership of Julián Medina. After Villa was roundly defeated at Celaya in April, and his fortunes began to wane, Azuela, with a few of Medina's soldiers who were fleeing from Carranza's approaching forces, moved northward, through Aguascalientes and the state of Chihuahua, to El Paso, Texas. It was during this retreat that he conceived and wrote *Los de Abajo* (*The Under-Dogs*), which first appeared serially in the newspaper *El Paso del Norte* (El Paso, Texas) in October, November, and December, 1915. The book attracted little attention for almost a decade but was destined to make him the most outstanding Mexican novelist of his day.

In 1916 Azuela moved to Mexico City, where he has since practiced his two professions, medicine and writing. A series of novelettes, employing the Revolution as a background, followed his establishment there: *Los Caciques* (*The Caciques*), 1917; *Las Moscas* (*Hangers-on*), 1918, which contains also two short stories, "Domitilo quiere ser Diputado" ("Domitilo Aspires to Congress"), and "De como al Fin lloró Juan Pablo" ("Why Juan Pablo Finally Wept"); and *Las Tribulaciones de una Familia decente* (*The Trials of a Genteel Family*), 1918. During the last two decades nine works of a fictional nature have come from his pen: three novelettes—*La Malhora* (*Ill-Fated*), 1923, *El Desquite* (*Tit for Tat*), 1925, and *La Luciér-*

naga (*Firefly*), 1932—all of which portray the low life with
which he as a physician came into contact in the capital; two
fictionalized biographies—the only works of Azuela that do
not deal with his contemporaries—*Pedro Moreno, el Insurgente*
(*Pedro Moreno, the Insurgent*), which appeared as a serial in
El Nacional (1933-34), and *Precursores* (*Forerunners*), 1935;
and five novels that present contemporary social problems:
El Camarada Pantoja (*Comrade Pantoja*), 1937, *San Gabriel
de Valdivias*, 1938, *Regina Landa*, 1939, *Avanzada* (*The
Advance Guard*),1940, and *La nueva Burguesía* (*The New
Bourgeoisie*), 1941. A volume entitled *Teatro* (*Drama*), 1938,
contains "Los de Abajo," "El buho en la Noche" ("The Owl
at Night"), and "Del Llano Hermanos S. en C." ("Llano
Bros., Inc."), which are dramatized forms, by Azuela, of his
celebrated novel of the same name, of *El Desquite*, and of *Los
Caciques*.

While Azuela's youthful sketches are rather puerile, they
reveal his interests and attitude at the time and certain literary
tendencies that are characteristic of his first longer works.
They express first of all a vital concern for the poor and oppressed, for the less favored in the scheme of life that existed
in the Díaz régime. "María Luisa," a sentimental sketch, was
inspired by the sight of a corpse of a beautiful young woman
in the dissecting room of the medical college. The girl had
been a mistress of one of Azuela's fellow students and had become a victim of tuberculosis and drink. "De mi Tierra,"
doubtless based also on observation, is a story of the violation
of a young peasant girl by the owner of the hacienda on which
she lived; and "Avichuelos" attempts to arouse sympathy for
a workman that had contracted tuberculosis in an unsanitary
factory and to express contempt for certain prejudices on the
part of the clergy and of so-called charitable organizations in
church circles. Another story, "En Derrota," in which poetic
style prevails, shows the influence of the *modernista* tendencies of the day. From the narrative point of view, "Lo que se
Espuma," which has a more involved plot, is the most enter-

taining of the five sketches; its milieu, certain aspects of the Guadalajara of Azuela's youth, is also attractive.

As in his sketches, Azuela expresses in his first group of novels his discontent with existing social conditions. While on the whole sentimental, with very little commendable in either plot or characterization, they depict admirably certain types and portray vividly certain aspects of Mexican society of the first decade of the twentieth century. The background in the four novels is varied: student life in Guadalajara in *María Luisa;* small town life in *Los Fracasados* and *Sin Amor;* and life on a country estate in *Mala Yerba.*

María Luisa, which Azuela developed into a novel from his early sketch, centers about a beautiful young woman who, as the story opens, was debating whether she would continue her humdrum existence in a factory or become the mistress of Pancho, a young medical student. A quarrel with her mother forced the issue. Then followed the same old story. At first life was idyllic for the two. But Pancho was poor; and after tiring of Luisa, he began to neglect her for another girl, Esther. Jealous, María Luisa sought forgetfulness in drink; when Pancho abandoned her altogether, she resorted to prostitution. Drink and disease led to her death in the very hospital where Pancho was an interne.

Whatever charm this novelette has lies outside of the commonplace story of seduction, which fails to arouse pity. Of greater artistic worth are the interlarded essays that portray certain aspects of life in Guadalajara: the two boarding-houses, one for medical students where there was much drinking and gambling, and one for theological students which was pervaded with an air of piety; the dance at Esther's house; and the diversions on a picnic at La Barranca and on a Sunday afternoon excursion to the Alameda. Also well done are the portraits of certain social types—María Luisa's mother, who kept a boarding-house; her old cousin, the falsely pious Doña Juana; Esther and her mother, somewhat light of virtue; and their protector Don Pedro. Not less interesting is the piquant dialogue, Azuela's principal stylistic forte, in which these personages express themselves. Nevertheless the work, done at the outset of his career, presents the chief weaknesses of Azuela as a novelist—his inability to tell an interesting and well-balanced story, and to integrate harmoniously the various elements of which fiction consists.

Likewise in *Los Fracasados* Azuela was less concerned with telling a story than with exposing the iniquity of certain inhabitants of Alamos, which has been identified with his native Lagos. The folk of Alamos of some thirty-odd years ago that are mirrored in this book are unforgettable—Dr. Caracas, the wit of the town; the landed proprietor Don Agapito Rodríguez, officious but ignorant; intriguing lawyers; priests, some worldly and others deadly serious; and office holders who indulge in endless literary discussions while humble people wait in vain for an interview. All come in for a good share of satire, especially Don Agapito and his family, who appear somewhat in the rôle of the newly well-to-do. Selfish, superstitiously devout, cruel at heart, lacking in true charity, they typify in every respect the materialistic bourgeoisie. There also lived with this family, but outside of its inner circle, the lovable and cultured Consuelo, whom Agapito, thinking her one of his natural daughters, had taken into his household in spite of his wife's hatred for her. But Consuelo was in reality the daughter of a priest who had lived in the town since his youth.

The setting in which the characters move, the town of Alamos, is developed fully from every angle. Even in the purely descriptive passages, for which Azuela's fiction is in general not remarkable, *Los Fracasados* is admirable. The natural scenery about the town at different hours of the day and in varying circumstances is portrayed, as are more restricted locales, such as the sitting-room in the home of Don Agapito. The social background itself, the most distinctive element in the book, is attained through a series of essays in which provincial life—with all of its foibles, jealousies, hatreds, and bickerings—is satirically but effectively pilloried. One of these essays describes a gathering of friends, at the home of the Rodríguez family, to welcome them on their return from a visit to Mexico City and to witness the unpacking of a new set of chinaware. The naïve remarks of the wife about the capital and what she had done there reveal her vanity, ignorance, and provinciality; and the tongue-lashing she gave Consuelo for accidentally breaking a dish betrays the baseness of her nature. Two other chapters, too, almost entities within themselves, are excellent for their insight into the social life of the town and the character of the townsfolk. One describes most effectively a dinner party at the Rodríguez home, attended by the élite, to honor a young priest, one of Agapito's protégés, on his elevation to the priesthood—the eating and drinking; the amusing remarks of Agapito and his wife that reveal their lack of culture; the piano performance by their daughter who had no feeling for music; and the conversations, banterings, and disputes among the guests. Equally vivid is the description of a great ball during the carnival season with the officious Agapito in charge of the refreshments, the women bedecked in all their finery, and the men completely ill-at-ease in their dress suits.

In all this detail, sight is often lost of the visionary and unselfish Reséndez, the protagonist who voices the ideas and sentiments of Azuela himself. As a young lawyer filling a secretarial post in the city, he saw at every turn the corruption of political officeholders, the prostitution of the courts, the abuse of authority, and the injustice to the defenseless. Although not rabidly anti-clerical, he believed that "under cover of all religions there were to be found two classes of people: those that exploited, and those that let themselves be exploited." Bold in doing what he considered right, Reséndez soon made enemies who brought about his dismissal. Disheartened, he went to Don Agapito's house with the hope of seeing Consuelo, for they had fallen deeply in love; instead he had an argument with Don Agapito and was wounded.

Some days later, he departed from Alamos, dejected but hoping still to find Consuelo, who had meanwhile disappeared from the town.

While *Los Fracasados* lacks much as a novel from a technical and artistic point of view, it is significant in that it portrays the intolerable conditions in a Mexican town that gave rise to the brutality of the underlings when they rose a few years later against their masters. The pessimistic tone found not only here but consistently in most of Azuela's novels, evidently voices his own attitude. How well a single incident illustrates this! The first day that Reséndez was able to be up after being wounded, he observed from his window that a statue to Juárez had been erected in a nearby park. While pondering over the irony of a statue to Juárez in a town as religiously fanatic as Alamos, he heard a child ask one of the crowd of Indians who had gathered about the new statue who Juárez was, and another reply that he was doubtless a great defender of the church. One day, he reflected bitterly, those Indians were shouting for Juárez and the next they were committing atrocities in the name of religion.

Also set in a small town is another thesis novel, *Sin Amor*, 1912, which portrays more pleasingly the same bourgeoise society. The bare mention of the new government under Madero suggests that no radical change had as yet occurred in Mexican social life. The well-developed narrative is decidedly a source of interest; the protagonist, a young woman, in comparison with Azuela's other characters who are generally of one fiber, is more complex; and the milieu, while amply set forth, is not overdone.

Ana María Romero, as we see her in the opening chapter of the book, is young, sensitive, well-educated, and courted by Ramón Torralba, the richest, and, therefore, the most sought-after young man in the town. The story then drops back to her antecedents. She was the daughter of Lidia Delgado, whose mother had kept a small shop. Poor but ambitious, Lidia had made the best marriage possible, and when her husband died he left her well-off, the owner of a small business. Iron-willed, Lidia directed all of her efforts toward giving her daughter every advantage and making her an equal of the best in the town. Not entirely without snubbings and opposition, Ana María attended the most select school, and in time its socially élite admitted her into their circle. To the detriment of her business, Lidia moved out of the shabby, shop-keeping district where she had always lived to a more aristocratic section; and when the richest girls went to an expensive school in Mexico City, Lidia contrived to send Ana María with them. Her schooling over, nothing remained but to make a good marriage, and that seemed in sight. To the untold anguish of Lidia, all did not go well during the courtship, for Ana María's preference was not Ramón, who was coarse and given to drink, but another young fellow, Enrique Ponce, who was attracted to her. As Ana María's coldness only inflamed him the more, Ramón finally married her; and Lidia, consequently, realized the ambition of her life.

From this point on the chief interest is the transformation in the character of Ana María. After her marriage, although she was discontented and unhappy, she remained true to Ramón. He loved her, too, but soon resorted to his old ways and, in time, became a confirmed drunkard; she lost her beauty and became fat and sloppy. Even more striking was the spiritual change in her; abandoning whatever ideals she had as a girl, she became, finally, a veritable Torralba, as sordid, as materialistic, as hypocritical as Ramón's old mother herself. A contrast to the main plot is presented by the subplot, which concerns the poor Enrique Ponce and his cousin Julia, who married for love and thereby found happiness—thus supporting Azuela's thesis that there are values in life greater than the possession of money.

In *Sin Amor* there is less portrayal, for their own sake, of manners and customs than in *Los Fracasados*, yet the philosophy of life of the social group common to both the novels— the middle-class folk of a fair degree of culture—is effectively revealed. One senses the great gulf between those that have and those that have not; the resentment of the latter toward the former; and the scorn of the wealthy for the poor. Both the men and the women are represented as uncharitable and mercenary; the latter are hypocritical, sharp of tongue, backbiting; and the men, who spend most of their time in the public bars and houses of prostitution, are debauched. Some of the minor figures embody in a high degree vices that are more or less characteristic of the entire social group: Lidia, who instilled mercenary ideas into Ana María; Don Salustiano, the falsely pious money-lender and miser; and Escolástica Pérez, a type of Mexican bluestocking who desired to reform society, but who deceived her husband and was fond of drink.

The accuracy of the settings of both these novels shows that Azuela's knowledge of small town life resulted from first-hand observation. Equally intimate was his acquaintance with rural folk, with whom he had come in contact in his child-hood on his father's hacienda near Lagos. It is from these, on the eve of the Revolution, that he chose his characters for *Mala Yerba,* 1909.

The lurid narrative centers about Marcela Fuentes, of humble stock, but possessed of charms irresistible to men. Her grandfather, with whom she made her home, had long been a trusted servant of the Andrade family, on whose estate they lived. She was in turn the mistress of the weak and degenerate Julián Andrade, of a North American engineer, and of Gertrudis, caretaker of Julián's race horses. Julián, who had already killed a peon that dared to look at Marcela, was by no means satisfied with their relations; Marcela gave herself physically to him, but refused him either love or esteem. Gertrudis, blind to her indiscretions, would have married her; instead she went to live in a neighboring village with the engineer. In his absence, Marcela again bestowed her favors on Gertrudis and then began a flirtation with Julián, who had by no means given her up. The caretaker was disposed of by one of Julián's tenants, whose own dead body, shortly after, indicated he had known too much. When Julián then rushed to Marcela, there arose within her at the sight of him such a feeling of revulsion that she lurched toward him, dagger in hand. Julián snatched it from her and stabbed her to death.

The most distinctive feature of the book is the excellent interpretation of the two types of people that it presents: the landed proprietors and the peasants on their estates. The former are the Andrades, descendants of bandits who had acquired large tracts of land and settled down like feudal lords, a law unto themselves. Heavy drinkers, ignorant and domineering, they were culturally not above their tenants. Nor are the peasants as a class portrayed idealistically. Although certain individuals are admirable, the majority are cringing cowards. At heart they hated Julián, but they fawned upon him; and to obtain his favor nothing was too base for some of them.

Marcela is the most interesting of the characters of her class; in her, there is a diversity of traits. She is a coquette; she has no sense of sex morality; but she can feel sincere remorse. At times impassive to wrong, at others she exhibits a determination to effect justice. Even with her servility toward Julián, her spirit is by no means entirely broken. When Azuela, in analyzing her feeling toward Andrade, says, "Her brain seethes and trembles with all the hatred that has accumulated within the enslaved race from which she sprang," he reveals a resentment that was smoldering, ready to burst into flames, in the entire peasant population of the country.

In brief but effective passages, Azuela throws in descriptions of the countryside itself, with its varying shades of color: the pasture lands; the fields of growing grain; and the wooded stretches, dotted with *huizaches*, mesquites, and cacti. In the dialogue, in which as always he excels, the peasants speak in colloquial language. Various phases of the social life of the region—the corrupt practices of the local courts, the weekly rationing of the peasants on the hacienda, funeral customs, the pastimes at the country taverns, and such diversions as the rodeo and the horse race—all enter into the picture.

In these stories Azuela has sketched the background of the Revolution; in the novelettes and short stories of the next decade, in which the portrayal of groups or of types rather than of individuals is also characteristic, he is to portray the Revolution itself. The first of these, *Andrés Pérez, Maderista*, gives a picture of life on an hacienda when the Revolution was brewing, and analyzes the motives of some of the participants. In the capital, despite its brilliant display of wealth, there was an ominous undercurrent; student riots were frequent and laborers received only thirty-seven cents a day. Yet the revolt under Madero in the northern part of the country was not regarded seriously by anyone, least of all by Andrés Pérez, reporter on *El Globo*, a partisan sheet of the Díaz government, when he accepted the invitation of his friend, Antonio Reyes, to spend several weeks on his hacienda near Villalobos. There the revolt proved an actuality, with Reyes and his wife in full sympathy with it.

At first both viewed Pérez with suspicion because of his disparaging remarks about Madero; but when local authorities accused him of being a revolutionist, they and their peons, thinking him a Madero agent, in spite of his protests to the contrary, placed themselves at his disposition. Especially friendly was the overseer, Vicente, who entrusted to Pérez a large sum of money. Among the zealous adherents of the Díaz government in the neighborhood was a Colonel Hernández, then in possession of property which had belonged to Vicente's family. The situation shortly became tense. Just as Pérez was about to escape to the United States, he was jailed. Then a battle occurred between the government forces and the *Maderistas*, in which the latter were victorious but Reyes was killed. Liberated from jail, Pérez was loudly acclaimed a patriot, only to discover that Colonel, now General, Hernández had become the leader of the revolutionists and ordered the execution of Vicente. Disgusted, Pérez snatched off the Madero insignia and made his way toward the train for Mexico City; but on passing the house where Reyes' widow was—for he was in love with her and had already quarreled with Hernández over her—he stopped, and then went in.

At this point the rather feuilletonistic story ends. Certain details are improbable, and the infatuation of Pérez for María is entirely out of key with the fundamental theme. The stir and confusion of the first armed struggles is well portrayed, and the varying motives of the *Maderistas* effectively contrasted—Reyes, honest and altruistic; Vicente, who had been robbed of his property; and Hernández, concerned only with securing high rank with the successful faction.

Like Colonel Hernández, the Llanos, in *Los Caciques*—a novelette of small-town capitalists, clerks, and shopkeepers—allied themselves with the *Maderistas* and thereby nullified all reform. The Llanos family—Ignacio and Bernabé, capitalists; their brother Jeremías, a priest; and Teresa, their sister, director of the local organized charity—were the "*caciques*" who dominated every phase of life in the town. A hardfisted lot were the four, but Ignacio especially was heartless and unscrupulous. Juan Viñas, owner of a small shop, undertook to erect a model apartment building and mortgaged his property to Ignacio to secure money; when he tried to get an additional loan, Ignacio was obdurate. Overworked and worried, Viñas fell ill, and Ignacio foreclosed on his holdings.

Another thread of the narrative concerns Rodríguez, one of Ignacio's clerks, who was in love with Viñas' daughter, Esperanza. Humanitarian in his principles, he had fruitlessly endeavored to warn the simple and trusting Viñas in regard to Ignacio. Nor was he blind to the political situation, for he saw quite clearly that the *caciques* throughout the country had allied themselves with Madero only to be in a better position to defeat his intended reforms; but when he stated as much to the Madero club of the town, he was instantly dismissed by his employer. Then came the assassination of Madero. Feeling that they were completely in the saddle again, the Llanos set to work, with police from Mexico City, to rid the town of all objectionables; among the first to be murdered was Rodríguez. But the rule of the Llanos did not long endure, for they themselves had to flee when Villa's soldiers arrived. Then it was that Juan Viñas' children set fire with their own hands to an imposing building lately completed by the Llanos family.

The pessimism with which *Los Caciques* is imbued—its sense of despair for the future—is that of Azuela when he wrote it. Yet, through the injustice that it lays bare, the book affords a vindication, in a measure, of those who committed the most shocking atrocities against the lives and property of the privileged classes when the Revolution broke. From the standpoint of good storytelling, not much can be said for *Los Caciques*; it lacks singleness of purpose and coherence. It does however present many scenes which throw light on the thoughts and attitudes of the shopkeeping and other middle-class elements in a small Mexican town. Types, too, of this society are excellently drawn: the covetous Ignacio, the worldly Father Jeremías, the self-sacrificing Rodríguez, and Juan Viñas, who took his cue in all matters from the Llanos.

It is the absence of idealism or principles in politicians and government employees that Azuela satirizes in *Las Moscas* and *Domitilo quiere ser Diputado*. In the interval that had elapsed between his last novel and these stories, the Revolution had progressed through various phases. Together, Villa and Carranza had brought about Huerta's downfall; but a breach had occurred between them, and they were now at each other's throats. Villa fled northward, definitely defeated. Certain particulars of that flight form the basis of *Las Moscas*. Fearing destruction at the hands of Carranza, both Villa's soldiers and the civil population hurried to entrain for the north. Azuela chooses certain individuals from this motley throng, and has them reveal through their own words their inner selves. Among them are General Malacara, a more zealous worshiper of Venus and Bacchus than of Mars; the Reyes Telles family, Don Sinforoso, and Donaciano Ríos, all government employees who had held office successively under Porfirio Díaz, Madero, Huerta, and Villa. The most parasitical and least sincere are the Reyes Telles—Marta and her two grown children, Matilde and Rubén—who, once they realized that Villa's sun had set, began to plan to ingratiate themselves with Carranza.

A wilier politician never lived than Don Serapio Alvaradejo, in *Domitilo quiere ser Diputado,* whose guiding principle in his long and successful career in Perón had been to adapt himself to circumstances. His first position as town treasurer resulted from youthful oratorical efforts in praise of Porfirio Díaz; a period of intense piety brought papal approval for a school in Perón; and in the time of Madero, his fanatical religious convictions led to still higher political preferment. Although Don Serapio had saved Perón from the various redeemers of the country, from Madero to the "First Chief" (Carranza), he was, when the story opens, in trouble with his fellow citizens. A certain Carrancista general, Xicotencatl Robespierre Cebollino, from whom Don Serapio desired certain favors, had demanded that the town raise a large sum of money; and its principal citizens, each of whom had been assessed according to his means, began to make life miserable for Don Serapio by accusing him of connivance. Besides, an anonymous writer had threatened to expose him to the General. Serapio concluded, and rightly, that his error consisted of having sent a telegram of congratulations to Huerta at the time of his coup d'état. But the General's record proved no better; for when drunk, he admitted publicly that he, too, had served Huerta and that, as an official under Díaz, he had hanged more *Maderistas* than Huerta, Blanquet and Urrutia together!

From a literary standpoint, these two sketches deserve a high place in Azuela's works. Essays rather than short stories, their title page rightfully describes them as "scenes and sketches of the Revolution," but it is their theme, not their narrative element, that is important. The technique employed is loose and discursive; the satire is keen and clever; but, without abuse or sentimentality, Azuela lets his characters condemn themselves through their own words and actions—lets them reveal their lack of principles or of loyalty to either party or leader, once their personal interests are endangered. It is this aspect of the Mexican Revolution that Azuela makes plain. Both sketches contain, too, some excellent descriptive passages. Very effective in *Las Moscas* is the scene at the railway station crowded with Villa's soldiers and his adherents— all in full flight before the approaching "Carrancistas." Not only can one see them rushing about trying to board a train, but the puffing of the engines, the clanging of bells, the screeching of whistles, and the switching of the cars is almost audible. Illustrative, too, of Azuela's artistic use of language are the concluding paragraphs, in which Villa, in all his strength, appears at the rear door of a Pullman car, on his retreat northward, just at the moment of a glorious sunset, which symbolizes the setting of his power and glory.

Politicians and government employees, as can be inferred from Azuela's works, felt the effect of the Revolution less than another class, the landed proprietors, many of whom were adherents of Huerta, in whom they saw a restoration of the Díaz government. But when opposition to him sprang up, and bands under Carranza, Villa, Obregón, and others began to pillage the country at large, many of these *hacendados* had to abandon their estates and take refuge in Mexico City. It is the trials of one of these families, the Vázquez Prado, that are recounted in Azuela's *Las Tribulaciones de una Familia decente*. Owners of a large estate near Zacatecas, they left it about the time of the fall of Huerta, to seek refuge in the national capital.

The members of this family are clearly drawn. The mother, Agustinita, had brought to the family their wealth; like many of the characters that Azuela satirizes, she favored the political chieftain through whom she could profit most. Procopio, her penniless husband, she considered of little consequence; yet for the saneness of his judgment, his honesty and sincerity, he was admirable. Two sons, Francisco José and César, were pampered, neurotic, incapable individuals unwilling to adjust themselves to any change that required effort; a daughter, Berta, was married to Pascual, a successful young lawyer.

While the Vázquez Prados, who did not have much ready money, were feeling the pinch of poverty in Mexico City, Pascual was ingratiating himself with Carranza; eventually he came to be highly favored by that chieftain. He and Berta then lived in luxury, but her family were in actual want. He did furnish them money, but it was on outrageous terms and with the intention of eventually taking over their Zacatecas property. Procopio vainly denounced him; but not until Pascual turned his back on them did Agustinita realize what a heartless rascal he was; and only slowly did she come to appreciate the genuine worth of her husband, who, through a position with a commercial establishment, was enabled to supply their necessities. Both men met death about the same time; the former, of a heart attack; the latter, in a brawl with his fellow "Carrancistas."

This novel will probably live, not for its story or its character delineation, although they are to be counted among Azuela's best, but for its depiction of certain phases of life in Mexico City in those unsettled years following the downfall of Huerta—the desperate condition of those formerly wealthy; the invasion of the capital by savage hordes; the rise of Villa to power; and finally the corruption and excesses of the Carranza régime. The novel voices one of Azuela's best messages —his praise of labor; for in individuals like Procopio, he sees the only salvation for such people as the Vázquez Prado.

Of all of his works, the book that carried his name beyond the confines of the Spanish-reading world is *Los de Abajo*. The period in which it is laid—two very dramatic years of the Revolutionary struggle—is itself one of the factors that contributed to its general popularity.

The story begins early in 1913, after Huerta had come into power, and traces the career of Demetrio Macías, then living with his wife and young child on a small farm he owned near Juchipila, Zacatecas. Although poor, Demetrio had dared to arouse the enmity of the *cacique* Don Mónico: as a result, he and his family had to flee and their hut was burned. After placing his wife and child in safety, Demetrio took refuge in the mountains with some twenty-five men who acknowledged him as leader. All were ignorant and more or less criminal, but united by a common bond—the hatred of the Federals, Huerta's soldiers. Although poorly armed, the band ambushed a far superior number of Federals and almost annihilated them. In the fight Demetrio was wounded, but the following day his men carried him "over bold and rocky plateaus and up steep slopes," until at dusk they reached a small settlement— a "few grass-thatched huts, scattered along the banks of a stream, in the midst of patches of corn and beans that were just coming up."

While tarrying there so that Demetrio's wound might heal, they took prisoner a certain Luis Cervantes, who was in sym- pathy with the Revolution and had deserted the Federals to join this band. A student of medicine, Cervantes cured Deme- trio's wound and, despite their prejudice against him, finally won the confidence and esteem of the men. With a far wider vision than his comrades, Cervantes endeavored to make them see that their problem was not a local one, that Demetrio's enemy was not just the *cacique* Don Mónico but the institu- tion in general that bred such *caciques;* and he advised them to move northward at once and unite with General Nátera's army.

Demetrio did move northward, fighting and defeating the Federals, and robbing and pillaging the towns, through Tepic as far as Fresnillo, where he joined Nátera. Honored by him with the rank of Colonel, Demetrio, with Villa and other gen- erals, had a hand in the siege and capture of Zacatecas.

Then followed the sacking of the picturesque city perched on the mountainside, with all its accompanying horrors and the ruthless destruction of everything that suggested culture or refinement. Demetrio was made a general and many sought admittance to his band. Among them were La Pintada—a bold, shameless woman who sought to win him for herself—and the vile Margarito, astute and wantonly cruel.

Again Demetrio and his band set out—this time in the direction of his former home, murdering and pillaging as they went. In Moyahua they burned the house of Don Mónico, his long-time enemy. Masters now where they had formerly played a very humble rôle, they whiled away their days at the public bar. To please Demetrio, Cervantes lured away from her home a young peasant girl, Camila, who had fallen in love with him.

Meanwhile the victorious revolutionists had split into factions—one favoring Carranza; the other, Villa—and were now fighting each other. Again there was activity for Demetrio, who proceeded with Camila and his band southward to Jalisco to fight Pascual Orozco. After sacking Tepaptitlán, they went to Cuquío, where the ferocious and jealous La Pintada stabbed Camila to death. Here Demetrio left his men while he, Cervantes, and a few others went to Aguascalientes where the national convention was being held. While the delegates were deeply engrossed in political chicanery, Demetrio and his band passed their time outside in carousals and displays of lawlessness.

There is a lapse in the story until May of the following year; then a letter from Cervantes reveals that he had left the band and was a practicing physician in El Paso, Texas. Demetrio and his men were back, not far from their old home, Juchipila. The region they were marching through had been stripped bare, and at their approach even the natives fled. It was then that Demetrio learned that his chieftain Villa had been definitely defeated. The men themselves were already disgruntled, and when they reached Juchipila, they found that it, too, had been sacked and burned, just as all the other towns they had passed through. Although Demetrio's wife begged him to give up his roving life and remain at home, he was soon off again—this time to pursue a band of Carrancistas in the neighborhood. But fate willed it that he and his men, in the very pass where two years before they had ambushed the Federals, should be trapped and cut to pieces.

Some nine years passed after the serial publication of this novel before its genuine worth was recognized, even in Mexico. Then, not only there but in the entire Spanish world, it was unanimously conceded to be the highest literary expression that the Revolution had inspired. Within the next decade it had been translated into all important languages of the world, and was rated as a classic. That it will continue to hold this esteem is more than probable, for its masterly interpretation of a certain phase of the Revolution combined with its literary excellence insure it a permanent place in literature. Among the qualities which contribute to its excellence is its intense and varied emotive power, for while the author arouses pity for the downtrodden peasants, he also horrifies the reader with the crimes that some of them, in their ignorance and bestiality, commit. Then, too, *Los de Abajo*, which was conceived and largely written in a period of great despair in the author's own life, is lyric in its expression of pessimism and hopelessness over the situation that existed in his country. Besides, the book is in general poetic rather than either historical or realistic. For while many of the incidents were doubtless suggested to Azuela when he was a physician in the Villista band, while he knew intimately the class of people from which he drew his characters, his creative imagination imparts to both character and incident a vividness transcending the mere realistic. This faculty also appears in his treatment of certain aspects of nature, which he himself had observed at first hand while fleeing with the remnants of the Villista band. With a few strokes he could paint the "sierras" of Jalisco as he, a revolutionist, saw them:

> The sun was bathing the plateau in a lake of gold. Down toward the gorge could be seen cliffs cut as smooth as a slice of bread; protuberances that bristled like fantastic African heads; *petayo* bushes like the stiff-jointed fingers of a colossus; trees that extended downward to-

ward the bottom of the abyss. And amid the arid rocks and the dry branches, the roses of Saint John whitened like a blanched offering to the sun that was beginning to spin out its threads of gold from rock to rock.

A further poetic charm of *Los de Abajo* is to be found in the language itself, which, despite its simplicity, its short and elliptical periods, its predominantly colloquial or vulgar tone, is decidedly rhythmical.

The characteristic that distinguishes Azuela as a literary artist in *Los de Abajo*, both in regard to the work as a whole and to its component parts, is his mastery of the art of selection and condensation. This method, whether he is describing nature, persons, or the man-made world, is to emphasize a few well-chosen characteristics concerning each. In Demetrio's *jacal* "a tallow candle lighted the one little room. In one corner lay a yoke, a plow, a goad, and other implements used in farming. Hanging by cords from the ceiling was a mould for adobe bricks, which served as a bed, and on some coarse cotton material and discolored rags a child was sleeping." Demetrio himself was "tall and vigorous; his face, a bright reddish color, without a single hair of beard; and he wore a shirt and trousers of coarse cotton cloth, a wide-brimmed straw hat, and rough sandals."

Nature is depicted briefly but with much imagination:

> The ridges of the mountain chain stretch out like drowsy monsters, with angular spinal columns; the hills look like the heads of immense Aztec idols, with the faces of giants, with awe-inspiring and grotesque grimaces, which at one time arouse a smile and at others inspire a vague fear, something like the presentiment of a mystery.

Within the various scenes or sketches that compose the story, Azuela compresses into a short paragraph incidents of a narrative nature that other writers would treat far more extensively. Here, for instance, is an incident of the closing weeks of Demetrio's revolutionary career:

Closing up the rear-guard, Demetrio and Camila came marching along; she, trembling, her lips white and dry; he, in a bad humor, on account of the monotony of the affair. Not a sign of Orozco and his men, and consequently no battle. Only a few Federal soldiers scattered about, and a poor devil of a priest with a few hundred deluded followers, under the ancient banner of "Religion and Rights." The priest continued swaying, as he hung from a mesquite tree, and from him there trickled off a rivulet of dead, each one of whom bore upon his chest a diminutive shield of woolen material and the words: "Stop! The Sacred Heart of Jesus is with me!"

While the language is poetic, there is certainly no idealization of the characters, who reveal themselves for the most part by what they say. Camila is the only one of them in whom human kindness predominates. The antithesis of all she stands for is the veritable she-devil La Pintada. Neither Demetrio nor any one of the grossly uncultured peasants that gathered about him near Juchipila was stirred by any patriotic motive. Nearly every one of them, on the contrary, had seized the opportunity to join the band on account of some difficulty in which he had already become involved in the community. Demetrio had incurred the enmity of the *cacique* of the neighborhood; Anastasio had killed an officer; Venancio had poisoned his sweetheart; and Margarito, who joined the band after the storming of Zacatecas and surpassed them all in downright cruelty, was a former jailbird. Less criminal than the others, Demetrio and Anastasio would have liked to be at home again and at work on the small farms they owned. The majority of the band, on the other hand, was interested only in the robbing and pillaging, for, as one commented, more could be gained in a few months during a revolution than could even be hoped for in a lifetime of peace. But, in the end, all were doomed to disappointment. Soon there was nothing left to rob, and in Demetrio's band newcomers ultimately held the important places. Anastasio—like the ignorant Juan Pablo, in the sketch "De cómo al fin lloró Juan Pablo," who had fought bravely and could not comprehend why others who had done nothing should reap the fruits of the Revolution— began to grumble when ex-Federals, their former enemies, superseded old revolutionists. Even Cervantes, at first a passionate partisan of the Revolution, through which he desired for the underprivileged ultimate benefits of which they had no conception, eventually deserted the cause to establish himself as a doctor in El Paso. Obeying not reason but an inner urge to push on, to encourage his men, Demetrio, who cared nothing for wealth, who cared for nothing more than physical gratifications, was the only one steadfast.

Certain stylistic qualities that distinguish *Los de Abajo* as a work of art—the fresh and striking imagery in regard to nature, the elliptical and suggestive, rather than direct, manner of narration, which makes heavy demands on the reader's imagination and factual knowledge—are often carried to the point of exaggeration in his next two novelettes, *La Malhora* and *El Desquite*, and in a longer work, *La Luciérnaga*, all of which portray some aspect of the Mexican society produced by the Revolution. Another common feature of these works is the central figure debauched by alcohol; besides they all reflect certain observations on Azuela's part as a physician in Mexico City in regard to abnormal and degenerate individuals.

Such was Altagracia, an addict of pulque and marihuana at the age of fifteen, to whom her associates of the underworld had given the sobriquet of "La Malhora." After she was deserted and her father killed by her lover Marcelo, also an habitué of the underworld, she swore vengeance. In this she was aided by Epigmenio, a young fellow in love with La Tapatía, a woman who kept a food stand in a pulque shop. But Marcelo, warned of his danger, broke into Epigmenio's butcher shop, murdered him, and brutally wounded La Malhora. Restored to health by a queer doctor and his charitable wife, and separated from her former associates, she became a decent individual. Then one day, after leading a very exemplary life for five years in the home of three devout women, she and her old rival, La Tapatía, met as they were coming from mass, and the result was a fight. When Altagracia returned home after the encounter and found the door locked, instead of knocking, she made a fatal decision and rushed off to her former haunts. The signs on the shops of La Tapatía and Marcelo awoke afresh all her old madness. She resumed her life of debauchery, but found no peace until she killed them both, and thus fulfilled the prophecy of the doctor—that the hatred that burned in her soul could be quenched only by blood.

Sordid characters and melodramatic incidents also characterize *El Desquite*. The central figure is Lupe López, who, following her mother's advice, gave up Martín, a poor student she loved, to marry the newly rich and profligate Blas, who was below her socially. Dissimilar in tastes, they were not happy, and there was no offspring from the marriage—a fact very disconcerting to Lupe's mother, who desired that nothing stand in the way of her daughter's inheriting Blas' fortune. Lupe, however, reared as her own a bastard half-brother of her husband, Ricardo by name. Later when the boy realized that she stood between him and a fortune, he tried to prejudice Blas against her. Instead, she succeeded in dominating completely her drunken husband and hastened his end by becoming his drinking companion. When accused of the death of her husband, she was successfully defended by her former sweetheart, Martín, now a prosperous lawyer. The two were then married, but too late for their happiness; for Martín, no longer young, was cold and calculating; and Lupe was a confirmed dipsomaniac.

Drink is again the theme in *La Luciérnaga*. The very violent collision of an autobus and a streetcar in Mexico City furnishes the owner of the autobus, Dionisio Bermejillo, good reason for drinking himself into a state of intoxication. The thoughts that passed through his befuddled brain reveal to the reader in a measure the man and his past. After he and his brother José

María had divided an inheritance between them, he had come to Mexico City from Cieneguilla to establish himself in business. Of a trusting nature, he had lost his money first to one trickster and then another; the demolition of his autobus was the last of a number of ill-fated business undertakings. His wife, Conchita, patient and hopeful, did what she could in the face of adverse circumstances. Their oldest daughter, adapting herself to the ways of the capital, secured employment from one who looked with favor on her. Desperate, Dionisio appealed to his brother in Cieneguilla for money, but no answer came.

To José María is devoted at least a fourth of the book, with emphasis on the depiction of his state of mind after receiving Dionisio's letter. Still in his thirties but in the last stages of tuberculosis, superstitious and devoutly religious, the incarnation of miserliness, José María was unwilling either to give his money to the Church or to aid Dionisio.

After the miser finally died and Dionisio—by fair means or foul—came into possession of his brother's hoard, he opened a shop in Mexico City; but fines for the violation of all kinds of city ordinances disheartened him. Next, he associated himself with La Generala in a pulque shop that for a time brought a good income but turned him gradually into a confirmed drunkard and a marihuana addict who associated with the criminal class and neglected his family. When one of the children died, Conchita took the rest of them back to her native Cieneguilla, where her upright conduct made her respected by the town. But when she read in the newspaper that Dionisio had been gravely wounded, she sold what she had, located Dionisio in Mexico City, and undertook to restore him to life and hope.

Between Azuela's first four novels and the group consisting of *La Malhora*, *El Desquite*, and *La Luciérnaga* there is a basic change in his technique. Those of the latter group are, in varying degrees, more or less obscure. Suggestive rather than direct in manner, they are subtle and tenuous; in spite of their brevity, they incline to discursiveness; and they are marked by an affected, over-wrought style whose extreme singularity attracts attention. These characteristics, except type of style, are less prominent in *La Malhora*, which in its singleness of purpose—that Altagracía would inevitably revert to the low social class from which she came and consummate her revenge—is the most unified of the three. It is also enhanced by strong contrasts in both characters and settings: the denizens of the underworld and their rendezvous, the "pulque shop," on the one hand; and respectable folk and their environment, on the other. In *El Desquite* there are also excellent descriptive touches, but as a whole it falls far short of being a well-knit work. What there is of a plot seems to be purposely concealed, so embedded is it in irrelevancies. In *La Luciérnaga*, the most pretentious work of the group, the description of the small town Cieneguilla and the impressionistic portrayal of certain parts of Mexico City are charmingly done. But this work, although to a far less degree than *El Desquite*, lacks proportion, singleness of effect, and compression. What, after all, is Azuela's aim in *La Luciérnaga?* Is it the glorification of the self-sacrificing wife Conchita, an illustration of the disastrous effects of alcohol on the simple and trusting Dionisio, or the characterization of the miser José María? The portraits of each of the three individuals are excellent, but the figures are not blended into an artistic group. The style of the three works is poetic and rhythmic, but the dialogue is often exaggerated and not in keeping with the characters. The debauched Altagracía, for example, takes leave of the physician that had befriended her in this fashion: "Doctor, farewell. I am leaving, weeping over my hopeless affliction and the hopes that I leave here interred." There is a superabundance of unusual words, of neologisms—"puericultura," for example —and of figures of speech which, rather than please by their beauty, shock by their strangeness or vigor. In the description of a cold wave one finds "a sky, as bituminous as the asphalt of the streets, had swallowed the sun [*La Malhora*]"; in the account of the pugnacious habits of the child Ricardo, "His tender hands were stained with the gold [blood] of his first victim [*El Desquite*]." Azuela's blended tone of pessimism, hopelessness, and fatalism pervades the three works. Particularly pessimistic is he in regard to dishonesty in the medical profession in Mexico City and among the politicians that had come into power with the new political order.

In two books only—*Pedro Moreno, el Insurgente* and *Precursores*—has Azuela turned from his own day to the past. The first of these tells the story of one of the lesser heroes of Mexico's struggle for independence, Pedro Moreno, like Azuela a native of Lagos. Although a well-to-do merchant when the rebellion under Hidalgo occurred in 1810, Moreno, who as a student had read Rousseau's *Social Contract*, was a liberal. He and other rebel sympathizers fortified a near-by mountain, known as "el Cerro del Sombrero," and with their families took refuge there. In 1817 they were joined by the celebrated Spanish liberal Javier de Mina and his followers. From their impregnable position the revolutionists preyed upon the royalist sympathizers in the surrounding country until finally the government took drastic measures and sent a large force against them. Surrounded and cut off from their water supply, the revolutionists decided to abandon the fort. Although Moreno and Mina succeeded in escaping through the enemy lines, they were later captured and shot.

It is civil strife itself, Azuela maintains in *Precursores*, that breeds brigandage in Mexico. A typical revolutionary force, he says, is made up in the main of professional job hunters and ignorant individuals who are useful as soldiers; but after the fighting is over and the politicians have divided the spoils among themselves, the others get no reward; all they can do is remain in the hills, with their rifles, and live by robbing and plundering. Only then does it become the interest both of victorious and deposed government leaders that the bandits be exterminated. In *Precursores* he traces the careers of three Mexican bandits—Eulogio Morales, better known as Amito; Manuel Lozado; and Antonio Rojas—all of whom, during the years of civil strife that followed the war with the United States, operated in Jalisco and the adjoining states. Although cruel and ignorant, each of the three possessed the quality of leadership, the most remarkable of them in this respect being Manuel Lozado, who made himself absolute master of the district around Tepic, in the present state of Nayarit, from 1857 until his capture and execution in 1873. Contending factions in the civil strife of this period sought the aid of the unprincipled bandit. Both the French, at the time they intervened, and later Maximilian, when he was emperor, honored him for his services.

While Azuela's biographical sketches of Pedro Moreno and the three bandits are based on documentary sources rather than his own experience, as in his purely fictional works, they are decidedly literary in style. Concise, for Azuela chose only the material necessary to characterize the central figure and trace briefly his career to its tragic end, the sketches are logical and artistic, each reaching, near the end, a very effective climax; information about the characters is presented through dialogue, which adds animation and secures dramatic effect; and, through the poetic language that characterizes them, Azuela succeeds in imparting to each some tinge of his own personality.

The implication in the word "precursores" is that the conditions that produced Amito, Lozado, and Rojas in the nineteenth century also gave rise to the bandits that flourished in the revolutionary period that followed 1910. Of the outright bandit, who has at least the virtue of being true to himself, Azuela is more tolerant than of that dishonest politician who, although his name be engraved on the national monuments of bronze and stone, has been untrue to the ideals he professed. It is the problem created by this type of individual—who, as Azuela sees it, has used his power solely for self-aggrandizement and thus frustrated the ideals of the Revolution—that figures conspicuously in the last five novels that have come from his pen.

In the first of these, *El Camarada Pantoja*, he inveighs particularly against the abuses that characterized the administrations of Obregón, president from 1920 to 1924, and his successor, Calles. The latter's term was especially marked by dissension: the conflict with the Church reached a crisis; the confiscation and partition of many landed estates, in accordance with the Constitution of 1917, took place; two prominent men who dared to oppose him, Francisco Serrano and Arnulfo R. Gómez, were murdered; and the Constitution was amended to permit the re-election of Obregón, whose assassination shortly after shocked the country and added still more to the general turmoil.

In the novel, however, it is not so much through a direct discussion of the major political questions—a knowledge of which it is assumed the reader has—that Azuela seeks to show the rottenness of the times as through the tracing of the rise to power of an incapable individual through most corrupt means. Celestino Pantoja was an ordinary workman in Mexico City when the novel opens. He participated actively in the labor unions that had come into power with the masses; he was a zealous adherent of Calles and ardently anti-Catholic; ignorant and vulgar himself, he hated those who had constituted the wealthy and cultured class even though they were now dispossessed. Pantoja was contented with his place in life, but his wife Chata, who was vulgar, too, but by nature astute, was ambitious for him, although she was forced to admit to herself his extreme stupidity.

A mere incident proved a turning point in Pantoja's career. One night a man sought refuge in their apartment; Chata concealed him and later helped him to escape. He proved to be General Calderas, a prominent figure in the Calles-Obregón clique, and he rewarded her by giving Pantoja a high place in the police department. Soon Pantoja came to know Obregón himself, who is presented in the book in a very unfavorable light. Later, when Calderas went with a company of soldiers to San Nicolás to kill "cristeros"—adherents of the Church or those accused as such—and to terrify and prey upon the town, he took Pantoja, who was cowardly by nature but inhumanly cruel to "cristeros," as one of his officers. He ingratiated himself with Calderas to such an extent that when the latter decided to be elected governor of a state he permitted Pantoja to be sent as a deputy to the national congress.

Back in Mexico City and a member of congress, Pantoja was only a figurehead, voting as the party leaders directed. Now rich, he and Chata lived handsomely, but she was not happy. For Pantoja had found a new love in a young girl, Cecilia, poor but of the old aristocracy. Although scorned by her at first, not only did he succeed in winning her but other honors too; finally the governorship of Zacatecas. When he was about to depart to assume his new duties, intending doubtless to take Cecilia with him, Chata, jealous and worried, sought out her rival and shot her to death.

Again, in *San Gabriel de Valdivias*, the time is the Calles administration; the theme, the abuse of authority for selfish ends; and the place, a small agricultural village, San Gabriel de Valdivias. The land around the town had belonged to the Valdivias, who still lived there, although most of their property had been partitioned among the peasants and they had been superseded in power by the agrarian leader Saturnino Quintana. Under his management a road had been built that brought the town into contact with the outside world, and a dam for irrigation purposes had been constructed. But Saturnino, at heart a selfish and unprincipled ruffian, proved an even greater tyrant than the Valdivias, and very soon the people realized that they had traded masters disadvantageously. Not only did he rob them of their crops, but he violated one of the girls of the village. Various factions finally rose against him. Among them were the "cristeros," under the leadership of a priest and one of the Valdivias; another was a band of peasants who were fighting for complete rights to

the lands they worked. After Saturnino was killed in an encounter, an army officer, Gonzalo Pérez, who had come with
soldiers to help put down the rebellion, persuaded the peasants
through promises to lay down their arms. The cleverer ones,
however, soon perceived that their situation was unchanged,
for Gonzalo Pérez, who was also a very sly individual, remained as the new dictator of San Gabriel de Valdivias.

While Azuela turns in *Regina Landa* from peasants to
white-collar workers in the government offices of Mexico
City, his purpose—to expose the contraventions, particularly
during the administrations of Calles and his successors, of what
he calls the ideals of the Revolution—remains in general the
same. Incidentally, he flays unprincipled turncoats, condemns
the persecution of Catholics by the organization "Camisas
Rojas," and satirizes hypocritical individuals who pose as
critics of literature, art, and music. The novelistic part of the
work centers about Regina Landa, a girl of twenty, orphaned
through the death of her father, and confronted with the
necessity of making her own way in the world. Upright like
her father—a general in the late Revolution who, strangely
enough, had not enriched himself while fighting to liberate his
countrymen from tyranny—Regina secured a position in a
government office in Mexico City; but the corrupt conditions
soon disillusioned her. The employees, concerned only with
retaining their positions, which depended entirely on the
whims of their superiors, were as a class disgustingly servile.
The heads of departments, political appointees, were as a rule
incapable, ignorant, and dishonest. Despite her refusal to bend
to the will of the department chiefs, Regina eventually secured
one of the most desirable positions in the service. Her superior,
Miguel Angel, who guarded carefully his private life, passed
for a very cultured man. Later, however, when Regina discovered that he was a very ordinary person whose pretentions to
culture were a mere show, she lost all respect for him. He grew
weary, too, of her chastity, and let her know, indirectly, that
he wished to be rid of her. Thoroughly disillusioned, Regina

quit her place and, intent upon being of some actual use to society, set up a bakery shop.

In character Regina Landa is in a measure the feminine counterpart of idealists like Reséndez in *Los Fracasados,* Antonio Reyes in *Andrés Pérez, Maderista,* and Rodríguez in *Los Caciques.* Of the same ilk as they, is Adolfo in *Avanzada.* The theme of this work at first seems to be the conflict between modern tendencies and reactionary methods. For, when Adolfo returned, after four years' study of agriculture in the United States, to take charge of the family hacienda in Jalisco, a clash occurred between him and his family. He disagreed, in the first place, with his father in regard to methods of farming; and gradually it developed that his opinions in general were opposed to those of his parents. Most disturbing to them was the fact that he neglected his cousin Margarita, whom he was to have married, for a much more modern girl in a near-by town. The affair with her terminated, however, when she learned his financial status. A bounteous harvest eventually paid off the indebtedness that Adolfo had incurred in buying modern machinery, but it also aroused the cupidity of the agrarians, who, during the Cárdenas administration, were particularly active throughout the country. Adolfo might have saved the property by paying what one of the agrarian leaders demanded; but, as he refused, it was confiscated and partitioned just as a crop was ready to be harvested. This loss led shortly to the death of both parents, but Adolfo, whose recent readings had produced in him a most philanthropic attitude toward his fellow man, felt no resentment toward those who lived on what was once his property. He remained in the old home and, with the help of a faithful servant, cultivated the small amount of ground that had been left him. His new neighbors proved lazy and indifferent; when their crops failed, they began to steal from him. On their part, too, there existed an undying class hatred, which becomes, from this point on, the paramount concern of the author.

Ultimately, after the hatred of his neighbors made his situation intolerable, Adolfo sought work as a day laborer in the sugar fields of Vera Cruz. Bound for the same region were many laborers and union leaders. The latter, Adolfo learned, always traveled in the Pullman; they never went by train if it were possible to go by airplane; they lived in a far more princely manner than the old *hacendados* had; and they were the new masters of the masses, who had merely changed rulers. On the train, Margarita, who had insisted on accompanying Adolfo in his misfortunes, attracted the attention of one of the labor leaders, a certain Torres, who recognized the superiority of both of them and later secured for Adolfo a good position as the operator of a machine used in cane harvesting. Although a labor leader, Torres was exceptional, for he was a man of culture and had been wealthy before the Revolution ruined him. They became close friends in spite of their opposing views, for the disillusioned Torres did not share Adolfo's enthusiasm for eradicating class hatred and dissensions among the labor unions themselves. Margarita and Adolfo, through their generosity and good fellowship, won many friends among the workers; but Adolfo nevertheless incurred the enmity of a certain labor faction, which ultimately murdered him.

The same reactionary tone that characterizes *Avanzada* is also found in *La nueva Burguesía*, the last work, to date, from Azuela's pen. The time of the book is 1939, when the political campaign was being waged between Almazán, of reputedly conservative tendencies, and the administration candidate Avila Camacho, who it was thought would continue to carry out the socialistic program of Cárdenas. There is much in the book regarding the economic situation, particularly the cost of living which had greatly increased, and, as in *Avanzada*, the dissatisfaction with labor leaders, who, far from having any altruistic ideals, were fattening upon the laboring classes. The bulk of the novel, however, presents a picture of social conditions in Nonoalco, a rather sordid district in Mexico City inhabited mainly by the working classes. The characters include men of various trades, such as Zeta López, a brakeman; Pedroza, a fireman; Campillo, a locomotive engineer; Roque, a section boss; Chabellón, a streetcar motorman; Benavides, a linotypist; and Bartolo, a shoemaker. There are many women characters too—Emmita, and the girls from two families, the Escamillas and the Amézquitas—all of exceedingly humble origin, who have come to the capital from the provinces and have succeeded in getting work of one kind or the other. Patrons of the beauty shops, regular attendants at the movies, and habitués of cabarets, they had become, indeed, a worldly, blasé, and sophisticated set.

The book can scarcely be said to have a plot at all. No one of the characters is of outstanding importance, and there is no central theme that connects the many episodes that make up its narrative element. Interesting in themselves and effectively presented in dramatic form, the episodes deal with various aspects of the life of the characters—their love affairs, their schemes to further their ambitions, their diversions, their political and economic beliefs, and their domestic tragedies. One of the incidents—a trip that Campillo, the locomotive engineer, and Rosa Amézquita made together to Guadalajara—reflects genuine feeling on Azuela's part—the outgrowth, probably, of nostalgic reminiscences of the Jaliscan city where he had spent his own student days. There awoke within Rosa a great love for the city of her childhood—for its mild climate, which contrasted with the cold of the national capital, and for the simplicity and sincerity of the people, which made her realize the emptiness of the life she had led. Disillusioned, she entered a church to pray, a thing she had not done for years; and when Campillo returned to Mexico City, she did not accompany him.

Azuela brought to *La nueva Burguesía* and the four novels that preceded it many years of observation and experience with disease; his diagnosis of the ills of his country is profound, but he knows no remedy. The disease from which Mexico suffers is still, like malignant cancer, incurable. He writes of it in these, as in all of his works, with a tone of hopelessness but with an earnestness of conviction that leaves no doubt as to his sincerity. On account of their theses these last novels have an especial interest. Yet, aside from their sociological interest, they have, decidedly, an artistic value. That lies—and what is said now applies in varying degrees to Azuela's work as a whole—not in the plots of his novels, which are rather formless, nor in any great character creations, although there is a very full gallery of excellent character types, nor in a realistically portrayed background, but in the fact that the author was able, at various periods throughout his own life, to analyze the motives which gave rise to the conflicts about him, to penetrate to the depths of the souls of the contenders, and to give to his findings both dramatic and lyric expression.

In spite of the fact that Azuela's fiction has a sociological and ethical basis, its poetic quality is its most distinguishing characteristic. For, except in the realistic detail of his earliest novels, he did not retain Balzac and Zola, for whom he admits a passion in his youth, as his models. On the contrary, his technique or approach to novel writing is far closer to that of the poet than of the purely realistic or naturalistic novelist. This is best exemplified in his masterpiece *Los de Abajo*. In many of his works he is both personal and imaginative, and the artistic use of language is often with him an end in itself. Like the poet, he centers on the points of high interest, leaving much to the imagination; as a result, the plots of his novels —consisting as they often do of sections almost complete in themselves—are in general difficult to follow.

But no other writer has pictured the Revolution in so many aspects. As an ominous cloud, he had seen it approach; in the midst of the hurricane, he perceived only destruction; and when the sky had cleared, he found that little of its gigantic force had been expended for the betterment of those who most needed help—the Indian and the downtrodden masses of Mexico. In his eyes, their problems still remain unsolved.

CHAPTER IV

CARLOS LOVEIRA
ADVOCATE OF A NEW MORALITY
FOR CUBA

❁

IN CUBA, as in most Hispanic American countries in the
twentieth century, the novel has been cultivated as a means
of effecting social reforms. To that end it is essential that both
background and characters be typical of the country and that
the plot grow out of local problems. Of these there were many
in Cuba, which was late in achieving independence from
Spain. Even after it became a nation conditions among the
laboring classes were deplorable; the Catholic Church still
had a firm hold on the people, especially the women; and corrupt politicians were in power. The first Cuban author of the
present century to set forth these conditions by using contemporary Cuban background and characters in a novel that
was both popular and literary, was Carlos Loveira.

A knowledge of the life of this writer contributes greatly
to a sympathetic understanding of his novels. Born in El Santo,
a village in the province of Santa Clara, Cuba, on March 21,
1882, Loveira lived through five eventful decades of Cuban
history. As a young child he experienced all the pangs which
servitude, poverty, and death could cause. His father, a Galician, died when the child was only three; his mother, reduced
by destitution to domestic labor, survived only six years. The
little orphan then remained as a menial in the home where

his mother had worked. When the revolution against Spain broke out in 1896, the family emigrated to New York and took the boy with them, but their straitened circumstances forced him shortly into finding outside work. For a time he sold fruits and candy on the streets and thereby learned the English language; then he was employed as a menial in one of the famous metropolitan hotels. Here he first came into contact with organized labor, whose cause he was consistently to champion, even at repeated personal sacrifice. His first experience came when the management of the hotel sought to replace striking waiters with other employees, and Carlos, already embued with the crescive militant spirit of labor, indignantly refused.

The boy showed character, even at this age, not only in his proletarian sympathies, but also in his patriotic devotion to the Cuban cause. While very young he had committed to memory the fiery discourses of the patriot Sanguily and these he declaimed with fervor; in New York he lived among Cuban émigrés whose one dream was independence. In the early part of 1898, with other impetuous young Cubans, he returned to his native land to join the insurgent forces which had, for the most part, been driven for refuge to the swamps and jungles. During his military service, spent partly in the field and partly in a military hospital, he rose to the rank of second lieutenant.

Loveira made no attempt to rise to political power on the strength of his military record, as did many of the insurgent officers; he contented himself with humble but useful occupations. For a time he was an interpreter in the United States army; then an overseer in railroad construction; later, after an apprenticeship as fireman, a locomotive engineer, in Cuba, Costa Rica, and Panama. It was while so engaged in his native land that he first awoke to the necessity of united action by which he and his fellow workmen might defend themselves against the hardships and injustices they constantly experienced. As a step to that end, he organized the first Cuban union of railroad workers, and promptly lost his own position.

For five years, from 1908 to 1913, he fought an up-hill struggle, learning the problems and suffering the discouragements that are the lot of any leader seeking reforms. In 1913 he went to Yucatan and took an active part in the social revolution which brought about the liberation of the Indians on the great estates, the partition of lands, the beginnings of public instruction, the dissemination of knowledge concerning birth control, and the organization of unions among many classes of workers. In 1916 he was chosen to head the newly organized Department of Labor of that state.

After a flying visit to groups of organized labor in Costa Rica and Cuba, he went to Washington, D. C., where Samuel Gompers appointed him secretary of the Pan American Federation of Labor, and in that capacity he visited the principal countries of South America.

It was in connection with his efforts to organize labor that he first used his pen. When discharged by the Cuban railroads as a trouble maker, he started a periodical, *El Ferrocarrilero* (*The Railroader*), at Camagüey; in Merida, he published *La Voz de la Revolución* (*The Voice of the Revolution*), as well as endless articles, leaflets, and pamphlets urging the working classes to action in self defense. In various Cuban papers he published many articles urging the organization of labor and other social reforms. In 1917 he published *De los 26 a los 35* (*Lecciones de la Experiencia en la Lucha obrera*) (*From 26 to 35: Some Lessons Learned through Experience in the Labor Struggle*), an autobiographical sketch which suggested the story-telling ability of the writer. Not until 1919, when he was trying to gain support for a divorce law in Cuba, did he resort to the novel as a means of propaganda. *Los Inmorales* (*Who Are the Immoral?*) gained immediate approval from a large class of readers quite indifferent to its message, and also very favorable comment from literary critics, most of whom recognized at once Loveira's great native ability as a writer of fiction. Three other novels followed in rapid succession: *Generales y Doctores* (*Generals and Doctors*) in

1920, *Los Ciegos* (*Those Who Will Not See*) in 1922, and *La Ultima Lección* (*The Last Lesson*) in 1924. So great was their success that he was made in 1926 a member of the Cuban National Academy of Arts and Sciences. The following year he published *Juan Criollo* (*Juan, the Creole*), which was unanimously acclaimed his masterpiece. It proved to be also his last novel, as he died in 1929.

In all of these works, except *La Ultima Lección*, there is a character, generally the protagonist, whose early life parallels more or less closely that of the author. In *Los Inmorales* it is Jacinto Estébenez, an orphan adopted by a family who emigrated during the Weyler régime to New York, where the boy soon began to shift for himself, learned English, which was to stand him in good stead later, read widely in the public libraries, and later worked in Costa Rica and Panama during the canal-construction era.

Such is the background, recounted in a few introductory pages, of Jacinto, who, when the story opens in 1906, was an engineer on the railroad connecting Camagüey and Santiago. There, in a second-rate hotel, his attention was attracted by two young and beautiful Cuban sisters on their way from New York to visit their parents in Caimanera, which they would reach by boat. To the elder, Elena, Jacinto was irresistibly and fatally drawn, not only by her physical beauty but by common intellectual tastes. Elena admitted that she was married to an ambitious young man of a well-to-do family, then studying medicine in Philadelphia, but not only was there no sympathy or understanding between them but he was utterly repugnant to her. Of this she had been convinced even before they were married, and forcibly so on their honeymoon trip from Cuba to New York, when he returned to the medical college. After some very unhappy months in Philadelphia, Elena, ostensibly to visit her parents but in truth to escape her husband, was returning with her sister Esperanza, who had accompanied them to New York. Although he did not admit the fact to her, Jacinto, too, was wedded to a young woman he had known in Costa Rica, but in whom, despite their infant daughter, he had lost all amatory interest.

Fully cognizant of the strong mutual attraction in spite of their brief acquaintance, Jacinto and Elena parted when the sisters embarked. The home in Caimanera to which they returned was, and had always been, wretchedly poor; the mother was gentle and lovable, but their father, an indigent carpenter, was lazy, given to drink, dictatorial in his home, and, although without honor himself, over-zealous in guarding the reputation of his daughters. After threatening Esperanza with physical violence to induce her to dismiss the young men he had found about the house late at night, the tyrant turned to abusing Elena, who had come to the defense of her sister; as a result, the young married woman quit the house. Failing to obtain lodgings in the town, because of the hesitancy of hotel keepers and landladies to receive an unaccompanied woman, she secured a room, but with difficulty, in nearby Guantánamo. There Jacinto happened to be, having lost his railroad position as the result of attending a meeting of a group of radical labor agitators.

Succeeding events drew Jacinto and Elena together, he abandoning regretfully a wife and child, she with no marital misgivings. After a pleasure trip together to the neighboring town of San Luis, the continued suspicions of the hotel manager forced Elena's departure. Then the two went to Havana, and after a most voluptuous night, which the writer delights in describing in all its sensual details, they set sail for Panama. Seasick, as she had been on her honeymoon trip to New York, Elena could not but contrast the behavior of her husband with that of her lover.

On their arrival in Panama, conditions for a happy life were most propitious. With building activity feverishly directed to the early completion of the canal, Jacinto secured immediate employment as a machinist, at excellent wages. Among the Panamanians they quickly made friends and acquaintances; and they continued to improve their minds by reading not only Zola and Eça de Queiroz, but outstanding writers on socialism. Their happiness was suddenly blasted by the arrival of some Cubans who knew of Jacinto's abandonment of his wife and child. When the report reached the ears of one of their acquaintances, a certain old Don Sempronio—a gambler but a devout Catholic, legally married but infatuated with his mulatto mistress—he forced his attentions on Elena, taking her to be a loose woman. Jacinto arrived on the scene unexpectedly and ejected him vigorously; for this he was arrested and, as the judge was a friend of the influential gambler, Jacinto was fined and sentenced to some months' imprisonment. Unable to secure reinstatement Jacinto took another position, only to discover that the influence of Don Sempronio was sufficient to prevent his holding any job very long, even that of editorial writer on an anti-clerical, socialistic sheet that the vigor of his articles had brought into prominence.

Driven from Panama, Jacinto worked in various places along the west coast of South America, and faithfully remitted a part of his savings for the support of his legal wife and daughter. But their secret was sooner or later discovered everywhere. At last, harkening to the call of country, they returned to Cuba to find Elena's parents and Jacinto's wife dead; her husband divorced, remarried, and enjoying an excellent medical practice; and Esperanza the discarded mistress of more than a half dozen men. In search of work, Jacinto tramped the streets of Havana, but without success, for everywhere it seemed his defiance of social customs doomed him to failure.

Thus society punishes those who violate its canons; but Loveira's sympathy is with the lovers, not with society. Touching lightly on themes to be developed later—the exploitation of the working classes, the development of labor unions, and anti-clericalism—in Los Inmorales he directs his shafts against the Christian conception of marriage as indissoluble. For him, far more immoral than Jacinto and Elena, who obeyed a natural law, are those who, out of consideration for their reputations, remain married, when no bond of love unites them. Especially does his sympathy go out to such a woman as Elena's mother, who, either because of the rigorous demands of society or because she had no other means of support, had no choice but to share poverty with a tyrannical brute for whom she had lost all love, if she ever had any, but to whom she nevertheless remained faithful. She endured all, he comments, for the sake of a respectability which he contemptuously flouts:

Respectability that goes with the washtub, the flatiron, the kitchen, and the sewing machine; that goes with bringing up children, putting up with an overbearing husband, and confinement within four walls; that goes with having just half enough to eat, dressing in rags, and sleeping little and badly. Respectability that is exalted in mere words, but is awarded few testimonials for its practical value or for any real recompense it brings.

Before woman's position can be dignified and a more liberal attitude toward the entire problem of marriage created, Loveira believes that certain inhibitions have to be broken down and certain practices abandoned; these Jacinto enumerated in reviewing with Elena the causes that contributed to their unhappy plight:

There will always be problems as long as in marriage, in the union of man and woman, there prevails through education, through law and custom, the idea of the "eternal vow." And problems there will always be as long as woman is reduced to consider love as a means of a livelihood, whether she sells herself for a title, for wealth, for family conveniences and interests, to escape poverty, or whether she sells herself, at a fixed rate, to satisfy some base lust. And so these problems will always be with us, as long as Christian morality, at variance with instinctive morality, at war with Nature, unable to cope with the realities of life, is the basis of education, of customs and laws; as long as love does not occupy its rightful place in

the world, in life, by being free and, as it should be, the
moving force of the world, the guiding star of life. Until
then, men will not be better, or more just.

In the last chapter of *Los Inmorales,* in a conversation between Jacinto and his socialist friend Romero, Loveira holds
up to scorn those who have ridden into political power or
wealth through hypocrisy, dishonesty, or a sacrifice of ideals.
These, so moral in the public eye but actually so immoral,
furnish a theme he develops more fully in his second novel,
Generales y Doctores.

Autobiographic in form and colored by many details culled
from personal experience, this is, in many respects, his most
admirable novel. The events center about Ignacio García y
Darna, born in 1878, of a Galician father, a commissary officer
in Cuba, and a Cuban mother, descended from a well-to-do
Spanish family. Ignacio spent his early boyhood in Matanzas,
where his parents lived with his father's brother, then the
prosperous owner of a general store. There, in the closing
years of the Spanish régime, Ignacio received his first schooling; there it was that he read stories of the Guerra Grande that
made him a pronounced partisan of the separatist faction.
His father possibly had leanings in the same direction, for in
1894 he was dismissed from the Spanish army. Without a position and forty-five years of age, he decided to gratify his life-
long desire to study medicine, but a few months after his
enrollment in a medical college in Philadelphia, he died of pneumonia. Ignacio and his mother, who had remained in Matanzas,
then went to reside with her father in her native Placeres, a
small inland town, where her family, for its wealth and position, was highly respected. As Ignacio had shown decided
talent in school, his mother planned to send him to Havana for
further study, but he had no such ambition, for he had fallen
in love with Susana Rubio, a modest and beautiful girl, who
lived with her family in the adjoining home. Already initiated
into some of the mysteries of life by Romira, a sensual, thirty-

five-year-old unmarried woman, he had also made the acquaintance of Nene, astute and wily, with whom Susana's
elder sister Mercedes was blindly infatuated. After stabbing
Ignacio in a quarrel, this rascal had to flee the town, but returned shortly afterwards as the captain of a band of maraud-
ers who passed as revolutionists. When civil strife made
conditions intolerable, many well-to-do families, such as that
of his grandfather and the Rubios, sought refuge in the United
States.

In a hotel in New York, frequented largely by Cubans,
Ignacio encountered the voluptuous Cuca, versed in all the
arts of coquetry, who sought to win him from Susana. Although attracted, and to an extent victimized by her unscrupulous wiles, he reserved his genuine love for Susana, whose
despair meanwhile was pitiful. When the rupture between
them seemed irreparable, Ignacio enrolled in a college of
dentistry in Baltimore, and after the completion of his course,
joined a group of Cubans returning to fight for the liberation
of their country. After a brief service in a guerrilla band, he
became ill, and was taken to a hospital in charge of Dr. Cañizo,
who proved to be an old friend he had known in Placeres;
under his care the young soldier remained until the end of the
war.

This part of *Generales y Doctores*, purely narrative, in a
direct and pleasing style, constitutes four-fifths of the novel,
which, from the artistic standpoint, should have ended here.
But Loveira, although he shows marked skill in narrative art,
is concerned less with pure literary artistry than with doctrines
and arguments, and it is in the concluding part of the book—
the action of which takes place twenty years later—that he
attacks conditions, especially the political, that had meanwhile
developed in Cuba.

The protagonist is reintroduced on a train bound for
Havana just after he has met his uncle, the former Galician
shopkeeper, now rich and influential; with him, Ignacio reviews his life. In the country town Placeres, happily married

to his boyhood sweetheart Susana, he had made through the years a modest living by the practice of dentistry. The sharpest thorn in his side had been the rascal that had stabbed him years before, for Nene had returned from the war a general and had established his home in Placeres, where, by making use of his military record and consorting with thieves, robbers, and cutthroats, he had become the mayor and dominant force politically and financially, despite the efforts of Ignacio and the better class of citizens. Ignacio was convinced that such generals as Nene, whose services to the country had been vastly overestimated, were parasitically sucking the country dry, while those prepared for the learned professions, instead of practicing them, were seeking riches and power through political preferment. In one pasage, Ignacio sums up the situation as he sees it:

> What has to be done is to put an end to all these licensed doctors and lawyers who never in their lives treated a single sick person or defended a single case, and who by reason of a university degree, together with the generals, grab for themselves all that there is. Here, if it isn't General John Doe, it has to be Doctor Richard Roe, and if not one of these, then it is General and Doctor So-and-So. In spite of the fact that a great deal is being said about work, that it has been said repeatedly that the Republic will be, or will not be, agricultural, all continue making lawyers and doctors of their sons. And as these gentlemen monopolize knowledge, intellect, and probity, the result is that they get into everything and take it all for themselves, leaving nothing for the rest of us to do save consider how the professional generals and the lawyers and doctors without clients or patients dispute among themselves over the prey and sometimes with revolutionary desperation.

As a deputy in the national congress, Ignacio pleaded, despite bitter opposition, for the establishment of a secretaryship of labor and for improved conditions among the submerged classes. In this vein he answered the argument that there was no labor problem in Cuba:

> There isn't any labor problem for those who, no matter where they have come from, once they feel themselves strong, happy, self-sufficient, don't think of going to feel the pulse of reality, to see the life of the unfortunate ones in those horrible tenement houses in the poor districts, where in a single room they go through with all the necessities of life: cooking, bathing, eating, procreating, in a horrible promiscuity of sexes and ages. When one considers that situation with humanitarian eyes, with heartfelt generosity, although it be with a clear-sighted spirit of preservation, he faces the facts of the social problem. Has Sir Deputy of the people, since he has had the office, gone to perceive at close range the physical and moral degradation of the tenement house, of the crib, of that human ant pile, whose inmates, undernourished, ragged, and preoccupied with a thousand fanaticisms, fill like chinches the narrow streets and the cabins, ironically called houses, in the districts of Jesús María, Cayo Hueso, and other sections of the city of Havana? Does this gentleman know the great lack of clothing, milk, light, and pure and breathable air in those districts where the candidacy of the fathers of the country is initiated triumphantly with corrupt and shameful dancing and music? Has this gentleman ever been in the hovels around a sugar mill? Does he know that these hovels still exist on sugar plantations? Does he know that the work goes on there twelve hours a day? That they still give "componte"? Has he ever been in an eating place at a sugar mill?

Just as, no doubt, Loveira had pleaded in actual life for the enactment of some tangible piece of legislation favoring the laboring classes, instead of palliatives and subterfuges, so did Ignacio as deputy plead with earnestness and vehemence, setting forth at the same time his opinion of the Roman Catholic Church as a social factor and of democracy as practiced in Cuba as a political creed.

To cling to the hope of a rebirth of religious sentiment, as some mystic souls endeavor to do, is to lose time and energy uselessly. Our country is a proof of the truth of that assertion. Here the only ones that continue believing —no, that continue going to the churches and supporting the cult—are the rich families that have need of the prestige of sending their children to schools of priests and nuns, just as they need the ostentation of the stylish churches for their showy weddings, baptisms, and funerals; and some old woman or other that, through atavism or ignorance, believes that a guano leaf that has been blessed turns aside lightning, just as she believes that the blood of a white child cures cancer and bewitchment. But the majority, the great mass of middle-class and poor people, are skeptical, profoundly skeptical. Each day the number of those that are married by the church or that have their children baptized is ever smaller, and it is possible to visit many houses, entire blocks of houses, without finding the image of a saint. No longer are satisfactions sought in a heaven that is very doubtful, but in the world of the living. The band of those that believe in the efficacy of charity is losing its partisans, for people are rapidly joining the ranks of those that believe only in justice.

And the same thing that is happening to religion is happening to democracy. The people no longer believe in it, whether it be because that which has been known as democracy has been nothing more than a hoax, a mere caricature of democracy, or because it is insufficient to secure the relative happiness to which all men on earth may aspire. In the countries that are reputedly the most democratic, the rich man has continued to mock the laws and the advantages of civilization. Only a few crumbs fall to the table of the poor. Instead of the people governing, the rich and they who aspire to be rich continue to govern, and they naturally, by the logical principle of self-preservation, have always looked out for themselves.

Aside from the question whether the novel should be a vehicle for the advocacy of social reform, *Generales y Doc-*

tores is, for its artistic treatment of plot, characters, and settings, probably Loveira's best novel. Set in the most eventful period of Cuban history, convincing in incident, replete with human interest, the story catches the reader's attention from the first and holds it to the end. Whether in Matanzas, Placeres, Havana, or the United States, the setting grows out of direct observation and personal knowledge. The best canvases in the book—those that portray bits of colonial Cuba—are unmistakably vivid, almost photographic in nature. One such is the school Ignacio attended:

> The school building was one of those old ancestral homes of Spanish days, which are seen now only in some of the towns of the interior.... There was a spacious entrance hall, adorned during class hours with a double row of caps and hats. The hall led into a large, airy antechamber. Then came a spacious, well-lighted room, with three large windows. The open court was paved with red and gray squares, with a tile border, and beds full of flowers, shrubs and vines. The back court was immense and was shaded by a grove of mangos, *anones* and *caimitos*. In the antechamber was installed the second year class, in charge of a hungry-looking, irritable, beardless young teacher. In the main drawing-room was the first year class, with Don Jacinto in charge. In the first chamber a primary class, taught by a daughter of the director, a tall, pale girl. The last room, in the minds of the pupils, contained Dantesque forms of images. It was the terrifying prison room, which to them teemed with goblins, snakes, bats, cockroaches, and rats. Between the front room and this jail lived Don Jacinto's undernourished family: his wife, the daughter already mentioned, his sister-in-law, and a little negress that had been taken into the family.

Even more detailed, in treatment more like the descriptions by Zola, whom Loveira greatly admired, is a description of the general store in Matanzas, owned by Ignacio's uncle:

> One end of a wooden counter stained green is given over to the bar, the upper side covered with a tack-

studded copper sheet. In this part, fenced off by an iron grating of pickets pointed like lances, stand rows of bottles varying in height and color—bottles of poison, and among them the bottle that contains the least poison, that containing pure cane brandy, of the color of drinking water, of a musty odor and a fiery taste. Then one of thick glass of checkered design, containing anisette brandy; a green one, containing a mixture of cane brandy, orange peel, and coriander seed; fat-bellied jars of murderous gin; cognac Moullón de Sagua la Grande; the Atella wine of Campeche wood; the Mistela wine, the genuine kept in the room back of the shop. All of the containers with their labels and stoppers fly-specked; the copper cover sticky from lack of cleanliness; and down below everything, the wretched tub, for the washing of glasses and spoons, with its water the color of stale coffee and milk, soapy, of foul odor, in which there floats an archipelago of corks, round slices of lemon and the legs of cockroaches.

At the other end of the counter from the bar is a showcase, containing all kinds of sweets and candies, in a happy Arcadia of bees, flies, and ants.

Between the bar and the showcase, on the counter proper, its surface crusty with spillings of salt, wine, lard, and kerosene, one sees a pair of thirteen-ounce balance scales and ream upon ream of coarse, yellow paper.

Opposite the counter, and against the wall that divides the two street doors, is another showcase cluttered with articles of hardware, postage stamps, prints of virgins and of saints, rosaries, catechisms, and "novenas." On one side and in the corner is the coalbin, made of boards, with its irregular-shaped spot of coal dust on the floor, and in the opposite corner some bundles of cane.

On the walls back of the counter stand dusty rows of chamber pots, jugs, jars, tins, bottles, casks, and bundles, with Bilbao, Catalonian, Galician, and Asturian labels. In the big drawers next to the floor, mixed with the rice, the beans, and the ground coffee, are the jerked beef, the codfish, the lobsters, fossilized in salt, and other poor and foreign foods of the dark days of slavery.

On the floor of the two rooms there is always a loathsome carpet of fruit peel, empty cigarette boxes, spittle, and papers, and in the corner of the house, extending along the sidewalk and draining toward the middle of the street the nauseating trickle of urine of some passers-by that still have the bad European habit of converting into an urinal, or something worse, the corners that are somewhat removed, the pedestals of statues, the steps of temples, and the bases of bridges.

In the room back of the shop in the midst of a veritable trail of objects that have been pawned by the undernourished customers; in the midst of barrels of lard, containers of sardines, pyramids of dried beef, walls of boxes of codfish, of candles, of soaps; in the midst of sacks of potatoes and more strings of garlic and onions; in the midst of chinch bites, the scampering of rats, the odors of fermentation, and the smell of the body itself in a chronic state of uncleanliness,...on two folding cots, innocent of clean linen, sleep my uncle and his clerk.

In like fashion, sensitive not only to sight but to smell and sound, Loveira describes the small town of Placeres as seen by Ignacio early in the morning:

On the sidewalk, on the shady side, water was still dripping from the eaves. In the middle of the street the recent rain had left its muddy trail—a mixture of sand, bones, papers, pebbles, fruit peelings, old cork tops, and all that the current collected and swept along those streets that only scurvy beggars cleaned. Before the door of a house, at which there appeared an old woman in a black shawl, a milkman in shirt sleeves was milking a cow, which, with her calf and a half dozen other cows and their calves, went through the town filling pitchers and jugs with white, foamy liquid. From a bakery issued the warm and pungent aroma of newly-baked bread. In a barber shop nearby, stretched out in the easy chair, a rustic dozed, his face being soaped by a barber whose feet were in slippers and whose hair stood out on top in tufts. When I passed by a shoeshop I heard a rasping sound from a showcase which was being moved by two men into one of the doorways. I passed by a drug store that was open early, and by a second-rate general store that a strapping villager in hemp sandals and unbuttoned shirt was sweeping. Finally I arrived at the square, with its cafes full of soldiers at their early morning drinks, who were shuffling, even at that early hour, the dominoes, while some native Cubans, in characteristic dress, were striking the floor with their cues in a game of billiards. On the few flat roofs—the pride of a few houses in the center of the town—on the laurels and the "framboyanes" in the plaza, the pure gold of the early morning sunshine glittered. In the foliage, still wet, the sparrows were chattering noisily. Underneath one of the blooming palm trees was a policeman in a faded blue uniform, who had come to leave a bony she-goat heavy with distended udder. The church bell was calling the faithful Catholic flock to mass, and some old women in mourning were entering the church. When I arrived at the entrance of the city hall, I let myself fall down onto one of the benches.

Graphic also, but not so minutely done, is the background of that part of the story that takes place in the United States— New York, Washington and its environs, Baltimore, and the country covered by a railroad journey to southern Florida. Against the background of New York City, the author contrasts the life of the rich Cuban émigrés with the struggles of the poor for an existence; points out the impressions made upon both classes by Anglo-American manners and customs; and stresses the imitative tendency of the Cuban women.

Some of the Goya-like portraits that the novel contains are unforgettable: Ignacio's uncle, the Galician shopkeeper, afterwards wealthy and influential; the sex-starved, middle-aged Romira, the youngest of five sisters, all spinsters and more or less repulsive; and the filthy Don Jacinto, Ignacio's teacher in the elementary school, who deserves a permanent place with

Squeers in the literary gallery of schoolmasters. As described by Loveira, Don Jacinto was

> ...a good Aragonese teacher, old but agile, testy, and distinguished by a very deplorable trait: the most absolute indolence in regard to everything that had to do with cleanliness and care of his person. Everything about Don Jacinto was filthy, foul-smelling, and repulsive. His everlasting suit, unclassifiable as to color on account of the spots and the shine from the most careless use—the vest so spotted by drivel that it looked like a map—with dirty ravelings at the edges and at the wrists. His scarf of the color of a glowworm, soiled at times by the yellow of egg, bits of spaghetti and grains of rice. His shoes, with elastic on the side, which had never seen a brush or polish, covered some rough, sticky socks that bulged out over the top with accordion-like pleats. He wore an ancient butterfly collar, edged with filth, and held by a blackish, poisonous looking brass button. His ears were waxy, and the nicotine from huge, yellow cigars impregnated his mustache, his tartar-covered teeth, the tips of his fingers and his furrowed nails, which had never known either soap or scissors.

But these, as well as others whose portraits fix themselves indelibly on the reader's imagination, are minor figures, sketched only in passing, of importance only as they come in contact with Ignacio, the protagonist and author's mouthpiece, whose development commands insistently the reader's attention. While other characters of Loveira may be delineated as fully, and their development be as interesting, Ignacio is the most lovable of his creations and the finest from an ethical standpoint. Commendable traits were manifested by him even in the elementary school: although intelligent, he was modest; retiring by nature, he did not lack courage to defend himself when the occasion demanded; and when it would have been more politic to have espoused the cause of the Spaniards, he brought trouble upon himself and his father by his sympathies for the oppressed Cubans. Differing, too, from Loveira's other characters, largely erotically promiscuous, Ignacio, in spite of repeated temptations, is remarkably faithful to Susana, whose love seemed to shut other women almost out of his life. It was his uprightness and sense of fairness that led him to practice his profession in Placeres instead of capitalizing on his few months of dubious military service, as did the unscrupulous Nene, whose oppression of his laborers Ignacio dared to combat, just as when a deputy he dared to attack the capitalistic interests in his plea for legislation favoring the laboring classes.

Set forth more dramatically than in *Generales y Doctores,* the conflict between labor and capital dominates a large part of Loveira's third novel, *Los Ciegos,* in which he advances also a Galdós-like thesis—the dire results of a Roman Catholic clergy meddling in the domestic affairs of man and wife. The man in the case is Ricardo Calderería, who as a youth in 1898, when peace followed the war for independence, set to work to improve his ancestral estate in the neighborhood of Matanzas, and to make a fortune for himself. Already on the road to wealth while still young, Ricardo—aristocratic, well educated, and intelligent—married Benigna Pedrosa, likewise of an aristocratic but poor Matanzas family, of which she and a brother, Cuco, were the only surviving members. A rather mischievous youth, but given to serious reading, especially of a socialistic nature, Cuco departed to broaden his education by travel. Although Benigna herself had been most carefully nurtured from a religious standpoint, having received all of her education in a convent, and Ricardo was entirely indifferent to its tenets, her confessor, the Jesuit Zorríñez, did not oppose the marriage, thinking that her influence would bring her husband into the fold. But Ricardo, more and more disgusted by the religious fanaticism of his wife, refused to be led. After two daughters, Alfonsina and Carlota, were born, a complete rupture ended all marital relations. While continuing to support his legitimate family in the luxury becoming his wealth, he set up another household in Matanzas, in which he placed

a young woman, Clara Herrera, whom he had brought from
Havana; in her he found an ideal love and she in time bore
him a son.

Such was the situation in this triangular affair at the end of
the World War. Through the high price of sugar, Ricardo had
become immensely wealthy, although he was kept, as were
other capitalists, continually in hot water by the repeated
strikes on the part of the laborers determined to fight for
higher wages and better living conditions. Doña Benigna, more
fanatically devout than ever, became practically an invalid on
account of a weak heart, but never ceased plotting with Zorríñez to break up the relations between her husband and Clara.
The elder of Ricardo's daughters, Alfonsina, had acquired a
very liberal education from such authors in her father's library
as Daudet, Eça de Queiroz, Tolstoy, Gorki, Zola, and Anatole
France, and had fallen desperately in love with a young machinist, Alfonso Valdés, a labor union leader. This love affair
was being carried on surreptitiously at Ricardo's country
house on his sugar plantation, where Valdés was employed as
a foreman of machinists, when it was discovered by Ricardo.
Although a liberal in matters of love, in so far as it concerned
himself, when it concerned his daughter, he was a dyed-in-the-
wool conservative. A violent scene ensued between father and
daughter, in which his arguments, voiced with a great show
of emotion, failed to convince her of the impropriety of her
behavior. Later he discharged Valdés.

At this crisis, Ricardo's brother-in-law, Cuco, returned from
his travels up and down the Americas and Europe, renowned
for a book he had written, in which he espoused the cause of
labor as opposed to capital. Trouble for all came fast. Overcome by emotion at the sight of her brother, Benigna died of
a heart attack. A series of strikes interfered with the work
on the plantation and in the sugar mill. In spite of Cuco's
appeals for the workmen, Ricardo resolutely refused to accede
to the demands of the strikers, and with the aid of government
police succeeded in restoring order. The strikers themselves

were divided according to the disposition of their leaders; some hoped for a sane adjustment of the conflict between the two factions, while others, led by such men as the Catalan anarchist, "El León," whom Ricardo caused to be sent out of the country, were determined to destroy capital completely. A few years elapsed, in which Ricardo continued relentless towards Alfonsina and Valdés, although he himself married Clara, his mistress all these years, and the two went to travel in Europe. On an inspection tour of his properties after his return, in company with Cuco, now in his employ, he came upon a man apparently sick. It was no other than "El León," who had trailed Ricardo with the determination of killing him; in the struggle that followed the recognition of the anarchist, both "El León" and Ricardo lost their lives.

The enmity between Ricardo and "El León" may be Loveira's symbolization of the struggle between labor and capital. The destruction of the latter he would have deplored as much as anyone, for, despite the fact that he championed the cause of the laborers and pointed out that the Cuban sugar plantation owners had extracted every possible cent from the industry, at the lowest possible cost, without improving the living conditions of the workers themselves, he did not advocate, as a remedy, the methods employed by "El León." Instead he included him among "the blind":

> To the first class belong the anarchists, the Bolsheviki, as that Catalan which is there, who will never see beyond the principles of the anarchism of the nineties. With his blind faith in a paradise of love, equality, and fraternity he will live until they kill him in some barricade, or until he is blown to pieces by some bomb that he himself has made to blow others to pieces.

Among the blind, Cuco continued, speaking for the author on this occasion, were Ricardo, unhappily estranged from his daughter Alfonsina through his own stubbornness and through ingrained traditions regarding family and position that pre-

cluded her marrying the honorable but poor mechanic who
had won her heart; and Benigna, who had lost her happiness
and died before her time, simply because her education, suited
to producing saints but not wives, had led her to follow the
advice of an interfering priest.

Serving as a vehicle for the three arguments, as well as for
propaganda directed to the improvement of working conditions on the sugar plantations, the novel as a whole lacks
artistic worth; the forging of the plot to serve an argument is
too apparent; the delineation of each of the characters for a
certain purpose, too obvious. With excellent descriptions of
colonial Matanzas, such as Ricardo's ancestral home, and of life
on a sugar plantation, especially the activities of the grinding
season, the background, which—in contrast to that in his
earlier novels—does not extend beyond Cuba, is perhaps the
best feature. Yet even local color is often made to serve one
of the writer's arguments, as in the following description of a
miserable hut only a short distance from Ricardo's more than
comfortable home:

A partition wall made of the bark of the palm, strength-
ened by interwoven rope and poles, divides the house
made of cane into two rooms. The palm-thatched roof,
dry, of unequal edge, hangs from the same style of
ridge-pole that the primitive tribes in Cuba invented. The
floor of red earth, hardened by the tramping of the dwellers, reddens everything that is near it: the feet of the
stools, the lower part of the walls, the table in the corner,
and the two boxes that serve as seats that are underneath
it. Opposite the front door, there is another that leads into
what was intended as a back yard. Here, in the drizzling
rain, some barnyard fowls are scratching; among them
strides with martial mien an old cock with a blood-red
comb and upright neck. Making the rounds with the cock
is a turkey whose spreading footprints are to be seen all
about the place; there is also a muddy hole, which gives
proof that some pigs are as much a part of the family
that lives in this hut as the turkey. From this back door

can be seen a smaller structure of cane, which must be the kitchen, for through the roof a bluish, fine smoke is filtering, arising and slowly thickening the heavy atmosphere.

With far less propaganda than *Los Ciegos*, characterized in general by the lightest tone of any of his novels, and with a new environment—the dance halls and night life of the city of Havana—*La Ultima Lección* is based on an incident in the life of the rich and respected Dr. Gustavo Aguirre, one of its best known physicians, a widower in his early fifties, whose two grown daughters were at school in Boston. As he planned to visit them, and had heard that dancing was the chief amusement in the United States, he decided to take lessons in the modern steps. On the advice of a friend, Arturo Pineda, a genuine representative of the man-about-town type, he went to a certain dance hall made popular by the beauty of one of its paid dancers, a certain Isabel, who posed as Russian. On their first auto ride together, she told him an improbable story of her life, spent in countless European and South American cities. From whatever cause—the mystery enveloping her, her beauty, or her resistance to his desires—Aguirre became enamoured and determined to marry her, in spite of the decided disapproval of Pineda. After Aguirre, under the pretext of taking lessons in Russian, succeeded in getting Isabel into his house, she confessed that she was not Russian but Cuban, although she had traveled extensively with a brother who had been in the diplomatic service; she confessed further that she had learned something of the language from a Russian who had initiated her into the secrets of love. With the promise of marriage, Isabel gave herself on this occasion to Aguirre, and thereupon followed a most passionate amour, carried on surreptitiously in various hotels in Havana. Honorable, however, in his intentions toward Isabel, Aguirre planned to put legally into effect his promise. He sought out her family, a mother and a sister, poor but honorable, who were overjoyed at the prospect of Isabel's marriage to a rich man, unaware, however, of the existent relations. While Isabel was busy purchasing clothes for her wedding, Aguirre, to escape the molestations of the Frenchman in whose dancing academy she was employed, decided to visit his daughters. During the journey by rail from Florida to Boston, he began to feel half glad to be free of Isabel, and sensed for the first time the inappropriateness of his projected marriage. At first they wrote to each other passionately, but the warmth of her letters ceased concurrently with a newspaper notice that Aguirre read by chance concerning a Russian violinist—the same Isabel had known—who had come to establish himself in Havana. A hurried return on the part of Aguirre followed, but his efforts to find Isabel were at first fruitless. Not until some weeks later —after he had completely recovered from his infatuation, had convinced himself that the incident had ended most fortunately for him, and had made resolutions never to be caught in a similar one—did he see her at a concert with the Russian.

Shorter than any of Loveira's other novels, *La Ultima Lección*, which could have been compressed into an excellent short story, is from a technical standpoint his nearest approach to a good modern novel. While the story itself is light and inconsequential, so unified is the plot and so definite the author's singleness of purpose that the reader's attention is held from the first to the last page; little is introduced that does not lead directly to the climax—the jilting of Aguirre. These two characters—ultra-civilized beings, who could scarcely be cited as models of conventional sex morality—are convincingly lifelike and do not fail to arouse interest. The mystery enveloping Isabel attracts the reader at once as it attracted Aguirre. After her identity is revealed, and she confesses she has lied shamelessly about herself, her presentation of the problems of the working girl, her attitude toward marriage, and her statement of the privileges of woman in matters of love command attention. Assuming that of all social prejudices the one in favor of virginity is the most stupid, she was nevertheless a person of refinement, with nothing in common, she insisted, with such a woman as Monique in Margueritte's *La Garçonne*. True to her principles, in the end she preferred the poor violinist to marriage with the rich Aguirre, although the latter was far from being repulsive to her. Amorous, but yet willing to pay for his amours with marriage, as he had promised, even when it would probably jeopardize his own and his daughters' happiness; sentimental, yet able to reason logically when his passion had cooled, Aguirre may be a rare *genus hominis* among Spanish Americans, but he is far from being an unreal or entirely imaginary character. Pessimistic but not bitter over the outcome of his love affair, determined to follow in the future the more realistic policy of his friend Pineda, Aguirre, probably speaking in the following passage the thoughts of Loveira himself, can pardon Isabel on the grounds that, as women had gotten the bad end of the bargain in the social world for so many years, turn about now and then was due them:

Havana is today a large, civilized city, with strong foreign influences. In it there exists, on the part of women, a spirit of rebellion, at once strong and in keeping with the time, which is not limited to those clubs that have been organized for the extension of women's rights, nor to articles and speeches by intellectuals. On the contrary, it appears to have been thought out individually, even in the case of poor women, who refuse to resign themselves to life in a tenement, to the washtub and sewing machine, to being only half clothed and shod, under the authority of a father or a husband that is poor and ignorant; and consequently they take up the struggle of existence outside of the home, in whatever way they can, in search of economic betterment, of more independence for themselves, and of a wider social vision. As many of them are worthy... they enter the shops, they operate accounting machines or typewriters, or they become manicurists. Those that become typists, in spite of being more efficient, assiduous, and diligent than the men, have the same experience that Isabel recounted; after learning stenography and typing, sometimes even English, their earnings are too meager to enable them to dress decently. The result is that not all of them are disposed to submit for the rest of their lives, and many seek—in a manner more or less hidden, with more or less tact and intelligence, with great or little risk, with the hope nearly always of finding something noble and redeeming—the means of having a well-provided house, presentable clothes and adornments, and in nearly every case a cultured, decent, and well-clothed mate. "And I don't blame them," is the comment one hears frequently in regard to the matter. Even with greater reason are they incited and urged on by the luxury and the corruption of some; by the atmosphere of inconsiderate selfishness that grows more intense each day, and by the advancing wave of sensualism, which in a great measure envelops us all, as a natural and inevitable consequence of greater general culture.

Pessimism of a far more bitter tone pervades Loveira's fifth and last novel, *Juan Criollo*, which is autobiographic in form, the title being the pseudonym of Juan Cabrera, the central figure of the book. Juan was born in Cuba, in the early eighties of the past century, of poor parents, his mother being Josefa Valdés, a native of Cuba, and his father a Spaniard from Galicia, first a soldier in the army and later a barber. Left a widow when Juan was still a young child, Josefa made a bare living doing the washing for a maternity hospital, a place she had secured through the pious Doña Juanita, wife of a prominent citizen of Havana, Don Roberto Ruiz y Fontanills. He, as amorous an old satyr as ever lived, had his eye on Josefa, at whose house his wife surprised him one day. So enraged was Doña Juanita that she caused the innocent Josefa to lose the miserable employment she had; unable to secure other work, without food for herself or her child, she had no other recourse than to accept an offer from a Galician shopkeeper to become his mistress. From a material standpoint, both Juan and his mother fared better, for the Galician was liberal; but, from a moral standpoint, Juan was warped, for from this time dated his initiation, street-urchin as he was, into all the vice of one of the worst quarters of Havana. Their freedom from want was of short duration, for one night the Galician was murdered near Josefa's door; although innocent of any connection with the crime, she was thrown into prison where she remained until Don Roberto secured her release and installed her as his mistress in a different residential district. Of a neurotic temperament, Josefa finally fell ill, and died a few weeks later.

Even before her death Don Roberto had taken Juan into his own home to serve as a sort of houseboy, for his food and keep. Don Roberto lived in an immense old colonial mansion in an aristocratic section; his household was numerous, consisting, aside from some eight or ten servants, of his wife Juanita and their five grown children, three sons and two daughters. The sons had graduated from the university, yet none practiced his profession. Domingo was a physician, Adolfo a lawyer, and Robertico a pharmacist. The last, the only one married, lived with his wife and their five children, three boys and two girls, in his father's home. Juan made himself liked by all except the pious Juanita, who never lost an opportunity to punish him. In addition to being generally useful about the house, he aided Don Roberto's sons by bearing messages to their various mistresses, for they were as amorous as their father. Don Roberto himself, a freemason and a partisan of Cuban independence, interested Juan in the same cause by giving him books to read on the lives of Cuban patriots. With Robertico's five children Juan played, but never as an equal, a distinction that rankled in the breast of the twelve-year-old boy. Among these children was a girl, Nena, about ten, already in the adolescent stage and conscious of the sex-urge. In playing together, certain intimacies grew up between her and Juan; together they read erotic passages in Paul de Kock, looked at suggestive pictures in magazines, and wrote letters to each other. Finally, Nena's uncle Domingo detected what was happening, and after consultation

with his father, without disclosing the affair to other members
of the family, decided to send Juan to their sugar plantation,
Los Mameyes, some distance from the capital, but attempted
first to recover Nena's letters. He was unsuccessful for Juan
had concealed them in a secret compartment of his trunk—his
only parental inheritance.

Juan was accompanied to Los Mameyes by Don Roberto
himself, who made an inspection tour of the property. On the
plantation there were two families. One, white, consisted of
Fidel Cabrero, his wife, Cándida, their six children, and an
orphaned relative, Rosa, whom, on this occasion, Don Roberto
added to his long list of feminine conquests. The head of the
other family, which was mulatto, was Rómulo, the overseer
of the plantation, in whose house Juan was to live. Rómulo's
family consisted of two boys by a former marriage, his wife,
Caridad, and her attractive sister, Petra. Gradually Juan was
initiated, cruelly at times, into the ways of country life. Except during the harvest season, when he was kept very busy
as weigher of the cane, he and one of Don Fidel's boys, Pepín,
amiable but roguish by nature, made excursions together into
the country. In time Juan and Petra found each other interesting, but carefully concealed their feelings from Rómulo,
who was secretly enamored of her too, for he was most brutal
and tyrannical toward his own boys and his wife. Another
whom Petra attracted was Don Robertico, the pharmacist,
Nena's father, when he came to spend a few weeks hunting
on the plantation. He attempted to use Juan in effecting a
conquest, but the jealous boy would do nothing to aid him.
Finally, however, he could not avoid taking Robertico to a
place from which he could see the women as they stripped to
go bathing in a stream. The lustful Robertico, when he saw
the well-shaped Petra bare of clothes, was scarcely able to
contain himself. Then, Juan, unable to repress his anger, let
loose some insulting remarks about Nena, Robertico's daughter, whereupon the latter fired at Juan twice but missed him.
Then with the idea of appeasing him and preventing him from

divulging what had actually happened, Robertico gave Juan various presents, including a revolver, and then left as soon as possible for Havana. Rómulo, suspecting in part how Robertico had seen the nude Petra, beat Juan brutally. The boy found sympathy in both Caridad and Petra, and the latter, who hitherto had yielded only kisses, at the first opportunity, surrendered herself completely. Two events which occurred at this time disturbed affairs at Los Mameyes considerably: Don Roberto died, and the Cuban insurrectionists again became active. Rómulo continued to make life unbearable for Juan, but—more serious still—Petra finally could not conceal that she was pregnant. When Caridad discovered her condition and felt that she must make it known to Rómulo, Juan fled the plantation and returned to Havana.

On his arrival there, after a trip in a third-class coach, he found that the Ruiz and Fontanills family had split into various units, on account of financial inability, occasioned by the insurrection, to maintain their large household. Domingo, the physician, a visionary and idealist, had been killed shortly after joining the insurgents. Robertico had opened a pharmacy in his home. Adolfo, more friendly toward Juan than the others, made him a general utility man in his house, in which he had set up a law office. Adolfo himself was very hopeful, for he was engaged to a well-to-do Mexican girl, Carmen, whose mother owned extensive property in the state of Yucatan, and he saw here a way of improving his own financial condition. On a certain occasion Juan was sent to Robertico's house, where he was received very coolly by the master, very haughtily by one of the sons, now a law student in the university, and very amiably by his old playmate Nena, now a handsome young woman, and very attractive to marriageable young men. Later both she and Juan, in spite of Robertico's opposition, accompanied Adolfo and his Carmen, after their marriage, to the large, comfortable country home her mother owned near Merida.

Nena one day asked Juan, who had referred to their childhood indiscretions, to return her letters. He agreed if she would go with him to his room; once there, he attempted to kiss her. She repulsed him haughtily; for while she might lure on an attractive young man beneath her socially, as was Juan, she was, after all, an aristocrat. The following day, Adolfo, who had began to eye Juan suspiciously, gave him some money with which to amuse himself for a day in Merida. There Juan met a companion of his childhood, Julián, formerly a leader of the street gamins in Havana, and now with other Cubans, all sympathizers with the insurrection, a worker in a cigar factory. It was the custom in such shops to employ a reader for the workers; and as the reader in Julián's shop was sick that day, he asked Juan to assume the task, which he did to the great delight of his listeners, for he was intelligent and had improved his mind by extensive reading. Late that same day Julián took Juan to see his lady love, a prostitute. The hour at which they arrived was known as that in which the "husbands" called on their "wives"—the period of the day in which there was little or no business for the prostitutes. Among these Juan met Julia, a blonde, the prettiest and the choicest of the house, who became so infatuated with him that she volunteered to support him if he would come to Merida.

Instead of accepting her offer, Juan was greeted on his return with orders from Adolfo to leave early the next morning for Peto, some distance from Merida, to work in the office of a hemp-producing plantation that the family owned. Now eighteen and with a grudge against the world, he repaired to Peto, whose inhabitants were for the most part mestizos and Indians. Although their food and manner of life were in general distasteful to him, he married Marta, a member of the mestizo family with whom he lived. In the town there was another Cuban, Cerilo Seijas, a barber, a musician, a reader of philosophical works, and an advocate of free love, who urged Juan to desert Marta, now pregnant, and establish himself in a more civilized region. These arguments, supplemented by a letter from Julia, induced his return to Merida under the pretext that Adolfo had summoned him. He secured employment in the cigar shop where Julián worked, and reunited himself with Julia, who, the author maintains, was as madly in love with him as if she had been a respectable girl of good family. So absorbed was she in him that she neglected her patrons and thereby incurred the ill will of the proprietress of the house, who appealed to her lover, known as the "Colonel," to warn Juan; and in the altercation that followed his attempt to do so, he was seriously wounded. For this offense, Juan was imprisoned; there the "jefe político," also one of Julia's admirers, was very glad to keep him. Although the Cuban émigrés were joyfully anticipating an immediate return to their country, for the intervention of the United States in 1898 had brought independence from Spain, all appeals to Adolfo proved fruitless. When Juan did secure his freedom, through Julia's influence, it was on condition that he proceed under escort directly to the boat bound for Cuba without seeing her.

Back in Havana, Juan was at first unable, since he had taken no part in the fighting, to secure any employment except manual; but he saw and heard of many of his old acquaintances. Nena, whose letters Juan finally destroyed, had married into one of the richest and most prominent families of Havana; Adolfo was now a judge; and Robertico, whose oldest son was finishing the law course at the university, had an excellent position. Although nonparticipants in the insurrection, they did not fail to sing aloud that their father had fought in the Guerra Grande and that their brother Domingo had been killed in the last insurrection.

With no aid from any member of this family, which was covertly hostile to him, Juan obtained a position in a secretariat, where through his own ability and the influence of Julián, now a politician, he earned enough to marry Julia, a stenographer he had become acquainted with in the office. Although they had two children, no spiritual unity bound them, for all Juan's interest had centered in reading, in making a cultured man of himself. Only too conscious of the sham,

pretense, and rapacity of those in high position, and the great
gap between the poor and ignorant and the more favored in
education and wealth, Juan followed Julián's advice and entered politics. Five years after this decision he took stock of
himself: for four years he had been deputy in the National
Congress, and was now starting on his career as senator; in
addition, he was rich; his cars were of the latest and most
expensive models; his mistress, a pretty blonde, was supported
in style; for his child by Petra, he had secured a government
position, and to Marta and his other child he sent money for
their maintenance. Any ideals he may have had at one time
had been completely shattered; entirely disillusioned he had
accepted the world about him.

The underlying plot—covering some forty years, from the
middle eighties to 1927—though diffuse, is kept well in hand.
Interwoven closely are the threads linking Juan, on the one
hand, with the Ruiz and Fontanills family, representative of
wealth, ease, and position; on the other, with the families of
Rómulo and Fidel—the underdogs, both black and white—
who typify want, exhaustion, and brutality. All are fully delineated, but without violence to relevancy, for it was the
writer's intention to pillory the social system that permitted
sons of the under-privileged, reared in ignorance and poverty,
to be subject to, judged by, and punished according to a code
suited only to those of higher moral development, while
worthless sons of aristocratic parents were awarded unmerited
positions of distinction.

Just as Juan is, from the first page to the last, the main figure
of the story, he is also the best developed character. In the
first place, he is very human, and for that reason enigmatical,
contradictory in attitudes, and neither entirely good nor entirely bad. Proud of his legitimate birth, acute of mind and
sensitive by nature, he was made to feel his social inferiority
from childhood; as a result, he developed early a grudge
against a world that had not treated him fairly as well as a sort
of inferiority complex. Yet he was something of a pícaro, for

he did not hesitate to steal, if he thought he would not be caught; and he kept Nena's letters—and she perhaps the only woman that he ever really loved—with the hope of extorting money from her or her family. While he did something ultimately for his two illegitimate children, he was absolutely unprincipled in regard to women, for if he could be excused for deserting Petra, he could not be for abandoning Marta. Although keenly sensitive to social injustice, instead of defending the downtrodden, he used his position of deputy to enrich himself, concluding that the one who has the opportunity to grab some worldly goods and does not do it, is less than a fool. A victim of his environment, he accepted, in the end, conditions as they were. For wealth and ease, he deserted the inarticulate poor.

This vivid presentation of life in Cuban government circles —valuable not only for emphasizing its effect on Juan as an individual but also as a documentary portrayal of social life in the twenties—is only one of a number in the book. On the whole, the milieu is presented very effectively, for it is generally closely related to the protagonist himself, and proves a factor that frequently contributed to making him the kind of man that he was. One such was the shabby district of Havana Juan and his mother lived in, with its street calls, its smelly food shops, its gambling places, its Chinese candy peddlers that Juan and his companions used to rob, and its houses of prostitution, through the windows of which they used to peep. From this street, the background shifts to Don Roberto's big household, the life of which, as well as the house itself, is pictured in detail. Though fairly comfortable there, Juan was made to feel that he was unescapably a menial, and in the games with the children, that he was a social inferior; but here it was, too, that he came in contact with culture, with books that started him on the road to educating himself. Life in this house contrasted so strongly with that of the people in Juan's next environment, the sugar plantation, that he could never quite forget their miserable state.

While preëminently Cuban in his interests, the influence of European novelists—especially French, Spanish, and the Portuguese Eça de Queiroz—is admitted by Loveira himself. In spirit and in practice he is closer to nineteenth than to twentieth-century ideals, for like Zola, Pérez Galdós, and Blasco Ibáñez, he is primarily a propagandist and a realist. Vitally interested in sociological problems, he sets forth his ideas regarding them in a vigorous, often oratorical, style, and—unlike many contemporary Spanish-American novelists—with little or no concern for literary embellishment. The many colloquial words and expressions that color his pages do not seem to be merely dragged in, as occurs in so many Spanish-American works of fiction; neither does he hesitate to coin a word when he has need of one. While he wrote, no doubt, with great facility, he is truly Spanish in that he gave little attention to revision or polishing. And this is to be regretted, for his novels would have gained much had the superfluous been trimmed away.

In spite of his faults as a literary artist, Loveira's works have permanent value. In the first place, they are genuine. The only period that he treats is that covered by his own life, an eventful and colorful era in Cuban history, marked first by ardent patriotism and later by wholesale political corruption. The background, pictured at times with photographic exactness, is not exclusively but preëminently Cuban; the atmosphere ranges from tropic languor to hurricane violence. The incidents are evidently taken in a large measure from his own experiences; although changed, no doubt, in certain instances, they are transmitted to the reader without the loss of a sense of reality. His characters are human, variable and contradictory, strange mixtures of good and evil, in the conventional sense. It is truth rather than beauty that characterizes his pictures of Cuban society; it is sincerity rather than artistry that marks his strokes. The ideas that he sets forth are of vital concern to him and it is with the fundamental problems of life that he deals. His main themes are labor, as a means to something more than a mere existence; and marriage, as a union growing out of love, congeniality, or common interests and aspirations. He looks to no future world for compensation for the miseries suffered here; he recognizes none of the peace which the Church promises its faithful; he sees Christian morality as tentacles which bind to unendurable misery much of the Latin world, especially the women. He sees Nature flouted and social institutions honored; integrity sacrificed to greed; and ideals trampled into dust.

For the truth and sincerity with which he paints his era, and for the implications to which his violent contrasts point, Loveira's novels will continue to hold a very prominent place in Cuban fiction.

CHAPTER V ✿

EDUARDO BARRIOS
PSYCHOLOGICAL NOVELIST
OF CHILE

✿

IN THE FIELD of fiction, Chile has particularly distinguished
herself: the number of her writers who have devoted their
energy to that literary form has been large, and the quality
of their work has been high. In the second half of the nineteenth century, the Chilean Alberto Blest Gana (1831-1920)
was unsurpassed in Spanish America as a novelist. A follower
of the realistic school, he mirrored in his novels the manners,
customs, and history of his country. He seems, too, to have
directed the trend of fiction in Chile; for a marked tendency
toward objectivity characterizes both his contemporaries and
those that followed him. Orrego Luco, in *Casa Grande* (1908)
and other novels, presented the follies, extravagances, and prejudices of the Chilean landed aristocracy in the last decade
of the nineteenth century; and in the present century, Mariano
Latorre in more than a dozen collections of short stories, and
Luis Durand in his excellent novel *Mercedes Urízar* and
other works have depicted Chilean rural types and life. Nor
have there been lacking in Chile adherents of the extreme
realistic school, who have preferred to depict the life of certain underprivileged and degenerate classes of the towns and
cities. Lillo, in two collections of short stories, *Sub Terra*
(Beneath the Earth), 1904, and *Sub Sole (Beneath the Sun)*,

1907, dealt with the hard lot of the coal miners in his native town, Loto; and Edwards Bello, notably in *El Roto* (*The Degenerate*), 1918, and Alberto Romero, in *La mala Estrella de Perucho Gonzáles* (*The Evil Star of Perucho Gonzáles*), 1935, have occupied themselves with the degenerate classes of Santiago. Also, in certain works of Eduardo Barrios, with whom this essay is principally concerned, there is ample evidence of the influence of French naturalistic writers; however, he owes his distinction as a novelist to his portrayal of the inner rather than the outer world.

Barrios was born in Valparaiso, Chile, in 1884, but his parents had been married in Lima during the occupation of that city by the Chilean army, in which his father was an officer. His mother, the offspring of a German father and a French-Basque mother, was born there, but she had spent her childhood and early youth in Hamburg. When Eduardo was five, his father died and his mother returned to her father's home in Lima, and there the boy went to school for some ten years. He then returned to his native Valparaiso, where his paternal grandfather secured for him an appointment in the national military school. Although he distinguished himself as a student, a military career was not to his liking, and after two years he withdrew from the college.

Angered by his disdain of the army, his outraged grandfather refused him further financial support. He was then forced to rely upon himself, and sought to make his living at first one occupation and then another—as merchant, bookkeeper, agent, rubber buyer, and mine prospector—in the nitrate fields of northern Chile, in the rubber-producing regions of Peru, in Guayaquil, in Montevideo, and in Buenos Aires. It was probably during his wanderings that he published in Iquique, Chile, in 1907, his first book, *Del Natural* (*In the Naturalistic Style*). He settled finally in Santiago, the Chilean capital, and in 1913 published there a volume containing two plays, "Lo que niega la Vida" ("That Which Life With-

holds") and "Por el Decoro ("For the Sake of Decorum").
The next ten years proved to be the period of his greatest pro-
ductivity. During that time practically all of his work appeared: *El Niño que enloqueció de Amor* (*The Love-Crazed
Boy*), 1915, a collection of short stories; *Vivir* (*Life*), 1916,
a play; *Un Perdido* (*A Down-and-Outer*), 1917, a full-length
novel; *El Hermano asno* (*Brother Brute*), 1922, a novelette
and his masterpiece; and a collection of short stories, *Páginas
de un pobre Diablo* (*Pages from a Poor Devil's Diary*), 1923.
Another collection of stories, *Y la Vida sigue* (*Life Goes On*),
was published in Buenos Aires in 1925; but these, with the exception of a dramatic skit in prose, "Ante todo la oficina"
("The Office First of All"), are reprints. Literary work, it
seems, was merely incidental in the life of Barrios, for he
held many important positions in Santiago. Aside from serving
in a secretarial capacity both in the university and the national
congress, he held between 1925 and 1931—the period of the
dictatorship of Carlos Ibáñez—such important posts as minister
of education and director of the national library. Since his
resignation from the latter post, he has been connected with
two newspapers of Santiago, *El Mercurio* and *Las Ultimas
Noticias*.

When Barrios published his first work, *Del Natural*, in 1907,
French Naturalism was still exerting a very profound influence
throughout literary Spanish America. In Chile, Augusto
Thomson published in 1902 *Juana Lucero*, a protest against
social conditions which were inducing prostitution; Joaquín
Edwards Bello, in *El Inútil* (*The Useless*), 1910, *El Monstruo*
(*The Monster*), 1912, and other novels, revealed the depravi-
ties of various strata of Chilean society; and Barrios himself,
in his preface, entitled "Algo de interés" ("Something of
Interest"), to *Del Natural*, admitted a great admiration for
Zola and other naturalistic writers who insisted on a frank
discussion of sex. The bent of Barrios' talent was not so much
in the direction of the externalities of Zola, which prevail in

the works of Thomson and Edwards Bello, as in that of the analysis of character of Paul Bourget, whom he also mentions in his preface.

For it can be said in general that background plays almost a negative part in Barrios' work. In the three short skits "Amistad de Solteras" ("The Friendship of Maidens"), "Lo que ellos creen y lo que ellas son" ("What They Believe and Are"), "Celos bienhechores" ("When Jealousy Works to the Good") and the novelette "Tirana Ley" ("Tyrant Law"), which compose the collection *Del Natural,* the setting is Iquique, although there is scarcely anything in them beyond the names of a few streets that is distinctive of that port. There is, on the other hand, in each an interest from the psychological point of view, which is the quality above all others that distinguishes Barrios as a writer.

That interest in "Amistad de Solteras" and in "Lo que ellos creen y lo que ellas son" is certain aspects of feminine psychology. The first of these tells of two young girls who, although rivals for the love of a young man, were such good friends that they did not let themselves become jealous of each other; but when the man finally chose between them and married one, the other, piqued and jealous, accused her former friend of disloyalty. The second piece shows very amusingly and by concrete example that it is useless to warn a woman against the seductive charms of a man, since it will have no other effect than that of attracting her all the more to him.

In the remaining two pieces in the collection, it is male psychology that is of interest. The shorter, "Celos bienhechores," presents a young man about to break with his mistress, a charming and talented girl. But when he was confronted with the possibility of losing her, on seeing her with another, he realized at once her great worth.

In "Tirana Ley," Barrios undertook to write a thesis novel. His problem here was to show that love is supreme—that it is stronger than social convention, that it will brook no barrier. Erotic in nature, the novelette tells in considerable detail of a great but illicit love, between two young people of Iquique: a painter, Gastón Labarca, and a well-to-do widow, Luz Avilés. She had made a marriage of convenience and had had, even before the death of her husband, love affairs with various men. With none, however, had she been so deeply in love as with Gastón, who was equally fascinated with her. An incident brought both great unhappiness. One of Gastón's pictures inspired by Luz won first place in a Santiago exposition, and he was awarded a government scholarship to study in Paris. Although unwilling to leave Iquique, for it meant a separation, Gastón, after much persuasion on the part of a friend, did break with Luz, assigning as his reason her former lovers.

In Paris he was so unhappy he could not devote himself to his work. Finally, he wrote to Luz and confessed the wrong he had done her; with the letter he sent an extract from his diary so that she might see what his thoughts were in regard to her. This part of the book recalls the analysis of the emotions of Hubert Liauran in regard to his mistress in Bourget's *Cruelle Enigme;* in it, too, is to be found the quality, the interest in psychology, that particularly characterizes Barrios' fiction. In these pages Gastón recorded both actions and his "soul states"; his boredom with life; his inability to work; his constant thoughts of Luz, whose picture he would contemplate by the hour; his repentance of the wrong he had done; and his speculations in regard to the paternity of a child—in fact his own—born after his departure. After these memoirs the book comes speedily to an end—Gastón returned to Iquique, and he and Luz were married. "Tyrant law," love, won in the struggle with social convention.

Barrios, it seems, has never been especially proud of *Del Natural*—only one of its stories, "Amistad de Solteras," which was revised under the title of "Como hermanas" ("Like Sisters"), has been reprinted—but in his next fictional work, *El Niño que enloqueció de Amor*, he found the direction in which his talent lay. This work and those that followed it—

Un Perdido, El Hermano asno, Páginas de un pobre Diablo—
have more or less definite characteristics in common. There
is in the main character of each work, according to the admis-
sion of Barrios himself, an autobiographic element; excepting
Un Perdido, each of these works is characterized by a confessional tone and a definite self-analysis by the main character
himself; not much attention is given to either background or
plot, the emphasis being on character; there is a conflict, certainly, in each work, but it is almost entirely within, not without, the person concerned.

So it is indeed in *El Niño que enloqueció de Amor*, which
consists supposedly of the jottings that a schoolboy made in
his notebook. On the verge of premature adolescence, hypersensitive and timid, as is the type of character of which Barrios
is most fond, the young boy fell deeply in love with a young
lady, Angélica, who often came to visit his mother. Her arrival
would throw him almost into a nervous fit. His legs would
tremble; he experienced sensations of cold; he would scamper
off to hide from her; but irresistibly drawn to her, he would
approach her in the manner of a timid animal. At times,
Angélica would take him for a walk; on one occasion they met
her sweetheart, Jorge, and the young boy became insanely
jealous. Unable to sleep at night, he would weep; and in order
not to cry out, he would bite the sheets on his bed. So absorbed was his mind with Angélica that he failed in his studies
at school, but he continued to make observations concerning
her in his notebook—of a dress she wore whose red color was
reflected in her face, of the manner in which she would open
and close her eyes, of her hair which was curly and of a reddish tinge at the end, and the smell of her glove which enthralled him. Hopelessly enraptured, he stole her picture,
which he would take out and kiss when alone.

His infatuation for Angélica and his queer behavior did not
go unobserved in his home. His mother was sympathetic, and
so was a frequent visitor the boy admired deeply, Carlos
Romeral, to whom he was tempted at times to tell his troubles.

His brothers teased him for trying to move his eyelashes as
Angélica did; and, manly fellows, all of them, they despised
him, for he was weak, had legs like toothpicks, and took no
part in their games. His grandmother pitied him for his weakness, but at the same time she could not avoid showing her
contempt for him. At school he puzzled the teachers, for he
would not run and play as the other children did.

Instead, he confessed in his diary, he preferred to read
stories, through which he created a dream world for himself
as the hero and Angélica as the princess. But when Angélica
ceased to visit his mother, his nervousness increased; he made
up his mind to visit her, yet when he neared her home such a
fit of trembling would seize him that he could go no further.
Desperate one day, he did enter with the intention of killing
that Jorge whom he had seen with Angélica; instead, when he
reached them, he stopped short like a fool and then was so
rude that finally Angélica had to put him out of the house.
Symptoms of his neurasthenic condition became more marked;
at times he would suddenly begin to weep. Then the final
break came; it was at Angélica's house, where his mother had
taken him. Jorge was there; and when the poor schoolboy saw
him, he fell to weeping bitterly and loudly. He gradually grew
worse; before death finally brought release, he was entirely
insane.

El Niño que enloqueció de Amor is, from the standpoint of
technique, one of the best short stories in Spanish-American
literature. The story itself is slight—not one of action, but of
psychological struggle; nevertheless, it grips one's interest and
holds it fast from the very first line to the last. No small part
of the charm of the story is due to the masterly manner in
which it is told. One of its most alluring qualities is its apparently simple but highly wrought style: the structure of its
sentences, which are short and childlike, but at the same time
rhythmic; its simple, even colloquial language, which by Barrios' magic touch has been rendered highly poetic; and its
original figures, which are not too numerous or exaggerated,

as in much of present-day literature in Spanish America. One
note, that of tragedy, rings through the story from beginning
to end; much is gained, too, through the diary form, by which
the protagonist reveals his innermost soul; and there is very
strict adherence to the theme. Although the setting is sketched
in with the finest strokes, it is by no means vague. In a single
sentence, minor figures are vividly delineated: the grandmother of the young boy, with her white lips and yellow
teeth, her vein-swollen hands and her face the color of dry
dirt; his good and pretty aunt, with plump, white hands, who
could tell stories in a soft and pleasing voice; and Angélica's
sweetheart with small, round eyes, and mustache like a tooth-
brush. Certain facts, too, are revealed adroitly in passing—for
instance, that Don Carlos Romeral is the lover of the boy's
mother and, incidentally, *his* father.

In the same collection with *El Niño que enloqueció de
Amor* were published two other short pieces, "Pobre feo"
("Poor Ugly Man") and "Papá y Mamá." Although less dramatic than "El Niño," they are in the same poetic and compressed style that characterizes it. In the first of these, which
is entirely epistolary in form, Barrios presents again an individual who is a misfit in society—this time, a young man,
physically sound, intelligent, and gifted, but so ugly as to
repel women. A veritable "tranche de vie," the brief stay of
the ill-favored José in a boarding-house in Valparaiso, where
on account of his gawkiness and unusual height he became
the butt of all the jokes, is pictured through the letters two
young sisters write to an uncle. One of the girls, Isabel, was
kindhearted and finally came to pity José so much as to consider marrying him in order to make him happy; but her
uncle, in reply to her letter, advised against such a course,
counseling her to marry only for love. The other sister, Louisa,
who took a fiendish delight in tormenting José, showed him
the letter. In a highly nervous state, he quit the house and
was seen no more.

"Papá y Mamá," the last piece in the collection, is rather

a dramatic skit than a narrative. An example again of Barrios'
interest in child psychology, it presents some children at play
who enact dramatically a scene they had doubtlessly witnessed
in their own home—that between a man and his wife when the
former, in a hurry to eat and be off again, arrived home and
found that the dinner was not prepared.

In striking contrast with the skits and novelettes discussed
so far, *Un Perdido* is the most completely rounded novel that
Barrios wrote. In a measure autobiographic, as Barrios himself
admits, it records undoubtedly much regarding his own family
and relatives as well as his experiences in Valparaiso, Iquique,
and Santiago, all of which figure as background in the book.
As in *El Niño que enloqueció de Amor*, the interest, which is
also psychological, centers again around the same sort of
individual—the weak, hypersensitive Luis Bernales, who was
incapable of adjusting himself to the world; but *Un Perdido*
is much more extensive, for Luis is studied not apart from his
family and relatives, but in connection with them.

He inherited much from his maternal grandfather of German extraction, Juan Vera, a lover of Heine and Goethe and
a thorough romantic whose motto was that the heart and not
the head should always be followed. After having traveled
extensively Vera married and eventually settled down in very
comfortable circumstances in Quillota, which is near Valparaiso. Their only child, Rosario, married an army officer,
Luis Bernales; but one of the conditions of the marriage was
that she should always live with her parents. For a time
Rosario was very happy; two children, Anselmo and Rosarito,
were soon born to her; then, on account of an indiscretion on
her husband's part, a rift occurred between them. Although
they continued to live together, the breach was never quite
mended, and when he was promoted and transferred to Valparaiso it grew even wider. Some five years after the birth of
Rosarito, another child, Luis, the protagonist of the novel, was
born.

Loved and petted by his mother, the older children, and his

grandparents, Luis received all the attention generally accorded the youngest child, yet even at the age of two, such traits of character as sensitiveness and susceptibility were clearly perceptible. He was very responsive to caresses, and when his mother or some of the children kissed him, he would return the kisses with a very evident emotion of satisfaction. He had, it might be said, a propensity for ease and softness. This was encouraged by the coddling he received from all the household except his father, who with his rough ways of a soldier would often unintentionally throw him into a fit of terror. Conscious of the barrier that existed between him and his infant son, the father attempted to break it down but was unable to do so. As he grew older Luis developed into a very quiet and sedentary child. Rather than romp with the other children, he would sit quietly and dream. The three children would often play in the family coach: Rosarito, with her dolls, as a mother; Anselmo, a boy of action, playing the part of a coachman, would lash with a great show of energy his imaginary horses; but Luis, sitting quietly, saw in fancy on the journey "fields of golden wheat, blue thistles, skies of blinding light, and great flocks of birds." Among strangers Luis was very self-conscious and suffered greatly from timidity. Later, in school, although not of a studious nature, he did passably well, for he had a great horror of the embarrassing situations he would otherwise have experienced. Through his grandmother he became fond of attending mass, not from any religious zeal but on account of the pleasing sensations he experienced on witnessing the celebration of the poetic liturgy.

The peaceful existence that Luis was leading in Quillota came to an abrupt end in the early years of his adolescence. A fall cost his grandmother her life; his grandfather lost his fortune and, in an attempt to recoup it, his life; and, saddened by so much misfortune, his mother died. A breaking up of the entire family followed. Anselmo, who was already a cadet in the national military school in Valparaiso, had found his groove in life; Rosario was sent to relatives in Santiago; and

Luis accompanied his father, who had recently been transferred to the garrison in Iquique.

There the boy failed to adjust himself to the changed manner
of life. His father—in a way a stranger to him—with whom he
now lived in the barracks, treated him on the whole kindly;
yet there still remained between them that old barrier, which
each of them desired to break down but could not, for it
seems that the father was in a way as timid as his son. Luis
attended school, but after failing in his examinations he withdrew and took a clerkship in the barracks. Without obligations
after certain hours, he was much happier in this position, since
it gave him more time to indulge himself in newly-acquired
pleasures. For, through the tutelage of two young lieutenants,
Blanco and Vial, he had come to know actresses, prostitutes,
and gambling houses. He had discovered, too, a great comfort
in drink; under its influence he lost his timidity and became
bolder. The favorite of Meche, a young prostitute of one of
the better houses of the city, he soon fell deeply and sincerely
in love with her. Luis was drawn to her, however, not so
much by sexual pleasure, which indeed he found in her, as by
the refuge she afforded him from an unkind world. For in her
embrace he experienced the same pleasure he had felt as a
child when his mother cuddled and petted him in her arms.

Luis' love, however, was of a bubble's duration. On the
death of his father, he had to go to the home of his paternal
grandfather in Santiago, through whom he was encouraged
to accept an appointment to the national military school in
Valparaiso. Although he did passably well in his studies, life
in the school was very boring to him. At times, to relieve the
tedium, he drank; and hungry for love, he sought prostitutes,
whom he found unsatisfactory, since they did not give him
the mental satisfaction he had experienced in Meche. When
finally unable to endure the irksomeness of military life, he
secured his release from the school by pretending to have
rheumatism.

Despised and berated in his grandfather's household, to

which he returned, Luis occupied truly the place of an uninvited guest. At times, as is characteristic of the timid, he would burst forth against the treatment he received from his relatives; at others, with Bohemian acquaintances he had made in Santiago, he sought consolation in drink. He came at this time into closer contact with his sister, Rosarito, who lived with other relatives; and through her he met a cousin, Blanca, a rich and beautiful girl with whom he fell hopelessly in love. But just when the future seemed brighter for him—for he had secured a position in the National Library, and Blanca seemed to respond to his love—his brother Anselmo, already an army officer, fell in love with her and they were married.

Some two years after this disappointment, Luis, who still held his position in the Library, met by chance, on the streets of Santiago, a girl in want, Teresa Bórquez, whom he befriended and helped financially. Teresa had experienced a terrible disappointment and had come to Santiago to forget herself. Although Luis furnished a house and took the girl as his mistress, troubles soon beset them. His salary was meager; already a confirmed drunkard, he spent much on drink; and Teresa, while she loved him in a way, was unfaithful to him. On the other hand, enamoured of her only as he had been of Meche, Luis was desperate when one of his fellow workers in the Library apprised him of her infidelity. A violent scene over the matter ended with his pardoning her, as he was unable to bear her going away. Ashamed to return to the Library, he increased his financial difficulties by giving up the small position he had there. But Teresa did not tarry in deserting him, and a blow indeed it was to Luis, who, cold, drunk, and stupefied, wandered over the entire district of ill fame in search of her. From this disappointment Luis never recovered. Although only twenty-seven, he was hopelessly lost—an outcast, a confirmed dipsomaniac, dependent upon his sister, who sent him a monthly income. How could one with so many excellent qualities sink so low, wondered his friend Blanco who saw him at this time, when others far less capable were fattening on excellent positions? His tragedy was due—as Barrios has gone to great length to show—to timidity, to lack of will power, to hypersensitiveness, and to an absolute inability to harmonize his inner world of dreams with an outer world of actuality.

Although the vivisection of Luis' soul is the main interest in *Un Perdido*, the outer world in which he moves is more fully treated than in any of Barrios' other novels. While not unique or particularly striking, since it is city life, which is more or less the same in Europe and America, it nevertheless presents an extensive panorama of the various levels of the society in Chile that Luis knew: the home of the well-to-do Juan Vera; customs prevailing in houses of prostitution, and in the garrison and port life of Iquique; the military school in Valparaiso; and, in Santiago, the homes of the wealthy, the National Library, and the haunts of Bohemian artists. There is in the setting, however, very little description of physical objects. On the other hand, there is an admirable interpretation of the spirit of each place as felt by Luis: the ease and comfort of his grandfather's home in Quillota; the bustle of port life and his pleasant hours with Meche in the brothel in Iquique; the rigid discipline of the military school in Valparaiso; the spirit of order that prevailed in his paternal grandfather's house; the want and deprivation of the period with Teresa; and the hand-to-mouth existence of the Bohemian artist colony in Santiago.

In this novel, consequently, the localities have no interest apart from the people associated with them. A great array of them and all drawn from life, constitute the minor characters. While a few of these, such as "Petitpois," the keeper of a house of prostitution, are described, or rather caricatured physically, the treatment is preponderantly of the inner characteristics rather than the outer. Outstanding among them are Luis' father, himself a victim of the curse of timidity; Papá Juan Vera, of an artistic temperament, kind and tolerant; Lieutenant Blanco, amateur psychologist and philosopher, who analyzes the mental make-up of Luis, his father, and Papá Juan. Unforgettable, too, are the portraits of characters of a lesser category: his grandfather on his father's side, materialistic, cold, and calculating; his Aunt Elena, fifty but still a spoiled and petted child; and the director of the National Library, Don Manuel María, thrifty and absorbed in the history of concerts in Santiago, although he could not tolerate music. Despite its numerous characters, *Un Perdido* is by no means a tedious book.

The factor that probably contributes most to this interest-holding quality is the ability of the teller of the tale, without injecting himself at all through comments or explanations, without the reader's ever being conscious of him, to present his story dramatically—the protagonist always in the center of the stage—and in language that is both euphonious and emotive. Yet in his next work, his masterpiece, Barrios abandons this method completely for the autobiographic, which seems entirely in keeping with his genius.

Much more limited in scope, *El Hermano asno* presents, in the main, the mental world of Fray Lázaro, a Franciscan in a monastery in the city of Santiago. When he began to write down his experiences, he was in a very perplexed state of mind, since he still feared, despite the seven years he had been there, lest he be unable to keep the vows of poverty, chastity, and obedience. For he had tasted of the fruits of the world, and had entered the convent as the result of a great disillusionment he had suffered when Gracia, a young woman to whom he was engaged, married another. Despite his doubt as to whether he could ever become a good friar, he was unwilling to quit the convent, as he felt he would soon tire of the world should he re-enter it.

But a graver matter than doubt arose at this time to vex his soul. It was a relationship that grew up between him and Gracia's younger sister, María Mercedes, whose resemblance to Gracia impressed him forcefully when by chance he saw her one day in church. She saw him too and recalled vividly his treatment by her sister. There awoke in María Mercedes a great interest in Fray Lázaro, and in order to see him and to talk with him she became a frequent visitor at the monastery. Realizing that he was falling in love with her, he determined, quite vainly, to discourage her visits. Fray Lázaro was no longer the ardent lover he had once been; Franciscan discipline seemed to have tempered his passions, and he had become philosophic and reflective.

Not only did he reflect about himself but about his fellow friars, particularly Fray Rufino, who of all the order was most zealous in his piety, humility, and obedience. For Fray Rufino scourged himself; he slept in the mud; he was unwilling to kill the worms that had bored into the frame of a portrait of Our Lady; he caused the buildings to be overrun with mice, for he taught them and the cats to live in peace; and when the convent's old dog became very ill of pneumonia, not only did he care for him but he even barked for him so that the dog would not injure his lungs. Reports of his saintliness and of miracles spread, and visitors began to come to the monastery to see the holy man. But Fray Rufino came to regret the renown that had come upon him. For, as he confessed to Fray Lázaro, a Capuchin monk had repeatedly appeared to him and rebuked him for pride and haughtiness; consequently, he expressed the desire to commit some deed that would bring the scorn of his brothers upon him. Some time after this conversation, Fray Rufino did in fact attempt to ravish María Mercedes. Her cries attracted the attention of Fray Lázaro, who went to her aid. Prostrate from excitement, Fray Rufino, after admitting his crime to Fray Lázaro, died. To preserve the reputation of his dead brother, the other Franciscan took upon himself the blame for the misdeed; as a consequence, he was sent by the provincial of the order to a distant town. So concludes the book, but Barrios has left us in much doubt in regard to the actual motive for Fray Rufino's crime. Was it to see himself scorned; or, as the title of the book leads one to suspect, did lust, or "el hermano asno" as St. Francis referred to it, actually get possession of Fray Rufino and cause him to attempt to ravish the girl?

El Hermano asno, truly a landmark in Latin-American fiction, has many of the characteristics of the new type of novel. Unlike *Un Perdido*, it is brief. In the plot, there is very little physical action; but the soul struggle in Fray Lázaro and particularly in Fray Rufino is intense. The background, which is limited to the Franciscan monastery, is impressionistically interpreted. Barrios attains in this work his greatest perfection of style. Poetical figures are frequent; and both the short sentence and the repetition of words, phrases, and sentences are used effectively. The quality, perhaps, that distinguishes it most from his other works is the clearly detectable vein of quiet humor which enters into the presentation of the overzealous Fray Rufino.

From a literary point of view, Barrios seems to have almost completely spent himself in *El Hermano asno*. In the collection *Páginas de un pobre Diablo*, of 1923, there are only three new stories. Of these, "Canción" ("An Idyl"), which bears no date, seems to belong to Barrios' early period. Largely poetical in nature, diffuse in its narrative element, it pictures scenes in the port of Valparaiso, in which figure Olga, a sheltered young girl, Ramiro Concha, with whom she is in love, and a friend of his, Gastón Labarca, a painter.

The remaining two stories—"Antipatía" and "Páginas de un pobre Diablo," the title story of the collection—bear the date of 1923 and were in all probability written in that year. Both stories are of a morbid nature, and in this quality as well as in their rhythmic prose recall very definitely certain aspects of the work of Valle-Inclán. Also, there is in "Antipatía" ("Antipathy"), in addition to a decidedly unethical bias, a certain heartlessness that is entirely out of keeping with the rest of Barrios' work. For, in this story, a young doctor gave an overdose of morphine to a boyhood acquaintance, not so much because he knew that he would die at all events and wanted to shorten his suffering, but because he had always had an inexplicable aversion for him. Then, while he was waiting for him to die, he set about entertaining the three sisters of the dying man, all of whom were ridiculous for their pronounced ugliness; and, as a result of a rather risqué joke, had converted their grief into hilarity just at the moment that one of the sisters went to her brother's bed and found him dead. A very droll figure in the same household was a young peon, who never in all his life had a pair of shoes; he, too, like the doctor, desired his master's death, as thereby he might get a pair of lately-bought shoes.

There is also a sense of the ludicrous in a rather gruesome situation in "Páginas de un pobre Diablo," which is by far the best of the three stories. Here, Barrios turns again to the confessional type of story and to his favorite character, a timid, hypersensitive, neurotic person—in this case a young man who wrote down his experiences and emotions during some months in which he was an employee in an undertaking establishment in Santiago. Among the excellent features of the story is the delineation of the undertaker who welcomed an epidemic and watched with great satisfaction a funeral procession if the coffin had been bought from him; if not, he turned aside in great disgust. There is throughout the story, too, a certain type of humor, which lies in the fact that the peculiar individual who wrote the memoirs was aware of his own peculiarity and of the incongruity between himself and the position he occupied.

With *Páginas de un pobre Diablo* Barrios' work came practically to an end. Although his place in Spanish-American literature is indisputably high, his entire literary output is small. His first book was published in 1907 and his last of any importance in 1923. In spite of the fact that literature has been an incidental matter in his life, it has been—on the other hand —a very personal matter. For Barrios' interest, literally speaking, is not in background or social problems, as is characteristic in general of Spanish-American fiction today, but in himself; and for his psychological analyses of those abnormal, self-centered characters in *El Niño que enloqueció de Amor* and *Un Perdido*, he drew, he confesses, upon himself. The latter novel contains much, too, of his own tempestuous life in Valparaiso, Iquique, and Santiago; and Fray Lázaro in *El Hermano asno*—disillusioned, tired of the empty pleasures of the world and now philosophic—seems to reflect the middle-age attitude of Barrios. In addition to his ability in psychological analysis, Barrios has a strong claim to fame for his style; in this, with the possible exception of Ricardo Güiraldes, he is without a peer among the writers of fiction in Spanish America. Nurtured on the rhythmical prose of the Spanish mystics, of the same literary tendencies as such contemporary Spanish "modernists" as Valle-Inclán, Ricardo León, Azorín, and Pérez de Ayala, Barrios attaches much importance to the pure music of style, without which "there are no sympathetic waves that enter the heart."[1]

[1] "Algo de mí" ("A Bit About Myself"), in *Y la Vida Sigue* (Buenos Aires, 1925), p. 87.

CHAPTER VI

A RENOWNED SHORT-STORY WRITER
HORACIO QUIROGA

✻

A MONG THE forms of fiction for which writers of Spanish America have shown a decided preference, particularly during the present century, is the brief prose narrative, or *cuento*. Nearly all of the outstanding novelists of this period —Gallegos, Güiraldes, Gálvez, Azuela, and Barrios—in addition to their longer works, have written *cuentos*. The word *cuento*, however, on account of its various connotations, is a nondescript and consequently unsatisfactory term. It is used, as an examination of any complete collection of *cuentos* will testify, to designate anecdotes and fables; legendary accounts, such as the *tradiciones* of Ricardo Palma; essays of manners and customs, in the manner of *Pago Chico*, a collection of *cuentos* by the Argentine writer Roberto J. Payró; prose poems, such as the *cuentos* by Amado Nervo, Díaz Rodríguez, and others, with emphasis on style rather than on other fictional elements; and short stories in the modern sense of the word—unfortunately rare both in Spain and Spanish America —such as "La Galleguita" ("The Galician Girl") by Hernández Catá, "El Milagro" ("The Miracle") by Mateo Booz, "El Alfiler" ("The Pin") by V. García Calderón, and "María del Carmen" by Francisco Espinola—all of which are in technique lineal descendants of the short story as created by Poe and Maupassant.

Their brevity, as in the case of poetry, has facilitated the publication, within the last two decades, of collections of *cuentos*. The first of these, *Los mejores Cuentos Americanos* (*The Best American Tales*), 1920, contains the cream of Spanish-American short stories—in the judgment of the compiler, Ventura García Calderón, an excellent critic. The only other collection of a general nature, exclusive of school texts, is the *Antología del Cuento hispano-americano* (*Anthology of Spanish-American Tales*), 1939, compiled by Antonio R. Manzor. Collections of the best *cuentos* of a single country or region— Mexico, Venezuela, Colombia, Chile, and the River Plate[1]— and of individual writers—Viana, Lillo, Blanco Fombona, Quiroga, López Albújar, and José de la Cuadra[2]—have also

---

[1] Among the most outstanding are *Antología de Cuentos mexicanos* (*Anthology of Mexican Tales*), 1926, by Ortiz de Montellano; *Los mejores Cuentos Venezolanos* (*The Best Venezuelan Tales*), 1923, by Valentín de Pedro and a recent two-volume work, *Antología del Cuento venezolano* (*Anthology of Venezuelan Tales*), 1940, by A. Uslar Pietri and Julián Padrón; various volumes in the collection *Biblioteca Aldeana de Colombia* (*The Aldine Collection of Colombian Literature*), 1936, compiled by D. Samper Ortega; *Los Cuentistas chilenos* (*Story-Tellers of Chile*), n. d., by R. Silva Castro and *Antología de Cuentistas chilenos* (*Anthology of Chilean Tales*), 1938, by Manuel Latorre, one of Chile's best *cuentistas;* and *Los mejores Cuentos* (*The Best of Tales*), 1919, by Manuel Gálvez and *Antología de Cuentistas rio-platenses* (*Anthology of the River Plate Region*), both of which include *cuentos* of the River Plate region.

[2] Only a few such writers can be mentioned here: Javier Viana, whose *Campo* (*In the Country*), in 1898, was followed by more than a dozen collections of stories; Baldomero Lillo's *Sub Terra*, 1904, and *Sub Sole*, 1907; Blanco Fombona's *Cuentos Americanos* (*American Stories*), 1904-13, 1920; Horacio Quiroga's stories concerning Misiones in *Cuentos de Amor, de Locura y de Muerte* (*Stories of Love, Madness, and Death*), 1917; López Albújar's *Cuentos Andinos* (*Andean Tales*), 1920, and *Nuevos Cuentos andinos* (*New Andean Tales*), 1937; and José de la Cuadra's *El Amor que dormía* (*The Love that Slept*), 1930, *Repisas* (*Brackets*), 1931, *La Vuelta de Locura* (*The Recurrence of Madness*), 1932, *Horno* (*The Furnace*), 1932, and *Los Sangurimas* (*The Sangurimas Family*), 1934.

been compiled. As compared with the best of modern short stories, the *cuentos* of these six writers are technically deficient; nevertheless the *criollismo* or vital concern of each for his native land and people has given them distinction. The degeneracy of the *gaucho* of Viana's Uruguay; the pitiless treatment of the unorganized workers in the coal mines of Lillo's Chile; the most intimate vices of the *montuvios*, a people of Indian, Negro, and white blood who live on the coast of José de la Cuadra's Ecuador; the ignorance and superstition of the people, the lack of sincerity on the part of revolutionary leaders, and the futility of democracy in Blanco Fombona's Venezuela; and not only the injustice of the whites towards the Indians, but also their own cruelty and viciousness in López Albújar's Peru are all brought out in these *cuentos*. Aside from their deep concern with these problems, Blanco Fombona and López Albújar sought beauty in style, both having been strongly influenced by the "modernista" movement. Although subordinate to the human element, the background —whether it be the plains of Uruguay, the coal mines of Chile, the forests of Venezuela, the Andean plateaus of Peru, or the jungles of the Ecuadorian lowlands—is an important factor with all these writers. In contrast, Horacio Quiroga, acknowledged peer of Spanish-American short-story writers, is less interested in people; instead, in the stories on which his high reputation depends, it is the background itself, the tropical Misiones of northern Argentina, on which emphasis is laid.

Into a full appreciation of the work of Horacio Quiroga, knowledge of his own life must enter. For it is his own life, rich in experience, which furnishes him the material for most of his stories; he himself is his own chief character; and in his work he reveals, to an extent true of few writers, his own character and temperament. He was born, December 31, 1878, in Salto, Uruguay, where his father was the Argentine consul. After the accidental death of her husband, Horacio's mother took him, still very young, and her older children to reside in Córdoba (Argentina). Some five years later she returned to

Salto, where Horacio attended the Hiram school, which was maintained by the Masonic order, and later completed the work of the Polytechnique Institute. Although he gave evidence of creative imagination and superior intelligence, he was an undependable, fractious, willful, and petulant schoolboy who shunned the society of others and found his pleasure in reading, especially books of travel and periodical literature. While enrolled in the University of Montevideo, he was a pronounced individualist who pursued only the subjects that interested him—history, chemistry, and philosophy—and sought the company only of those of similar interests. Outside of the university he distinguished himself for his hobbies—bicycling, photography, and the manual arts, especially carpentry and ironwork. Narcotics, too, fascinated him; not only did he take chloroform to allay suffering from asthma, but he experimented on himself with hashish. Besides being interested in the theater and in music, he was passionately fond of nineteenth-century French literature, particularly the works of the Parnassians. Pronouncedly influenced by these writers are his own first articles, which appeared under the pseudonym of Guillermo Eynhardt in two literary periodicals, La Revista, in 1897, and Gil Blas, the following year.

Experiences around the turn of the century, when he reached his majority, deeply influenced Quiroga's later life. With some of his youthful companions in literary interests, he visited Leopoldo Lugones in Buenos Aires, in 1898, and became an ardent admirer both of the man and of his verse. That same year, in keeping with his visionary and unrestrained nature, Quiroga fell desperately in love with a girl he met in Salto, María Esther; but he was doomed to bitter disappointment, for the girl's mother objected to him as a suitor. In September of that year he established a literary periodical, which lasted but five months; in this his work, influenced to a marked degree by Poe and Lugones, is decidedly modernistic. The following year brought the realization of the great dream of his life—to see Paris; but lack of funds while there entailed great hardships and shortened his visit to a few months. Back in Montevideo in 1900, he was for the next two years the moving spirit in one of the most important literary groups of the city, the "Consistorio del Gay Saber." His own writings for this period are to be found in the records of this society; in his first book, *Los Arrecifes de Coral* (*Coral Reefs*), 1901; in the daily newspapers; and in two literary periodicals, *Rojo y Blanco* and *La Alborada*. In 1902 he accidentally shot and killed one of his best friends, Fernando Ferrando, who had been closely associated with him. Shaken by the tragedy, Quiroga left Montevideo for Buenos Aires.

Through friends Quiroga soon found means of earning a living there, and early in 1903 he secured a position as teacher of Spanish in the Colegio Nacional. When he resigned shortly to join a historical commission that was leaving for Misiones in northern Argentina, he took a step that led directly to his fame as a *cuentista*. The commission, of which Lugones was in charge, had been appointed to study the ruins of the Jesuit settlements, which had given the name to the region. One of the most important of these was at San Ignacio on the banks of the Paraná River, in the midst of dense forests which covered an area remarkable for its fertile soil, heavy rainfall, and many streams subject to frequent and rapid rises. In this hot, sultry region the Jesuits for almost a century and a half maintained missions, but the native Indians wandered away after the expulsion of their spiritual leaders. Only the ruins of the cathedral, the college, and living quarters remained—mute witnesses in stone of Catholic attempts to Christianize and civilize the people of the region.

With all that he saw in Misiones—the broad expanse of the Paraná River, the tropical forests, the strange animals, and the deadly serpents—Quiroga was enthralled. He had known of them from childhood, but only through the eyes of others. On his return to Buenos Aires early in 1904 he published a volume of stories, *El Crimen del Otro* (*Another's Crime*); but the urge to return to the tropical jungle was strong within him. It was easy, consequently, for a friend to persuade him to join in the purchase of a tract of land in the Chaco, some seventy miles from Resistencia, for the purpose of growing cotton. The undertaking failed, and early in 1905 Quiroga returned to Buenos Aires. That same year he published a short story, *Los Perseguidos* (*The Haunted Ones*), and became closely connected with the leading literati of the city— Lugones, Roberto Payró, and the dramatist Florencio Sánchez. His contributions to various literary periodicals—*Caras y Caretas, El Hogar, El Atlántida*—also began that year. In 1906 he was appointed to a professorship of the Spanish language and literature in the Escuela Normal. Teaching, however, was not his forte, and the fact that he purchased at this time 185 hectares of land near San Ignacio in Misiones is evidence of his intention ultimately to return there. During his vacations he made the 800-mile journey up the Paraná River to improve his property. His dream of a small, lovely cottage in the midst of this vast virgin forest had never left him, and now he sought to make that dream a reality. By the end of 1908, which saw the publication of his novelette *Historia de un Amor turbio* (*An Ill-Fated Love*), he had built with his own hands a rough cottage in this untracked wilderness. He had feverishly hurried its completion, for he was deeply in love with Ana María Cires, one of his pupils in the Escuela Normal; and his dreams included marrying her and taking her to Misiones to live. Although Ana María's parents objected to Quiroga as an erratic individual, they finally gave their consent to the marriage, which took place on December 30, 1909.

Shortly afterward Quiroga and his bride set off up the Paraná for the wilds of Misiones. At once he began improving the house, which leaked copiously—for the unseasoned lumber had shrunk. The outdoor life and the opportunity of making his living with his hands delighted him; and in 1911 he broke with civilization by resigning from the Escuela Normal. He was not without a remunerative position, however, for the governor of the territory of Misiones, in appreciation of his literary work, had appointed him justice of the peace and also official recorder for the district of San Ignacio; but, intensely occupied with his own undertakings, he was very remiss in the execution of his public duties. While he enthusiastically embarked during the next few years on various enterprises—a stock company for the growing of *yerba mate*, the distillation of alcohol from oranges, the utilization of a particular wood for the making of charcoal, and the manufacturing of pottery —all proved, aside from furnishing him material for some of his best stories, unprofitable. He spent much time hunting, fishing, sailing his boat on the Paraná, and listening to stories and tales about the district.

Two children were born to him and Ana María: Eglé, in January of 1911, and Darío, in Buenos Aires, the following year. Eglé was born in Misiones without the aid of a physician, for Quiroga held that childbirth should be entrusted to Nature alone, and Ana María almost died. For the birth of her second child, she returned to Buenos Aires. Although Quiroga and Ana María loved each other, their lives came to be a long succession of quarrels and reconciliations. She was very excitable and easily provoked; he was irascible and headstrong. His ideas on rearing the children—for he wanted to bring them up like young animals, in what he regarded as Nature's way— particularly irritated her. In one of her fits of anger she took poison to end her life and, after much suffering, died in December, 1915. Quiroga then had to occupy himself with the duties of his household, for he was unable to keep a servant on account of his irritability; but at the end of a year he abandoned Misiones and returned with his children to Buenos Aires.

The next nine years seem to have been one of the most active and productive periods of his life. In 1917 he made the collection of stories *Cuentos de Amor, de Locura, y de Muerte;* he was given a position in the Uruguayan consulate; and he and three friends, in a boat he had made with his own hands, sailed the long way up the Paraná to pass their vacation on Quiroga's place in Misiones. Back in Buenos Aires he took a house in Agüeros Street, where he lived for more than seven years. His most distinctive work, *El Salvaje* (*The Savage*), 1920, was followed by *Cuentos de la Selva para Niños* (*Tales of the Jungle*), 1921, *Anaconda* and *Las Sacrificadas* (*The Sacrificed*), 1923, and *El Desierto* (*The Wilderness*), 1924. During this time his contributions to various periodicals and dailies—*La Nación, La Prensa, Caras y Caretas, Fray Mocho, Atlántida,* and *El Hogar*—were also numerous. Those were pleasant years, too, it seems. He spent hours in his shop working with his beloved tools; his house, although by no means pretentious, was visited by the literati of the city; and, devoted as he was to his children, he spent much time on their education, although in sudden fits of anger he would sometimes punish them severely. Through prominent friends in the federal government in Montevideo, he received promotions in the consular service and in 1922 was appointed secretary of the Uruguayan delegation that was sent to Rio de Janeiro to the centenary celebration of Brazil's independence. But Quiroga, subject as he was to whims and caprices, could not remain in any one groove. Obtaining a leave from the consulate in 1925, he left Buenos Aires suddenly and returned to Misiones, where he resumed his old life, working his farm and visiting his neighbors at odd times. Although the house and furniture brought back memories of his dead wife, they did not prevent him, now in his forty-seventh year, from falling desperately in love with a young girl in the neighborhood, again Ana María by name, whom he had known some eight years previously as a mere child. The girl responded to his prince-charming love, but her parents put an end to the affair by sending her away. He, too, left Misiones.

Back in Buenos Aires early in 1926, with his children, his menagerie of wild and tame animals, his souvenirs of Misiones, particularly the skins of the snakes and animals he had killed, he moved to Vicente López Street. Again a city dweller, he renewed acquaintance with his literary friends; he indulged himself in his favorite diversion, the "movies," of which he was a confirmed habitué; and in addition to publishing a series of sketches of types in Misiones—*Los Desterrados* (*Exiles*), 1926, and a novelette on his own recent ill-fated love affair, he wrote extensively for periodicals—articles, animal stories for children, and reviews of moving pictures. There was time too, unfortunately, for another love affair, with María Elena, a girl of twenty, whom he married in July, 1927. Differences early arose between the two. He was jealous; and she, it seems, had not married him for love but was interested in him only as a successful writer. The birth of a child did not help matters. Again weary of the life he was leading in Buenos Aires, Quiroga decided to seek contentment once more in Misiones. He succeeded in being transferred as consul to San Ignacio, for which he embarked, with his family and all his belongings, early in 1932. He himself was delighted with returning to his old way of living; but his wife, in spite of his efforts to content her, grew so weary of life in the tropics that he finally let her return to Buenos Aires. It was in those dark days of domestic friction that his last book, with its foreboding title, *Más Allá* (*The Great Beyond*), 1934, was published. Other difficulties also beset him. The closing of the Uruguayan consulate in San Ignacio left him without a position. In 1935, through the influence of friends, he was appointed honorary consul, but more than a year passed before he received any salary. Then ill health, caused by cancer, set in. When medical aid became imperative, he sailed down the Paraná, for the last time, in September, 1936, and entered a hospital in Buenos Aires, more or less as a charity patient. In the following February he ended his life by taking a deadly poison. The body was interred, at the expense of friends, in his native Salto.

Quiroga was, to say the least, a strange individual. Ill health was probably one of the causes of his fractiousness, for various diseases beset him at different periods in his life—asthma in his childhood, dyspepsia in his early manhood, and later prostate trouble. Inherently, too, he was capricious, morbid, and introspective. In school he was undependable, and as an official very remiss in his duties; yet he was capable of great energy and endurance in the prosecution of some plan or scheme that struck his fancy, whether it was building a house or a boat, clearing land, working his farm, or engaging in some agricultural or chemical experiment.

Between Quiroga the man and Quiroga the writer there is an inseparable bond. In many of his stories, he himself, faithfully delineated, is the principal character, and events from his own life—his disappointments in love, his experiences in the wilds of the Chaco and Misiones, his scientific experiments—provide him with the narratives. Highly imaginative by nature, he reveals, like the true romantic that he was, his obsession for the supernatural, particularly the thought of an existence after death, on which hinges a goodly number of his stories. Although he was indifferent toward religion, his observations in certain essays and allegories on human conduct bespeak a truly high and noble soul. His writings during his youth and his last years reveal that his mind was often occupied with thoughts on insanity, suicide, and murder.

His fondness for such morbid subjects appeared at the outset of his literary career. That he was very deeply impressed by d'Annunzio's *Il Trionfo della Morte* is evident in "El Guardabosque comediante" ("The Actor Forest-Guard") and "Sin Razón, pero cansado" ("Without Reason but Tired"), two stories in his first book, *Los Arrecifes de Coral*, 1901. This novel of d'Annunzio traces the progress of insanity in the protagonist, Giorgio Aurispa, who, bored with existence, murders his mistress and takes his own life. Under the spell of this book, the central figure in "El Guardabosque comediante" lets himself be devoured by a pack of wolves. There is no reference to d'Annunzio's novel in "Sin Razón, pero cansado"; its influence, however, is evident, particularly in Luciano, a bored individual, who, like his prototype, Giorgio, murders his mistress when he tires of her.

Quiroga admits also, in his early writings, an absorbing passion for Poe, who, as Englekirk observes in his *Edgar Allan Poe in Hispanic Lands,* had a very definite influence on him. "El Crimen del Otro," the title story of one of his collections, is admittedly inspired by "The Cask of Amontillado." The two characters in the story are insane; infatuated with Poe's tales, each reveals their effect on him; and, finally, one of them, following Poe's story, buries the other alive. Insanity is the theme of "La justa Proporción de las Cosas" ("Things in Exact Proportion")—another story in the collection—and also of *Los Perseguidos.* The latter is unique in that it is a sort of case history, purportedly written by one suffering from a persecution complex, of another victim of the same malady. Two other stories in the collection seem to derive their inspiration from Poe: "El triple robo de Bellamore" ("A Triple Robbery by Bellamore"), a very lame attempt at a detective story, and "Historia de Estilicón" ("The Story of Estilicón"), in which the destiny of a man, a woman, and a gorilla are fatally interwoven—a queer story surpassing Poe in certain abnormalities.

D'Annunzio and Poe were not the only writers that influenced Quiroga. In his youth in Montevideo he was one of the leaders of a group of admirers of modernism. Particularly in the sketches in *El Crimen del Otro,* such as "La Princesa bizantina" ("The Byzantine Princess"), Quiroga was endeavoring to write in the modernist manner and striving for effect through rhythmic and figurative language. In his third work, *Historia de un Amor turbio,* he is not concerned with refinements of style but with psychological analysis. The influence of Dostoevski in this novelette Quiroga acknowledged some years later, and he added that the Russian was one of very few writers in whom he still retained an interest.

In all this early work, in which Quiroga was endeavoring to find himself, individuality was lacking; but nevertheless the direction his later work was to take, in technique and subject matter, is clearly indicated. Like his more mature productions, they are, first of all, impressionistic; for Quiroga aims primarily at creating in the mind of the reader a mood, to which the action of the story is entirely subservient. The prevailing tone is one of gloom, although, as in "La Muerte del Canario" ("The Death of the Canary"), there are occasional touches of humor. In the subject matter utilized to produce the desired effect, he shows a decided preference for mental abnormalities. Nor in his study of abnormal beings does he overlook himself, a by-no-means well-balanced person. This highly personal element that definitely characterizes Quiroga's writing appears very early. In "Hashish," a sketch in *El Crimen del Otro*, he recounts an experiment upon himself with that narcotic; in "Los Perseguidos," he himself appears by name as one of the abnormal characters, his recent journey to Misiones is mentioned, and his friend Lugones plays a minor rôle. Much of *Historia de un Amor Turbio* is probably based on his own experience. The central figure—the dyspeptic, romantically minded Rohán—is Quiroga himself. Like Quiroga, Rohán had been to Paris, and he had abandoned the city to work on a country place, just as Quiroga was himself contemplating doing when he wrote the story. It will also be recalled that Quiroga's daughter, born a few years after this novelette was published, was named Eglé—the name of the character that as a child, and later as a young woman, became so passionately enamoured of Rohán. Another story, "Historia de Estilicón," suggests not only the prominent rôle animals were to occupy in Quiroga's later stories, but his passion for the tropics, the background of his Misiones tales.

The stories he wrote in Misiones between 1910 and 1916 brought him a very enviable reputation as a *cuentista;* and it was fifteen of the most representative that he republished in *Cuentos de Amor, de Locura y de Muerte.* According to content they fall roughly into three groups. "Nuestro primer Cigarro" ("Our First Cigar"), "El Meningitis y su Sombra" ("Meningitis and its Delusion"), "Una Estación de Amor" ("A Season of Love"), and "La Muerte de Isolda" ("The Death of Isolde"), have an intimate tone that connects them at

once with Quiroga himself. The first of these is a humorous
account of a boyish trick. The second reveals the wildly imaginative and romantic side of Quiroga's mind; it concerns a
young girl who during a severe illness fell deeply in love with
the narrator of the tale, but—and here the fanciful element
enters—was conscious of her infatuation only when delirious.
"Una Estación de Amor," of which *Las Sacrificadas*, 1923, is a
dialogued version, is based without a doubt on his first disappointment in love—a very bitter experience which he seems to
have nursed all his life. A youthful couple who are romantically in love are separated by the young man's father; when the
two meet years later the man is married and the young woman
has been forced by poverty to degrade herself. Urged by the
girl's mother, a drug addict, the man takes her as his mistress;
but the relationship proves unsatisfactory, for both feel they
have been false to their former love. The theme of this story,
the futility of attempting to recapture love, is somewhat similar to that of the last story of this group, "La Muerte de
Isolda," which is motivated by unavailing remorse for having
spurned a sincere love.

Four stories of a very morbid nature, in which critics have
detected the influence of Poe, constitute the second group in
the collection. Technically, these stories vary considerably.
Two relate mere incidents: the suicide craze of a crew that
had manned an abandoned ship, "Buques suicidantes" ("Barks
that Lure to Death"); and the pining away of a young bride
caused, as was discovered after her death, by a loathsome para-
sitic animal in her pillow, "El Almohadón de Pluma" ("The
Feather Pillow"). The remaining two stories of this group,
however, "El Solitario" ("The Solitaire") and "La Gallina
degollada" ("The Beheaded Hen"), come as near meeting
the requirements of an artistic short story as anything that
Quiroga wrote. Both are told in a very direct and straightfor-
ward manner; each creates a very definite mood; the plots,
though simple, are well constructed, each having a very definite climax; and the characters—each facing an impending

catastrophe—are well delineated. Particularly effective is the contrast, in "El Solitario," between the poor, plodding, and patient jeweler, Kassim, and his vain, frivolous wife. He, sick and weak, worked long hours at his trade to gratify her whims; she, ungrateful and dissatisfied, continually rebuked him for their poverty. In time, too, she was possessed by an inordinate desire for gems which her husband's trade gave her an opportunity to see; on one occasion she became so envious of a beautiful diamond that Kassim was mounting on a scarf-pin as to fly into an ungovernable fit of anger, in which she unwittingly revealed her unfaithfulness. When calmer, she re-tracted what she had said; but Kassim, as if unmoved by it all, continued his work on the scarf-pin. When he finished it late in the night, he took it to her; then, as she lay asleep, he thrust it into her heart and quietly left the house. The most tragic story that Quiroga wrote, however, is doubtless *La Gallina degollada*, in which some idiot sons, imitating the cook whom they had seen behead a chicken, kill their sister, a beautiful child and the only normal one of the children. Both these stories have an urban background and derive dramatic effect from the startling ending and from the dialogue in which the characters reveal themselves; but in neither, as is true of all Quiroga's stories so far discussed, is the setting a vital factor.

On the other hand, the most important element of the seven stories which constitute the third group from this collection is setting or background. With these, twenty-two others—five in *El Salvaje*, seven in *Anaconda*, two in *El Desierto*, and three in *Los Desterrados*—must be considered, for all are concerned in one way or another with the Misiones territory that borders the Paraná River. The source of the passion that was aroused in Quiroga when he visited the region for the first time, and that swayed him for the rest of his life, lies in the contrast that the tropical forest region presented to the level, open, and less picturesque country around Montevideo and Buenos Aires. Not only did the spirit of the tropics enthrall him, as fre-quently befalls those that enter that realm, but he was converted at once from an urban resident apparently indifferent to Nature into her worshipful student. His passion for the region—its climate, its topography, its animal life, the human derelicts that had taken refuge there—found expression in this group of stories, which constitute his greatest achievement and give him his main claim to distinction as a writer.

In reading these stories, one senses first Quiroga's own imaginative personality and next his very close personal contact with Misiones. Particularly real and vivid are the details in these stories in regard to climate, topography, and animal life; the extremes of heat—"La Insolación" ("Sunstroke") and of cold; the droughts and torrential rains—"El Simún" ("The Simoom"); the Paraná River, both at flood stage and in a normal state, with its dangerous rapids and high banks of black stone; and the broken terrain covered by forests in which lurked deadly snakes and other animal life hostile to man, such as army ants—"La Miel silvestre" ("Wild Honey"). True to life, also, are many of the events in those tales in which Quiroga himself is the chief actor—such as "Los Fabricantes de Carbón" ("Charcoal Burners") and "Los Destiladores de Naranja" ("The Distillers of Oranges"), which bring to light certain of his unfortunate business ventures and which emphasize his love for scientific experiments; "El Desierto," which is autobiographic in a number of details, particularly those in which the principal character is left in Misiones with two children after the death of his wife; "El Techo de Incienso" ("The Roof of Incense Wood"), which is reminiscent of Quiroga's life as a public official in that territory; and "Polea loca" ("Off Balance"), which centers about a person, like Quiroga, averse to answering, or even opening, official correspondence.

So real as to be unforgettable are the people of the region, in some thirteen stories of this group. Some of these are types found along the Paraná River in the Misiones section. "Los Mensú" ("Hired Hands"), which is undoubtedly one of Quiroga's best stories, recounts the experience of two laborers who, after contracting to work in a lumber camp where they faced enslavement and death from malignant fever, succeeded in escaping and, after untold hardships on a raft on the Paraná at flood stage, reached the town of Posadas. The story is remarkable, too, for its unexpected ending. For the laborers, after spending their first night of freedom in a state of drunkenness, signed up the next morning for the very sort of work from which they had just escaped. Other tales intimately connected with the Paraná and those that dwell along it are "Los Pescadores de vigas" ("River Thieves"), which presents those who steal the valuable logs being floated down the river; "El Yaciyateré" ("The Sinister Call"), which tells of the riverfolk and their superstitions; and "En la Noche" ("In the Night"), which recounts a horrible experience of a European and his wife on the Paraná. In other sketches and narratives of this group, types peculiar to the region appear, with all of whom Quiroga had doubtlessly come into direct contact: day laborers, particularly one that had probably worked on Quiroga's own farm ("El Peón"); an overbearing landlord who paid dearly for an act of arrogance—"Una Bofetada" ("A Slap"); European immigrants who had come to take up land in Misiones—"Inmigrantes" ("Immigrants") and "La Voluntad" ("Will Power"); a promoter who, after repeated failures, is finally successful—"El Monte negro" ("Black Mountain"); an ailing and drunken justice of the peace, of whose corpse the widow had a photograph made, probably by Quiroga himself—"La Cámara oscura" ("The Dark Room"); and other human flotsam and jetsam that had found a haven in the region ("Los Desterrados," "Van Houten," and "Tacuara-Mansión").

While there is abundant evidence of a keen power of observation in the remaining stories with a Misiones background, realism is somewhat held in check and a freer rein given to romance and imagination. These stories are "El Salvaje," "Anaconda," "El Regreso de Anaconda" ("The Return of Anaconda"), and possibly two short sketches, "A la Deriva" ("Down Stream") and "El Hombre muerto" ("The Dead

Man"), which are identical in theme and technique, and in having a dying man as a single character. In "A la Deriva," he had been bitten by a venomous snake, and the effects of the deadly poison, which Quiroga had no doubt observed, are described in detail. By sheer will power the afflicted man got into his boat to go down the Paraná to seek medical aid. The great pain he was suffering finally ceased, and his mind became clear. Then, by virtue of Quiroga's imagination, the reader is enabled to know the thoughts that passed through the mind of the doomed man. He recalled various friends in the town to which he was going, friends he had not seen for years, and he anticipated the joy he would have in seeing them again. But suddenly a convulsion seized him; his mind again became cloudy; and, there in his boat on the Paraná, he died. In "El Hombre muerto" is a man mortally wounded by falling on his machete as he was crawling through a fence. Again, in this sketch, the interest is in the train of thoughts that passed through the man's mind as he lay dying, out of reach of help.

The play of imagination is far greater in "El Salvaje," which, despite the lack of unity between its first and second part, is to be numbered among Quiroga's most original tales. The background is the upper Paraná, above Iguazú Falls, a region of dense forests and heavy rainfall. Tired of civilization, an educated man—no other than Quiroga himself—had taken refuge there, set up a meteorological observatory, and begun sending in reports to Buenos Aires. According to those that he sent in one season, the rainfall was so excessive that an inspector was sent from the central office in Buenos Aires to verify his figures. Shortly after his arrival the rain began to fall as the man had never seen rain fall before, and he had to spend the night with the amateur meteorologist—a tall, thin, pale man with a long black beard and a strange look in his eyes that suggested an unbalanced mind. Rather uncommunicative at first, the meteorologist suddenly asked the inspector if he had ever seen a dinosaur, and when the newcomer acknowledged he had not, the refugee told a long, impossible story of his experiences with one there on the Paraná River. The next morning when the inspector was going down the river he was overcome by the humidity of the air and the stench of the forest after the deluge. This convinced him that the story-teller had experienced in a dream the reality of that past age as fully as if he had actually lived in it.

"La Realidad" ("Reality"), as the second part of "El Sal-vaje" is entitled, is a unit in itself and, despite the fact that it deals with the Tertiary period, one of the most dramatic stories that Quiroga wrote. The principal character is a tree-dweller; his habitat is a humid, forest-covered, tropical region such as that of the upper Paraná; and what happens to him— his progress from a herbivorous to a carnivorous animal, from a tree-dweller to a cave-dweller, and from insecurity to secur-ity after he accidentally pushed a huge stone against the en-trance of the cave—is the story of several stages in the slow upward progress of man.

If one of Quiroga's best stories deals with primitive man, it is not at all strange that he also writes about animals. Two stories of the Misiones group, "El Alambre de Pua" ("Barbed Wire") and "Yaguai," show an intimate understanding of domestic animals. Of the animal kingdom, however, snakes fascinate Quiroga most. In many of his stories they appear, very realistically, as actual snakes. But in "Los Cazadores de Ratas" ("Rat Hunters"), "Anaconda," and its sequel "El regreso de Anaconda," they are endowed with the power of speech and certain other human characteristics. "Anaconda," his masterpiece, pictures the consternation that ensued when the snakes in a certain district in Misiones learned that their natural enemy, man, had invaded their kingdom. A group of scientists, the serpents discovered, had come to catch veno-mous snakes, which abounded in that region, in order to extract their poison and make with it a serum that would ren-der their one dangerous weapon ineffective. Preferring to die rather than to submit to such degradation, the snakes con-vened to discuss means of combating the intruder. In the

convention there were two factions, the poisonous and non-
poisonous snakes, whose leaders—a large cobra and Anaconda,
a huge boa—moved as much by the natural enmity between
them as by the differences in viewpoint, almost came to the
point of attacking each other. The cobra's plan, that the
snakes in a body should attack the men, was finally adopted;
and Anaconda, putting aside personal prejudice, yielded to the
general will. The result was disastrous, for the snakes were
routed and many were killed. Then followed a terrific battle
between the two leaders who had survived; and although
Anaconda killed the cobra, she herself at the end of the struggle lay senseless from his deadly poison. The men saved her,
however, as they saw in her an ally against the poisonous
snakes; and she lingered among them for a year, "nosing about
and observing everything," before she returned to her natural
habitat further north.

She was in that region, along the upper Paraná, when
Quiroga writes of her again—this time in "El Regreso de Anaconda." "A young serpent she was then, some ten meters in
length, in the fullness of her strength; and in all her vast hunting range, there was not a deer or a tiger capable of with-
standing with a breath of life in his body one of her embraces."
It was at this time, during a great drought, that she conceived
a plan of damming the river itself in order to shut out man,
who had already begun to invade the district. Aided by the
other animals whom she would win over to her venture, it
could easily be done, she thought, when the rains came, with
all the debris that the flood would wash down. Finally the
great hoped-for deluge came; and down the river with it there
descended a vast army of birds, insects, snakes, alligators,
tigers, and other dwellers of the forest. Anaconda herself was
on a huge cedar tree that had been uprooted. Later, she
crawled upon a floating island, on which she found a house
and in it a dying man. Whether he excited pity in her or
whether she saw in him a place to lay her eggs, as she did do,
she did not destroy him but protected him from the poisonous

snakes that swarmed about. But Anaconda's plan failed; no dam was formed, and she herself met death, through a bullet of a high-powered rifle that one of the crew of a steamboat on the river sent through her head.

In these two stories, "Anaconda" and "El Regreso de Anaconda," Quiroga appears at his very best. In nothing else that he has written can there be found such a large number of excellent qualities. Here, imagination and observation have joined hands to make them the little masterpieces that they are. The background, particularly the Paraná River at flood stage, is intensely individual. The stories themselves are told with dramatic effect. The characters, whose psychology and bodily movements have been recorded with masterly precision, are interesting for themselves, that is as snakes, not solely, as in nearly all animal stories, for the human characteristics that have been attributed to them. If there is a supreme quality of excellence in these two stories, however, it is the feeling of admiration and of compassion that Quiroga arouses for the great boa herself. The style is very effective, being simple, unadorned by figures of speech but rhythmical.

The only remaining stories with the Misiones background are eight fables (*Cuentos de la Selva para Niños*) that deal with certain animals of that region. One of these, which tells of the alligators who erected a dam in order to keep man out of the Paraná River, recalls "El Regreso de Anaconda." The story of the lazy bee is the only one that has a definite moral: in general Quiroga's aim in these fables is primarily to amuse. In nearly all of them, nevertheless, certain moral values are presented more or less indirectly—for instance, the consequences of disobedience on the part of young animals of the forest, and the gratitude that some animals show man in return for kindness. Certain qualities of these stories—their easy-flowing, chatty style, and the free hand that fantasy takes—recall *Alice's Adventures in Wonderland*.

On the other hand, six apologues—five in *El Desierto* and one in *Más Allá*—differ from the fables in that their purpose is not so much to amuse as to exemplify some philosophic truth. In "Los tres Besos" ("The Three Kisses"), the only one of the stories in which animals do not figure, he shows that a desire which is long deferred on account of some other consideration finally ceases to be a desire. Liberty, even with hunger—and no one could have said this any more sincerely than Quiroga himself—is preferable to luxury that brings with it a false and circumscribed life—"El Potro salvaje" ("The Wild Colt"). "La Patria" ("The Homeland") decries, through a story of discord that arose among the animals of a forest, the establishment of political boundaries between countries. The tenor of the three remaining stories—"Juan Darién," which has points of similarity with Kipling's "Tiger! Tiger!," "El León" ("The Lion"), and "La señorita Leona" ("The Young Lioness")—is that animals are in many respects superior to man. In each story a wild animal, after coming under the influence of human civilization, abandons it for the animal kingdom.

Motifs of an ethical nature are to be found also in the "Cuadrivio laico" ("The Lay Cuadrivium"), which is the general title of four stories in El Salvaje. One of these, "Reyes" ("Kings"), may be dismissed at once, as it is only a short prose poem in the "modernista" manner. The remaining three, which are genuine narratives, are significant in that they contain the only references in all of Quiroga's works to any phase of the Christian religion. Slightly ironical, "La Navidad" ("Christmas") and "La Pasión" ("The Passion of Jesus") recall the style of certain stories of Anatole France; both claim to be incidents in connection with Jesus Christ. When Herod sought Jesus, says the first story, and threatened to slay all the infants of a certain age unless the place where He was born were revealed, Salome, a Jewish girl, disclosed that information to her Roman soldier-lover. Later, to the dismay of Saint Peter, Salome was admitted to Heaven on the ground that she had shown a great tenderness of heart in preferring the betrayal of her God to the death of so many innocent infants. According to "La Pasión," reunions were held from time to time in Heaven at which Jesus showed His absolute goodness by pardoning all that had taken any part in His crucifixion. Finally a man appeared whom Jesus refused to pardon, and thereafter no hymn to His absolute goodness could be sung. The man was Ahasvero, the wandering Jew, who, in this version, refused Christ water when He begged for it on the cross. In the last story of the group, "Corpus" ("Corpus Christi")—which tells of the persecution and burning, in Geneva at the time of Calvin, of a young German for having made an image of Christ—there is a ring of true feeling. For Quiroga, although unaffected by religion, hated intolerance in any form.

The material in the collections that has not been discussed up to this point is of a heterogeneous nature. Especially is this true in the case of *El Salvaje*, which contains an account of a man that was stung to death by his bees—"La Reina italiana" ("The Italian Queen"); an essay picturing a scene in Belgium during the World War—"Los Cementerios belgas" ("Belgian Cemeteries"), one of the few instances in Quiroga's writings of references to contemporary events; five brief narratives—"Estefanía," "La Llama" ("The Flame"), "Fanny," "Lucila Strinberg," and "Un Idilio" ("An Idyl")—all rather plotless, thin in substance, and, if not downright wildly imaginary, at least inconsequential; a humorous skit on the tactics of the Buenos Aires "masher"—"Tres Cartas y un Pie" ("Three Letters and a Foot"); and a tragi-comic account of a squabble between a man and his wife, probably based on an actual event in Quiroga's life, when their baby waked them at night by its crying—"Cuento Para Novios" ("A Story for the Betrothed"). Of the remaining items in *Anaconda*, there are two articles dealing with climatic phenomena of tropical Africa—"El Simún" and "Gloria tropical" ("Tropical Glory"); a ludicrous tale of the sad experiences of a young man who married the daughter of an expert in dietetics—"Dieta de Amor" ("The Diet of Love"); and "Miss Dorothy Phillips, mi Esposa" ("Miss Dorothy Phillips, My Wife"), which, aside from being a rambling, highly fanciful story of a young Argentine who went from Buenos Aires to Hollywood and married his favorite "movie" star, contains much light satire on Hollywood actors and actresses. Another story of "movie" actors, also highly improbable, is "El Espectro" ("The Spectre") (*El Desierto*), in which a deceased husband fascinates, through a picture in which he had had a part, his widow and her lover and prevents them from marrying. The same collection contains also a droll account of a woman's scheme to get an author to read a novel her husband had written—"Una Conquista" ("A Conquest"); a story of two souls that met in an outer world and became enamoured of each other—"El Síncope blanco" ("In Another World"), whose supernatural quality predominates in Quiroga's last book, *Más Allá;* and, lastly, "Silvina y Montt," which foreshadows, in that it tells of a love affair between a middle-aged man and a young girl, a later event in Quiroga's own life.

Of that ill-fated love affair in Misiones in 1925 with Ana María, he has left a record in his novelette *Pasado Amor (Bygone Love)*, which is mainly of interest as his most personal and definite confessional. Many of the incidents in the life of the chief character, Morán, have been clearly established as autobiographical—his return to Misiones, where everything reminded him of his dead wife; his falling madly in love with Magdalena, whom he had known as a child; and the opposition of her family, who succeeded in thwarting him. Another character, perhaps fictitious, is Alicia Hontou, who took her own life because she was deeply in love with Morán but unable to attract him.

The characterization of Morán is nothing more than a delineation of Quiroga himself; intensity of feeling is the quality that distinguishes him. It reveals itself in that inner force that drove him to work hard physically at the things that interested him: the clearing and cultivation of his fields, boat making, rowing up and down the Paraná River with its dangerous rapids. High-strung, over-wrought, verging on madness, in his love affair with Magdalena he acted more like an adolescent than a middle-aged man. So immoderate is his sentimentality as to arouse disgust in readers.

In this work Quiroga pays more attention than usual to the setting. Here, it is the country itself, the "mate" fields and the Paraná River, and the people of the region, rather than the animals and snakes, with which he concerns himself. An insight is afforded into the lives of three families of different social levels and points of view. There are comments, too, on the public dances, on that inevitable social institution, the bar, and on labor unions—organizations which had come into existence since Quiroga's earlier residence there. Interesting in themselves, these details of manners and customs fail, however, to contribute to the artistry of the novel; rather than being fused with the story, they seem entirely extraneous.

To the troubles that marred the last years of his life—domestic dissensions, financial difficulties, and ill health—are traceable in a measure the somber themes that characterize in general his last collection of stories, *Más Allá*. In at least seven of its eleven stories the preoccupation of the author with death, suicide, insanity, and an existence beyond the tomb seems not only to indicate an unhealthy state of mind but to presage his own tragic end. "Más Allá," the title story, tells how the souls of two lovers who had committed suicide were united on this earth for three months but then had to separate without knowing what awaited them in the great beyond. Two stories, probably the most absurd that Quiroga wrote, hark back to his interest in the "movies": "El Vampiro" ("The Vampire"), which tells how a devotee of occult science created from a screen picture of a deceased movie star a real, living vampire, which finally destroyed him; and "El Puritano" ("The Puritan"), which portrays a straight-laced married man who went night after night to see a picture featuring a woman he had loved but spurned until he, too, took his own life, in order to join her in ghostland.

Quiroga returns to the theme of insanity, the predilection

of his early stories, in "El Conductor del Rápido" ("The Conductor on the Flyer"), which describes the symptoms of incipient madness in a locomotive engineer, pictures his distress when he began to suspect that he was losing his mind, and narrates graphically, when the crisis did come and the engineer became a raving maniac, how he brought his train safely to the end of his run; and in "El Llamado" ("Voices") a woman in an insane asylum reveals that the tragic death of an only child, of which she had been warned by voices of the dead, had brought about her own mental derangement.

Two short sketches, "Las Moscas" ("Flies") and "El Hijo" ("The Son"), present very vividly states of mind: the former, that of a man, who, having fallen and broken his back, knows by the large green flies that begin to swarm about him that death is nigh; and the latter, the mental anxiety of a father shaken by a premonition of the death of his young son. Both of these sketches are very similar in technique to "A la Deriva" and "El Hombre muerto."

A tone of levity, rather than of gloom, characterizes the three remaining stories in *Más Allá*. Based on a lapse of memory, one of these, "La Ausencia" ("A Case of Amnesia"), has the best plot in the collection. Roldán Berger, an engineer, finds himself one day with no knowledge of the last six years of his life but engaged to a very beautiful and intellectual woman who had been attracted to him by a renowned philosophical work attributed to him. The matter-of-fact engineer would have broken the engagement at once, but his physician counseled otherwise. Terribly bored, after his marriage, by the intellectuals who pursued him, he confessed to his wife that he had not written the book. As he had succeeded in making himself loved for his own sake, she did not forsake him; instead, before an open fireplace, they tore the leaves from the book and cast them into the flames. The theme, that love does not depend on literary accomplishments, appears also in the far less interesting "La Bella y la Bestia" ("Beauty and the Beast"), in which a young woman of literary interests sets out to find a husband of similar tastes but finally decides in favor of an ordinary business man. "El Ocaso" ("Sunset"), the last story in the volume, relates an incident in the life of an old *roué* and of a young girl none too chaste. Somewhat risqué in nature, it is entirely out of keeping with the general tone of the author's other works.

Quiroga's entire literary output is not extensive—one narrative in dialogue, two novelettes, and some ninety-six short stories, sketches, and articles. The total impact, too, of his work is slight. Thin in substance in general, it is on the whole not much better than the usual type of journalistic material that fills the pages of the literary supplement of Sunday editions of newspapers or of weekly periodicals such as *Caras y Caretas* and *El Hogar,* in which much of it appeared. The influence of Poe on Quiroga in regard to themes and motifs is indisputable, but not in regard to his short-story technique, for only a few of his stories—"El Solitario," "La Gallina degollada," and "Los Mensú"—can be cited as examples of fair narration. His forte, however, does not lie in narration or in the analysis of human character. It is his ability to transfer to his pages the atmosphere of Misiones, the scene of so many of his joys and sorrows, that catches the attention of his readers and gives him distinction as a writer. Of the many stories that have Misiones as their background, those that are outstanding are very limited in number. For only in three— "El Salvaje," "Anaconda," and "El Regreso de Anaconda"— does his genius find its highest expression. But they are enough to entitle him to international fame as a short-story writer.

CHAPTER VII

THE SECRETS OF THE
SELVAS OF COLOMBIA UNFOLDED BY
JOSE EUSTACIO RIVERA

❋

IN THE FIELD of prose fiction, which has been cultivated in Colombia since the third decade of the past century, two figures tower like giants among many others who as novelists did not acquire full stature. One of these is Jorge Isaacs, whose *María*, 1867, is indisputably the most outstanding romantic novel written in the Spanish language; the other is José Eustacio Rivera, whose novel *La Vorágine* (*The Vortex*) has stirred the Spanish world as deeply during the present century as *María* did in the past. Two novelists of lesser height deserve mention in this connection. One is José María Vargas Vila (1860-1933), probably the most prolific Spanish-American novelist, whose works are also widely known. Of less fame, but of more enduring worth as a writer, is Tomás Carrasquilla (1858-1941), celebrated for the purity of his prose in a series of novels that deal with the manners and customs of Antioquia, his own native province.

But it is with the life and work of Rivera that we are particularly concerned here. He was born in 1889 in Neiva, a port of some consequence on the Magdalena River about one hundred and fifty miles south of Bogota, and there his childhood and early youth were spent. In the capital, where he was sent to finish his education, he completed a course in a normal school at the age of twenty, and eight years later a law degree was conferred upon him by the national university. Entering zealously into the political life of Bogota, he soon won for himself a place of high distinction. His interest in writing was equally keen, as is evidenced by the publication there in 1921 of *Tierra de Promisión* (*The Promised Land*), a volume of sonnets inspired by the tropical region around Neiva and noteworthy for their perfection of form and rhythm.

Two positions that came through his political prestige served to take him for several years to wild and uninhabited regions in Colombia. One of these was the chairmanship of a congressional committee appointed to study certain problems relating to the oil lands in the country; the other was the appointment as secretary of the commission that was named in 1922 by Colombia and Venezuela to settle their boundary controversy. The group to which Rivera was assigned was charged with the establishment of the boundary in the south-eastern part of Colombia, a swampy, forest-covered region drained by scores of tributaries of two great rivers, the Orinoco and the Amazon. On this expedition Rivera became thoroughly familiar with that inhospitable region, and wit-nessed there the mad rush for rubber, which had become in the early years of the twentieth century a very valuable commodity. In the barbarous methods to obtain workers em-ployed by both individuals and companies engaged in the gathering of rubber, and in the inhuman treatment to which they subjected laborers once they were in their power, he found the message of his celebrated novel *La Vorágine*. Many sections of the novel were written while he was still in that wilderness, but he did not complete it until after he had dis-charged his duties in connection with the boundary commis-sion and returned to Bogota. This book, which was published in that city in 1924, was received most enthusiastically throughout the entire Spanish-reading world. Up to 1928 four editions had been published, and a fifth had just been issued in New York City in 1928, when Rivera, weakened by a disease that he had contracted in the tropics, died there from pneumonia. It has since passed through many editions and has been translated into English, German, and Russian.

Written in the form of memoirs and impressions, *La Vorágine* records the experiences of its central character, Arturo Cova, through the trackless plains—the Casanare—and the dense forest areas of southeastern Colombia, the region Rivera had himself just traversed. Despite its great interest, the book, if regarded purely from the standpoint of technique in novel writing, is formless and unintegrated. The source of its interest is not in his description of a strange and weird district, for travelers had already described it fully; but rather in his imaginative treatment of it, as perceived through the senses of Arturo Cova.

Cova, a youthful poet of Bogota, is an uncertain character. Irascible and impetuous, blasé and sophisticated, he had sought in vain for a love that would move him deeply. He thought for a time he had found it in Alicia, who was of a respectable family of the capital; but, realizing later that he had not, he refused to marry her; yet when her parents turned her out and he himself was forced to flee or be jailed, he took her with him.

Traveling slowly on horseback and fearing arrest, the fugitives reached the Casanare region. Alicia, unaccustomed to the hardships of primitive life, grumbled continually, and Cova longed at times to be rid of her. At the village of Cáqueza, where they tarried a week because Alicia was sick, the inconstant Cova sought another conquest in love. On their way again, they were accosted by a very wily individual, Pipa, who had been deputized to arrest them but instead made off with one of their horses. At another village, Villavicencio, they had difficulties with a drunken army officer who decided he would like to have Alicia. Of great assistance, on the other hand, was an old peddler and trader, Don Rufo, who served them as a guide. For the strange region filled both Alicia and Cova with awe: the boundless plains which spread before them at daybreak; the scorching and dazzling sun of midday; and the wooded oases, where birds abounded, wild animals lurked, and alligators and huge water snakes lay concealed in the dark, leaf-covered pools.

After some weeks in the Casanare the travelers arrived at the Maporita ranch, where they found lodgings. Here they encountered other characters typical of the region: Fidel Franco, owner of the ranch, formerly an army officer, who had taken refuge in the Casanare with his mistress, the fascinating Griselda; the servants—an old mulattress, Sebastiana, and her son Correa; and a wily contractor for labor in the rubber-producing region, Barrera, who had electrified the entire neighborhood with tales of the high wages paid there. At the Maporita the situation grew tense. For not only had Barrera lured away Franco's helpers on the ranch but he was paying court to Griselda, and after Alicia's arrival he began to play the same game with her, incurring thereby also the enmity of Cova.

Barrera and his gang passed much of their time drinking and gambling at Hato Grande, the headquarters of Zubieta, an astute and vicious old rancher who owned an extensive tract of land and great herds of cattle. Franco, Don Rufo, and Cova bargained with him for a certain number of cattle, which they had hoped to sell at a good profit in Bogota. While his partners were hunting men to help in rounding up the cattle, Cova remained at Maporita to protect the women. Here old Sebastiana told him tales and superstitions of the plains; Alicia, for whom his love returned when he thought of losing her, quarreled with him; and Griselda and he made love, although consideration for Franco somewhat restrained him; until finally, crazed by liquor, he, too, went off to Hato Grande. There he took part in the drinking; he was lucky at gambling; and when he found that Barrera was trying to cheat him with loaded dice, a fight took place between them. In the general melée that followed, Cova was knifed, but Barrera and his gang were driven out. A medicaster, Nanco, treated Cova's wound, and a good-hearted prostitute, Clarita, cared for him. The descriptions of two events of his stay at Hato Grande— a cock fight and the stampeding of a herd of cattle—add much local color.

As soon as he was able to travel, Cova set out to search for Franco on the plains. Here he met and misdirected a corrupt judge who he discovered was on his trail; he experienced the horrors of a storm and a torrential rain on the shelterless plains; and he witnessed the goring-to-death of a cowboy by a wild bull. Unable to round up the cattle, he and Franco returned to Maporita, only to find that Zubieta had been murdered and that they were suspected of the crime; that Barrera had departed with his laborers for the rubber-producing region, and that Alicia and Griselda had gone with him. To kill them for their faithlessness, Cova and Franco accompanied by Correa and Pipa, whom they had found on the plains, set off in the direction of the forests.

The crafty Pipa, who had grown up with the Indians and knew the region thoroughly, led the party to the banana groves of Macucuana on the Meta River. They tarried for some days in the jungles with the semi-civilized Indians, whose queer customs are described in considerable detail; and in a great swamp abounding in herons and egrets they collected some beautiful feathers which they sent back by Indians to be sold. On the march again, they proceeded south, through swamps and through forests, harassed by insects and threatened with insanity, to the Vichada River, where they met a friend of Franco's, Helí Mesa. He had set out with Barrera but escaped when he realized that all with him had sold themselves into worse than slavery. Barrera's destination, he told them, was the rubber region of the Yaguanarí, which lies in Brazil between the Negro and Amazon Rivers; and Barrera had proceeded with his party down the Vichada River toward the Orinoco, from which he would reach the Negro through the Casiquiare. On learning that Alicia and Griselda were still alive, Cova and Franco determined to continue their pursuit but to take a shorter, if more perilous, route. They planned to proceed south to the juncture of the Vúa and Inírida Rivers; then ascend the latter some distance, and cross over to the Isana, down which they could float into the Negro. Versed in the lore of the region, Mesa told them, as they neared the Vúa River, the legend of Mapiripana, a sprite of the woods, rivers, and lakes, who lured a missionary to her cave, where she kept him a prisoner for some years and by whom she had twins, both monsters.

Finally the party reached the Inírida River. Sick with fever, Cova suffered from hallucinations; in the rapids they lost their boat and two Indian guides; but they came upon an old man, Clemente Silva, a Colombian, covered with worm-infested sores. He was a guard in the service of El Cayeno, a rubber baron who exploited the Inírida region and defended it by force against his competitor, the notorious Colonel Funes, of San Fernando del Atabapo, Venezuela. Clemente offered to conduct his compatriots to Guaracú, El Cayeno's settlement on the Isana.

Little by little Don Clemente told them his story. He was from Pasto (Colombia); for sixteen years he had been searching through the jungles for a son. He had spent years along the Putamayo River, which was controlled by another rubber baron, the Peruvian Araña; there he had worked in various capacities, had suffered unbelievable indignities, and had witnessed terrible crimes. Araña finally sold him to a woman trader who plied the Amazon and all of its waterways—the voluptuous Zoraida Ayram, or La Madona, as she was called. In her launch Don Clemente journeyed through the Amazon to Iquitos (Peru), where he sought in vain for a Colombian consul to whom he might appeal for redress of the wrongs done him. Then, in Iquitos, when he was just about to set out over the same route for Manaos on the Negro River, he learned that his son had been killed and buried on a certain spot near the Yavaraté, a tributary of the Negro. To be nearer his son's bones, Don Clemente persuaded the Turk Pezil, who operated along the Negro, to purchase him from La Madona. Some months later he succeeded in escaping, with some six others, from Pezil's jurisdiction; but in attempting to make their way through the forest, not daring to follow the river route, they suffered horribly from poisonous insects, army ants that destroyed everything in their path, and from a form of madness that the monotony of the forest induces. Of the seven, only Don Clemente survived; he finally succeeded in finding his son's grave but was unable to get all of his bones, for the flesh had not fallen from some of them. He was then captured by El Cayeno, in whose service Cova found him.

With difficulty Don Clemente led his countrymen to Guaracú—a settlement of half-starved wretches. Here they found El Váquiro, a drunken lout, in command, for El Cayeno was away; Ramiro Estévañez, a talented young man whom Cova had known intimately in Bogota, now half blind, who told Cova the particulars of the massacre he had witnessed of the inhabitants of the town of San Fernando del Atabapo by Funes; and La Madona, Don Clemente's former mistress, whose real business there was buying stolen rubber, although she claimed that it was otherwise. Greedy and lustful, her love for money was of the two passions the greater. Cova ingratiated himself in her favor as a lover, but her main interest in him proceeded solely from hopes of gain, for he had led her to believe that he was connected with a banking house in Manaos. On the pretext of needing to communicate with his firm, Cova obtained through her a boat in which he dispatched Don Clemente and Correa to Manaos to beseech aid of the Colombian consul.

With great surprise Cova observed one day that La Madona was wearing Griselda's earrings, and only a short time later Franco discovered that his former mistress was in the neighborhood. She was in the service of La Madona, on a boat concealed in the river, which had come to take away rubber that had been stolen from El Cayeno. In this boat, Cova and his friends saw a means of escape, which they were quick to seize.

A reconciliation had taken place between Griselda and Franco, and when she told Cova that Alicia had left him through jealousy and had not submitted to Barrera, he was filled with a great desire to go at once to the Yaguanarí to rescue her. At this time El Cayeno appeared at Guaracú, and in a fight that followed he was killed. Cova and his group then proceeded down the Isana and the Negro, and at Yaguanarí they came upon the Colombians who had been lured away. There, too, was Alicia. Without stopping to talk to her, Cova ran in search of Barrera, whom he found bathing. The two grappled in a desperate struggle; but Cova, who succeeded in freeing himself, pushed Barrera into the river, where he was instantly devoured by caribe fish. Fearing a contagious disease that had attacked the Colombian workers, Cova and his friends, together with Alicia and her baby, withdrew into the forest. Some time later, Don Clemente received a letter from Cova outlining the route he proposed to follow. The old man then set out to find them and searched diligently through the Yaguanarí for his friends; but it was all in vain. For, like a monster, the great forest had swallowed them up.

Unquestionably of unusual merit and interest, *La Vorágine* is marked by certain characteristics—its epic-like nature, the vast territory it covers, and its time element—which do not make for unity or a well integrated plot. Interest is largely centered on one character, Cova, and his wanderings through an almost impenetrable region. His own story, which constitutes the main plot, covers only some seven months of the year 1920, but the relations of Don Clemente Silva and Ramiro Estévañez carry the novel back in point of time to the early years of the century. Such details and other circumstances that affect the action of the main plot are entirely out of proportion. One feels, too, that those details were the principal concern of the author and not the story of Alicia and Cova, which seems to have been invented merely as an excuse to lure the reader into the forest regions and to reveal to him the appalling conditions that exist there. The main story is probably fictional, but its setting, as Mr. Eduardo Neale-Silva has clearly demonstrated, is based to a very large degree on fact. The geography of the two regions is presented with great fidelity; Cova's journey through them can be accurately plotted; the life of the people that is portrayed, whether of the plains or the forest, comes first-hand; the mistreatment of the workers in the rubber-producing districts, of which Don Clemente told in great detail, is substantiated by reliable documents; and many of the characters—Julio César Araña, the rubber baron of the Putamayo; Colonel Funes, who massacred the inhabitants of San Fernando del Atabapo in 1913; and others less notorious—existed in actual life.

While through these and many other realistic details in the setting a sense of actuality is attained, and while the treatment of certain aspects of nature contributes greatly to its artistry, the main charm of *La Vorágine* is enhanced by a certain dramatic presentation of the narrative itself. For the story unfolds largely through a series of scenes, of a nature so dramatic and vivid that one feels in reading them that he is witnessing an animated play; and, too, as at a play, he judges the characters by what they say and do. The scenes in the first third of the book are particularly effective. Almost in the very opening pages, Cova and Alicia disclose in a quarrel not only the relation that exists between them but also their very natures. And so it is with all the other characters that are introduced in this part: the crafty and thieving Pipa; Don Rufo, the wise old peddler; the mulattress Sebastiana and her son Correa; Barrera, wily and oily-tongued; Franco, faithful and upright; Zubieta, the wary old rancher; and the corrupt judge of Orocué, whom Cova, when he found him lost on the plains, sent in the opposite direction to that of his destination.

In the second third of the book, that dealing with the experiences of Cova and his comrades in the jungle, the narrative moves forward through a series of vivid pictures rather than dramatic scenes. Cova describes graphically the effects of the tropical fever which attacked him and the manners and customs of an Indian tribe on the Meta River. Later, Helí Mesa pictures to him and his friends the horrors of the enslavement of the Colombian laborers that Barrera had lured away with rosy promises. Then in a series of lurid pictures Don Clemente recounts his sufferings in the jungles for sixteen years. The dramatic scene is, however, by no means entirely absent in this section. There is dialogue between Cova and his men, between them and Helí Mesa and Don Clemente; and the latter often drifts from pure narrative into a dramatic scene in order to present more vividly some ghastly situation in his past.

After the conclusion of the stories told by Don Clemente and Ramiro Estévañez, the interest in the third section again centers on the difficulties of Cova and his comrades. Here again, as in the first part, the story moves swiftly forward through a series of scenes, in which Cova, La Madona, Váquiro, Griselda, and many others take part. Here there are two very memorable examples of pictorial skill: the description of the half-starved beings around the huts of Guaracú, and of the hand-to-hand conflict in which Cova disposed of Barrera on the banks of the Yaguanarí. With his destruction— the denouement of this human drama—justice triumphs, at least temporarily, in its struggle against wrong and oppression, for the impulsive Cova, with his many faults, was ever a "friend of the weak."

But the struggle between human beings is not the only one that is enacted; it is paralleled by another, that between man and nature, which brings with it a poetic and lyric tone. Nature, as it impresses Cova, is, if not actually terrifying, always astounding: whether sunrise, sudden storms, or torrential downpours on the limitless plains or that most awe-inspiring aspect of nature—the *selva* itself, its foliage so dense as to shut out the sun, its insects so poisonous and destructive, its sounds so appalling! Always the forest is hostile to man, and Cova feels its menace as he apostrophizes it:

Oh forest, forest, spouse of silence, mother of solitude and of shadows! What evil spirit left me a captive in thy

green prison? Like a great vault, the canopy of thy huge
branches stretches always above my head, between me
and the bright heavens for which I long, of which I catch
a glimpse only at the sad hour of twilight when the
trembling tops of thy trees move like billows. Where is
the beloved star that frequents the hill? And those hues
of gold and purple with which the west adorns itself,
why do they not shimmer in thy canopy? How many
times—as I looked over in the direction of my land, with
its unforgettable plains and its snow-capped peaks on
whose summits I have stood at a height equal to the cor-
dillera itself—have I not sighed, O forest, imagining across
thy labyrinth the reflection of the moon coloring with
its purple shadows the distances! Where does that
heavenly body now shed its placid and silvery light?
Thou, forest, hast robbed me of those pleasant fancies I
had when I beheld the horizon; for my eyes now there is
only the monotony of thy zenith, over which passes a pale
light which never penetrates the dense foliage of thy
damp recesses.

Thou art the sanctuary of sorrow, where unknown
gods speak in a whisper, in a murmuring language, promising long years to the imposing trees, which are as old as
heaven itself, which were already venerable when the first
tribes appeared, and which await impassively the passing
of the centuries to come. Thy vegetation forms upon the
earth a powerful family, among whom there are no trai-
tors. The embrace that thy huge branches do not give to
one another, is received by the winding vines and lianas.
Thou art as one, even in the grief of the leaf that falls.
Thy numberless voices blend, on weeping for the dead
trunk of a tree that gives way and falls, in a single echo;
but in each breach thus made new germs speed their ges-
tation. Thou hast the gravity of cosmic force, and in thee
is embodied the mystery of the creation of the world. My
spirit, nevertheless, borne down by the weight of thy
immortality, yearns for the transitory; and it has come
to love, not the tough oak, but the languid orchid; because, like man, its life is of short duration and it passes

away like a dream. Let me flee, O forest, from thy sickly gloom, formed by the dying breath of all the beings that yielded up their lives within thy desolate realm. A vast cemetery thou seemest in which there is everlasting decay and rebirth. Let me return to the realm where the unknown frightens none, where bondage is unknown, where the view is clear, and bright light surrounds the spirit. Let me return to the land whence I came on this pilgrimage of blood and tears, when, through the caprice of a woman, I pressed on through woods and desert realms, in search of vengeance, an implacable goddess, who smiles only upon tombs.

And finally, when the forest—like a dread monster—devours the group, it is Nature, after all, that has conquered man.

Rich in information about strange and little-known regions, abounding in emotion that is deeply felt, endowed with a high and noble purpose, *La Vorágine* is, in spite of its shortcomings, a great book. In it the forest and the jungle have been masterfully interpreted. Here is a Colombia unknown before in the annals of literature.

CHAPTER VIII

RICARDO GUIRALDES
STYLISTIC DEPICTER OF
THE GAUCHO

✤

T HE MOST distinctive of all Spanish-American literature—
the literature linked most directly with the country and
the people—is the so-called "gaucho" literature of the River
Plate region. Pioneers of this type of literature were three long
narrative poems—Ascasubi's *Santos Vega*, 1851, Estanislao del
Campo's *Fausto*, 1866, and José Hernández's *Martín Fierro*,
1872—all of singular merit. Worthy writers of prose inspired
by the *gaucho* did not appear until the turn of the century.
Of these, two deserve mention: Roberto Payró, an Argentine,
celebrated for his novelette *El Casamiento de Laucha*, 1906,
and a volume of sketches, *Historias de Pago Chico* (*Stories of
Pago Chico*), 1908; and Carlos Reyles, a Uruguayan, who,
although he knew Europe thoroughly, owes his distinction
to his realistic as well as naturalistic depiction of the rural life
of his country in such novels as *Beba*, 1894, *El Terruño* (*The
Home Place*), 1916, and *El Gaucho Florido* (*Florido, the
Gaucho*), 1932. Two other writers of the present century
have cultivated successfully this type of literature: Benito
Lynch, who has written novels somewhat in the conventional
style on Argentine farm and ranch life; and Ricardo Güiraldes,
who, cosmopolitan like Reyles, is generally conceded to have
written most artistically about his native surroundings.

Although born in the capital of Argentina, on February 13, 1886, of a very distinguished family, Güiraldes knew country life intimately, for during both his youth and manhood he spent much time at "La Porteña," a large *estancia* which his family owned in the province of Buenos Aires. Also, from infancy, he spent long intervals in Europe, particularly in Paris, and in 1910 with his bride he visited the Orient, which had for him a singular fascination. While writing was merely a diversion for Güiraldes, as he was wealthy, and his literary work is very limited in extent, it is of a very superior type. Most of it was published during his lifetime: *El Cencerro de Cristal* (*The Glass Cowbell*), a volume of verse, and *Cuentos de Muerte y de Sangre* (*Stories of Death and Blood*), a volume of sketches, in 1915; *Raucho*, a novel, in 1917; *Rosaura*, a novelette, in 1922; *Xaimaca* (*Jamaica*), a travel account, in 1923; and *Don Segundo Sombra* (*Shadows on the Pampas*), a novel and also his masterpiece, in 1926. In 1924 he was associated with Jorge Luis Borges in the establishment of a literary periodical, *Proa*. After his death in Paris on October 8, 1927, three very slender volumes were published: *Poemas solitarios* (*Poems of Solitude*), *Poemas místicos* (*Mystic Poems*), and *Seis Relatos* (*Six Stories*), whose content, except five stories in the last, was hitherto unpublished.

Güiraldes reveals himself both as man and writer in his very first work. Although a cosmopolite, his creative impulse springs entirely from the Argentine. Of the first nineteen prose sketches in *Cuentos de Muerte y de Sangre*, four relate incidents in the life of its military chieftains; three recount happenings in the wars of independence; and some twelve narrate occurrences in connection with Argentine ranch life. Of particular interest among these are "Al Rescoldo" ("Embers"), in which Güiraldes's celebrated character, Don Segundo Sombra, appears for the first time and narrates one of the tall tales for which he is famous; and "La Estancia vieja" ("The Old Ranch"), based on an old theme—the punishing of the image of a saint for refusing a request. In this case an old rancher brought a downpour by punishing an image of Our Lady after she had steadfastly failed to bring rain during a long drought. A group of four stories, entitled "Aventuras grotescas" ("Grotesque Adventures"), deals with Argentine urban life. Three of them—"Máscaras" ("Masks"), "Ferroviaria" ("A Train Trip"), and "Sexto" ("The Sixth")— are notable for their salaciousness, not a striking element in Güiraldes's works but one that particularly appeals to the Argentinean, as Manuel Gálvez comments in his *Hombres en Soledad*. The last three stories in the collection, "Trilogía cristiana" ("Christian Trilogy"), deal, as the title suggests, with the Christian religion and are noteworthy for their rhythmic flow of language. Quite sincere in tone, "Güele," one of the stories, tells of the miraculous conversion of an Indian chieftain of the Argentine; the two remaining stories, one caricaturing a scene in Heaven ("El Juicio de Dios") ("Divine Judgment") and the other portraying the struggles of Saint Anthony against the flesh ("San Antonio"), are quite in the spirit and manner of Anatole France and thematically quite at variance with the general tone of the collection.

Two stories from *Cuentos de Muerte y de Sangre*, "Al Rescoldo" and "Trenzador" ("A Leather Worker"), are reprinted in *Seis Relatos*. The remaining four, thoroughly Argentine in background, are: "Diálogo y Palabras" ("A Dialogue and Words"), which exemplifies in a dialogue between two ranch workers Güiraldes's mastery over dialectical peculiarities of the River Plate region; "Esta Noche, Noche Buena" ("This Christmas Eve"), an amusing tale that portrays certain Christmas customs among the lowly folk of the Argentine; "La politiquería" ("The Knack of Politics"), an account of a peon that had a charmed life; and "Telesforo Altamira," a story of a down-and-out individual in Buenos Aires that had once been somebody.

In general, however, in these early *cuentos* Güiraldes does not appear in the light of a teller of stories, but rather as an artificer in words. Tropes abound, many of which strike the reader for their surprising air of freshness. A winding road is compared to a lasso that has been carelessly cast aside; the travel of gossip is likened to the spread of grease in a hot frying pan; and the nimbleness of a pig's snout is compared with the quickness of an eye. Some of the figures are very poetic, for instance the metaphor in "Al Rescoldo" in which embers are described as velveting themselves in ash. But his poetic fancy takes at times a Gongoresque turn, as the conceit in the description of a young girl in "Arrabalera" ("Suburban"):

> On her neck she wore a ribbon of black velvet, and, harmonizing in color with it, down near her mouth, was a mole of surpassing beauty, which was black—perhaps from striving to be the pupil of an eye, in order to contemplate in ecstasy the coquettish passing of her little moist tongue over her lips.

Quite different from the *Cuentos* is *Rosaura*, which comes nearer to meeting the standards of the short story of Poe or Maupassant than anything else that Güiraldes wrote. The setting is a small town in the Argentine pampas, Lobos, in the early years of the present century. When the story begins, the railroad, which had recently connected Lobos with Buenos Aires, had already jarred the town from its long, peaceful slumber. Infected with idle curiosity, if not absolute restlessness, many of the townspeople had acquired the habit of gathering at the station each day at train time in order to catch a glimpse of the outside world.

Among such was the young and pretty Rosaura Torres, who, one day, in company with two girl companions, attracted the attention of a very handsome young man on the train. When they stared at him, he was irritated by their rudeness and attempted to shame them by fixing his gaze intently upon Rosaura, who remained completely unperturbed. Recovering his good humor as the train was leaving, he bowed pleasantly to the girls, evidently dismissing them from his mind. Rosaura, however, unmistakably affected by the stranger, returned home somewhat in a daze. In the weeks that followed she saw again and again the same young man on the train, and her love increased, for although he made no advances, he showed clearly an interest in her. If he came near her, as he sometimes did when he got out of the train and walked up and down the platform, poor Rosaura almost swooned, so great was her emotion.

Still greater was her concern when she discovered that he was far above her socially. She was in very comfortable circumstances—her father was the owner of the best livery-stable in Lobos—but Carlos Ramallo was the son of an extremely wealthy landowner and had been educated in Europe. Self-conscious, by nature quiet and unassuming, Rosaura bore her anguish silently. Finally, at a dance given in the town to honor Carlos, Rosaura met him formally; and he showed clearly that he preferred her to all the other girls in Lobos. Their acquaintance improved, for when he stopped in Lobos, as he frequently did, the two saw each other and talked. Although poor Rosaura was now considerably occupied with dress patterns and the fashioning of new clothes, her mind was in a constant swirl, so possessed was she by her infatuation for Carlos. A fatal day it was for her when he told her he was going to spend six months in England, where his father was sending him to study certain methods in farming.

How slowly those months dragged by for Rosaura! Then one day when she and her dearest friend, Carmen, were at the station, they saw Carlos again. A woman, evidently his wife, was with him on the train. He saw Rosaura, but bowed very coolly to her. In deep despair, she returned home. A few days later, accompanied by Carmen, she went again to the station. She was wearing the dress she wore on the night she met Carlos at the dance, and in her bosom she had tucked a brief note that he had written to her at one time; Carlos was on the train and with him was the same woman. Visibly moved, Rosaura walked away along the track; but when the locomo-

tive neared her, she uttered a scream and threw herself under
its wheels.

In *Rosaura* the various narrative elements are exceedingly
well developed and unified. One tone, that of tragedy, dominates the plot, which moves swiftly and without interruption,
incident by incident, to its tragic culmination. But by far the
outstanding quality of the story is its portrayal of the modest,
sensitive village girl Rosaura under the spell of a great love,
which she repressed and yet inwardly nourished until the
realization of the utter futility of her dreams broke the barriers of her will and led her to destroy herself. Güiraldes pro-
ceeds impressionistically in sketching in the background
against which the tragedy is enacted. Without actually saying
much about Lobos, with only a remark here and there about
any of its inhabitants—such as Doña Petrona, who sometimes
spoke to Rosaura as she was on her way to or from the station
—he succeeds in leaving a very definite impression of the town
and its people. A very important element of the setting is the
train itself; the locomotive appears as a sinister force from
the beginning of the story to the end. It is to be regretted that
Güiraldes, with the inimitable style that characterizes everything he wrote and the mastery of the technique of the modern short story that he exhibits in *Rosaura*, did not write other
stories like it.

The main characters in Güiraldes's longer works are, as in
his *Cuentos*, distinctively Argentine. Represented as well-to-
do ranch owners, the Galváns, who might very well be
Güiraldes's own family, appear in all of his longer works. In
Xaimaca the central figure is Marcos Galván; and in *Don
Segundo Sombra* Leandro Galván and his son Raucho appear
as minor characters. These last two characters figure largely in
Raucho. The story itself begins with the sorrow of Don
Leandro over the death of his wife, but it soon centers about
Raucho, whose life might be regarded as typical of a wealthy
young Argentine. In a magically poetic style, Güiraldes re-
creates the scene of Raucho's childhood, the headquarters of

the Galván ranch, with its family residence, its stables, other outhouses, and corrals; and he animates that scene with descriptions of the activities of the workers on the ranch, of the pastimes of Raucho and his brothers, and of such incidents as the arrival from time to time of peddlers with wares to sell. Then follows an account of Raucho's schooldays in Buenos Aires, attended with love affairs and his first acquaintance with prostitutes. Those days over, Raucho returned to the ranch, with whose activities he had long been familiar; there, for some months, freer than ever in his life from the authority of his father, he was very active, helping with the management of the property. Particularly impressive, in this part of the book, are poetic passages descriptive of the four seasons of the year, and the realistic touches that color the rounding up and branding of the cattle, the shearing of the sheep, and the invasion one year of the entire countryside by great swarms of locusts.

Then, little by little, Raucho grew weary of the country. He began to read, especially the French writers—Lorrain, Maupassant, Verlaine. He went frequently to Buenos Aires to talk to French women about Paris; finally he went to live there permanently, joined the Jockey Club, and took a mistress. Not until the eve of his departure for Europe did he return to the ranch, where for a few days he amused himself with a buxom girl of the countryside, and with shooting birds out on the edge of a lake, a spot that fascinated him peculiarly, for there—with only wild birds of all sorts about—he felt quite removed from the rest of the world.

Then came at last the long anticipated journey to Europe; and with it his impressions of the sea, of Río, of Lisbon, of Paris, which he already knew thoroughly from his reading. There, he abandoned himself to all the sensual pleasures the city afforded; and when his father commanded him to return home, he refused, his mind being deranged by drugs and drink. When Raucho finally fell sick, his brother made the trip and brought him home. Whatever love Raucho had had for Paris, faded gradually away as he neared America. His joy on the way from Buenos Aires to the ranch was unrestrained; but he was not entirely at peace until he went out and sat down under a willow near the river bank, where "the whistling duck pierced the night with his shrill cry," and then on his own native soil he "fell asleep, flat on his back, his arms outstretched—crucified thus by the calmness that had pervaded and possessed his soul."

Even more convincing than *Raucho* that the experiences it records are absolutely genuine is *Xaimaca*, Güiraldes's second novel and his most poetic work. This sense of reality arises from the fact that *Xaimaca* is a travel book—one of the most delightful in Spanish-American literature—in which, even to the names of boats and hotels, there is a scrupulous regard for fact. Entirely in keeping with the exaltation of the central figure, Marcos Galván, who jots down his impressions while on a journey, is the highly imaginative treatment of the material.

Scarcely had Marcos begun his journey by train from Buenos Aires to Peru when he became interested in a young woman, Clara Ordóñez, who was accompanied by her brother, Peñalba. The places through which the travelers, who soon become friends, passed are poetically described: the Argentine plains, the city of Mendoza, the Andes, and the city of Santiago with its lofty, picturesque mound of Santa Lucia on which the three travelers took tea. Journeying by automobile from Santiago to the port of Valparaiso, they were forced by an accident to spend a part of the night in a Chilean village, where they witnessed native dances and other quaint rural customs.

The bond that united the three travelers grew stronger. Clara responded to the interest Marcos had taken in her, and his love for Kipling endeared him to Peñalba. Consequently, shortly after they had embarked for the voyage northward along the west coast of South America, Marcos decided to abandon his plan of stopping in Peru and to continue with his friends to Jamaica. He was delighted with all that he saw from the boat—a shoal of fish, a shark, a whale, and the interesting birds of the region; the Pacific itself awakened in him all that he had read, probably in Loti, of the distant Orient, which is repeatedly brought to mind. Wherever the boat stopped, Marcos and his friends went ashore: in Iquique they ate crabs; from Arica they went by train to Tacna, where they ate river-shrimp; and at Paita, Peru, Marcos was charmed by the Indian venders, descendants of the indigenous race, who swarmed with their wares into the boat.

For Marcos all of these sights and experiences were highly colored by his intense emotional state—by his love for Clara, for between the two there already existed a very intimate, personal relationship. Of a very rich Argentine family, she had married according to dictates of her parents for money and position, and the marriage had turned out badly. Genuine and without restraint, however, was her love for Marcos, whose account of the ecstasy into which he was transported by his passion is truly a glorification of carnal love.

In time the travelers came to Panama, with its lighthouse and beautiful bay; they suffered from the heat as they passed through the Canal; in Colón, whose negroes and Oriental shops fascinated Marcos, they spent several days at the Washington Hotel; and then in a few days reached their destination, Jamaica. The beauty of the tropical region struck them all, especially Marcos, who, "his mind carbureting perfectly," likened the island to an immense avocado on a great blue tray, the botanical garden to a piece of the forest that the English had disciplined and shaved, and the sound of the impact of the rubber tires of the automobile against the wet pavement as "a sticky, whistling" noise.

All went gloriously for Marcos and Clara until Peñalba discovered the relation that existed between them and forced him to leave Jamaica. Dejected, truly lovesick, Marcos set out for Buenos Aires by the same route he had come. His melancholy was apparent to the passengers, particularly to a North

American girl who became enamoured of him and would have given herself to him; but, romantically true to Clara, he declined her love.

Episodic, and in this respect like *Raucho* and *Xaimaca*, Güiraldes's masterpiece, *Don Segundo Sombra*, consists of a series of incidents that trace the development of an Argentine boy to early manhood. His name is never mentioned, but the reader suspects from the very outset that he is the illegitimate son of Fabio Cáceres, a rich ranch owner, who had sent him to a small country town to be educated. Already weary of school when we see him for the first time, and weary, too, of Cáceres's two maiden sisters with whom he lived, the boy had become a loafer about the public places in the town. He came to admire intensely an individual he saw from time to time—a roaming ranch worker, an expert breaker of horses, Don Segundo Sombra by name, a man of great courage, physical strength, and probity. One evening in a tavern the boy rendered Don Segundo a service that probably saved his life, and the two became friends. It was then that the boy decided to run away from home, to attach himself in some way to the man he admired; and the next morning he set out on his pony for a ranch to which he knew Don Segundo was going.

When the latter arrived at the ranch, he took the boy, who had already found employment there, definitely under his protection. For five years he was directly under the tutelage of Don Segundo; at the end of that time he was an expert cowboy and horse-breaker; he was proficient in leather work and in the treatment of the diseases of livestock; he knew how to play the guitar and to dance the popular dances; and, from the standpoint of moral conduct, he had learned to show "endurance and fortitude in the struggles of life; to accept fatalistically and without grumbling whatever happened; to have moral force in sentimental affairs; to distrust women and drink; to be prudent among strangers; and to be true to his friends."

Even after his probationary period the boy continued with

his mentor. The two went to work on a ranch on the seacoast, the owner of which was half-crazed; here the boy saw strange sights, among them an enormous colony of crabs that filled him with awe. In the same neighborhood, in a great round-up in which the two took part, the boy's horse was gored and he himself suffered a broken collar bone. After attending to his protégé's injury, and placing him in the home of a rancher in the district, Don Segundo left to follow his work elsewhere. But a fight with a jealous suitor over a girl, both of whom lived at the ranch where he was recuperating, soon terminated the boy's stay there. He joined Don Segundo again, but ill fortune continued to pursue him, for at a horse race he lost both his money and several of his horses. Other experiences as a cowboy followed. At a ranch where he took a job of breaking horses, the owner took a fancy to him and invited him to remain; at a country tavern he witnessed a brawl in which a man was killed; and on the pampas at night he was faced with a stampede of the herd of cattle he was helping drive to market.

Then one day while he was reflecting on the adverse fortune that had lately attended him, he received a letter from a lawyer in the town where he had lived a as young boy informing him that his erstwhile protector, Fabio Cáceres, recently dead, had acknowledged the boy in his will as his legitimate son and left him a large estate. Irritated by the deference all his friends began to show him, he would have refused the property, but for the advice of Don Segundo. After he assumed his new rôle as proprietor, he acquired through the influence of Raucho Galván, the son of his guardian, a taste for literature, and frequent visits to Buenos Aires transformed him in a measure into a cultured person; but he did not lose his democratic attitude toward those of lower social rank. Don Segundo remained with him for more than three years; then, feeling that his work of moulding a man had been completed, restless again for his old life, he took leave of his protégé and returned once more to the pampas.

The two main characters, like the tale itself, are a bit romantic. Somewhat shadowy, as befits his name, Don Segundo
Sombra, who possesses so many virtues—courage, endurance,
moral and physical strength, leadership, the art of entertaining
in various ways, and unusual skill in the work in which he
made his living—and none of the vices which afflict humanity,
is an idealized rather than a real character. We know him only
through a source that is prejudiced in his favor, his protégé,
who tells us what he is and what he does. The boy is also
idealized, but he is less of one cloth than Don Segundo. Skilled,
first of all, in everything that pertains to life on the plains,
finally a cultivated man with a love for reading, he stands as
an exemplar of Güiraldes's own ideal of a man. Of him there
is, too, a side that we never see of Don Segundo, and that is
his inner world, his thoughts and reflections on life, which
in his rôle of autobiographer he constantly reveals.

The very effective portrayal of the background for these
Argentine characters has contributed probably more than any
other feature to winning for the book the high praise that has
generally been accorded it. When Don Segundo's ward takes
stock of himself at the end of five years, he enumerates a long
list of towns and ranches, all of the province of Buenos Aires,
which had seen them pass many times, "covered with dirt and
mud, behind a herd of cattle." Of the appearance of this region, with the exception of the dunes and crab-infested bogs
of the seacoast, there is in the book practically no description.
Certain phenomena of nature, on the other hand, particularly
in reference to their effect on the teller of the tale, are frequently commented upon: the cold; the heat of the summer's
sun; the rain, as he is driving a herd of cattle; or the night, as
he is sitting with others by the campfire.

The part of the setting, however, that is really striking is the
varied panorama of rural and small-town life in the province
of Buenos Aires. While there is some detailed description of
places, the salient characteristic in nearly all of the various
scenes is the human element, which imparts, through its lively,

natural vernacular, a decidedly animated tone—whether it be the coarse joking in the tavern where we first see the hero of the tale; or the bantering of the cowboy at the ranch where he obtained his first job; or the raillery of the "tape" Burgos when he tried to pick a quarrel with Don Segundo; or the love-making between Paula and our hero, when he was recuperating at the ranch. In this connection, too, mention must be made of two tales that Don Segundo tells in quaint, dialectical language: one, a supposed incident in the life of our Lord when He was on this earth; the other, a veritable fairy tale of demons, witches, enchantments, and disenchantments.

In addition to vernacular speech the author attains local color through the description of certain manners and customs with which Don Segundo and his pupil come in contact in their wanderings. Some of these portrayals are veritable essays in themselves: the account, for instance, of a country dance, which among a diversity of details includes certain popular songs as an accompaniment to the dances; the description of a cock-fight, at which our hero had the good fortune to bet on the winner; and, later, of a horse race, at which he lost almost everything he had; the account of a Sunday spent at a country saloon, where a friend was forced in self-defense to kill a man; and the portrayal, probably the most masterful in the book, of a great round-up, which is made so vivid that one almost smells the dust, hears the lowing and bellowing of the cattle, and sees the cowboys, in mad pursuit, racing after and lassoing them. Many passages in the book, such as the following, reveal the keenness of Güiraldes's observation in regard to cattle:

> Without moving, I let the herd of cattle pass. Some, as they looked toward the ranch houses, bellowed. Weary, the yearlings went by slowly. From time to time, when one would hook another, a hollow space for some meters about would form; but it would soon fill up again, and then the march would go on, slowly, relentlessly.

In a measure this passage reveals how the chief aesthetic value of the book is attained—by rendering into poetry, through the use of rhythmical and figurative language, experience which is generally regarded as common, prosaic, or even sordid.

Güiraldes, however, with all of his excellent qualities as a writer—now that we have come to a final evaluation of him—is not the truly great novelist that some enthusiastic critics would have us believe. His novels, after all, are limited in scope, rather one-sided. For, while his style is poetic, while his sharp-toned pictures of certain strata of Argentine society remain with one long after his books are read, he is sadly lacking in two essentials of a great novelist: he gives no evidence of ability to develop character or to weave a plot that is much beyond that of the picaresque novel.

In spite of these shortcomings, *Don Segundo Sombra* has entered the ranks of international literature in both German and English translations and has received high praise from other than Argentine and Spanish critics.

CHAPTER IX

ROMULO GALLEGOS, INTERPRETER OF THE *LLANOS* OF VENEZUELA

❀

URING THE second and third decades of the present century three novelists of first-rate ability made their appearance on the literary horizon in Venezuela. One of these
was Ana Teresa Parra Sanojo, who, although stricken by
death when her talent was in its first bloom, wrote in *Ifigenia*
the most outstanding psychological novel of her country, and
of Spanish America with the exception of the work of Barrios; the second, Rómulo Gallegos, whose masterpiece, *Doña
Bárbara*, ranks in the highest category of Spanish-American
novels; and the third, Arturo Uslar Pietri, whose *Lanzas
Coloradas* (*Crimson Lances*), 1931, like the novels of Gallegos,
is firmly rooted in Venezuelan soil. The oldest of the three and
by far the most productive is Rómulo Gallegos, who was born
in Caracas in 1884. Without completing his university course,
he began to earn his living as a teacher. In 1912 he was made
director of the Colegio Federal in Barcelona (Venezuela); in
1918 he returned to Caracas to serve in like capacity the
Escuela Normal; and in 1922 he became director of the Liceo
"Andrés Bello." Elected senator for the state of Apure in
1929, he soon resigned on account of disturbed conditions in
the country. In 1932 he went to Europe, where he remained
until 1936. On his return to Venezuela he was appointed

Minister of Education, a post he occupied for a year. Later he was a candidate for the presidency.

His interest in literature manifested itself early, for in 1909 he established a literary review, *La Alborada*, and in 1912 and in 1914 he was contributing short stories to one of the most outstanding Spanish-American literary periodicals, *El Cojo Ilustrado*, published in Caracas. In 1913 he issued a collection of short stories under the title of the first story, *Los Aventureros (The Adventurers)*. Another short story, *Los Inmigrantes (Immigrants)*, appeared in 1922, as the initial issue of *La Novela semanal*. His first novel, *El Ultimo Solar (The Last of the Solars)*, whose title was changed in a later edition to *Reinaldo Solar*, was published in Caracas in 1920. Since then four other novels have come from his pen: *La Trepadora (The Climber)*, 1925; *Doña Bárbara*, 1929; *Cantaclaro*, 1931; *Canaima*, 1935; and *Pobre Negro (Poor Negro)*, 1937.

In these novels converge various currents that had appeared in Venezuelan fiction before Gallegos began to write. While all of his novels are autochthonous, there already existed numerous sketches on native manners and customs, notably those by Bolet Peraza and those in Romero García's novel *Peonía*, 1890, which is very rich in descriptions of life on the ranches in the plains region of Venezuela. The satiric style of *Reinaldo Solar* had already been employed by M. E. Pardo in *Todo un Pueblo*, 1899, and in a most masterful manner by Blanco Fombona in his *El Hombre de Hierro* and *El Hombre de Oro*. Before Gallegos dealt with the breaking down of class distinctions in Venezuelan society in *La Trepadora* and *Pobre Negro*, Urbaneja Achelpohl had essayed the same problem in *En este País (In This Country)*, 1916; and before *Canaima* and *Cantaclaro* pointed out the impositions of military and political bosses on defenseless citizens, Picón-Febrés had done so in *El Sargento Felipe (Sergeant Philip)*, 1899, and Pocaterra in *Vidas obscuras (Obscure Lives)*, 1916. Nor did Gallegos escape the influence of the modernista school, exemplified most strikingly in Venezuelan fiction by the novels of Díaz

Rodríguez—*Idolos rotos*, 1901, *Sangre patricia*, 1902, and *Pere-grina ... (The Pilgrim Girl)*, 1922, for his first book, *Los Aventureros*, as well as his last three, is more notable for its stylistic qualities than its content.

Characterized by lyricism, by rhythmical prose, and by lack of objectivity, the seven stories Gallegos published in 1913 give little hint of the charm of *Doña Bárbara*. For they do not differ essentially from stories by Pedro Emilio Coll, Alejandro Fernández García, and Carlos Paz García—all more or less contemporaries of Gallegos—who followed the literary pattern of Díaz Rodríguez. One device that Gallegos employs so effectively in the greater number of these stories as to distinguish him in a measure from his contemporaries is that of contrast, as is clearly evident in *Los Aventureros*, the first and, as a short story, the best of the collection. Here, we see Jacinto Avila, a poor and insignificant young lawyer, paving his way to wealth and power through a revolution to be effected with the aid of Matías Rosalira, a bandit of twenty years' experience. Jacinto's eloquent language persuaded Matías to lend his support but not the latter's followers; only when Matías urged them, in his rough, vulgar fashion, were they inspired with the necessary enthusiasm. For the accomplishment of their purpose, the two men, differing completely in education and native talent but possessing individually peculiar abilities, complemented each other admirably.

In "El Apoyo" ("The Prop"), the second story in the collection, the author contrasts, through letters in which each confesses his innermost thoughts, two boys whose intimacy dated from their student days. After their separation Francisco entered a monastery; Manuel remained in a seminary. Influenced by Francisco, Manuel eventually elected the priesthood, and struggled faithfully against doubt and worldly desires. Always before him was the example of his friend, who apparently suffered no such temptations. After taking the vows came the shock of discovering that Francisco, calm only from apathy and indifference, had abandoned the convent. When Gallegos incidentally describes in this story the interminable plains with their herds of wild cattle; the water-holes in the great desert stretches; and the drowsy, poverty-stricken towns of the region, he foreshadows that interpretation of nature, cruel and inhospitable, which characterizes his *Doña Bárbara, Canaima,* and *Cantaclaro.*

Lacking that essential of the short story—an outstanding dramatic incident that claims predominantly the reader's attention—and written in rambling but poetic prose, the third story, "Estrellas sobre el Barranco" ("Stars Over the Gorge"), presents a weird d'Annunzio-like picture of a poverty-stricken pair—a brother mentally and morally diseased and struggling against an insane lust for his sister, who, unable to earn a living, faces prostitution as inevitable. Far better as a short story, "La Liberación" ("Escape") contrasts two friends of opposing temperaments: Valentín Branto, strong and dominating, and Ricardo Fariña, physically weak and submissive by nature. They became acquainted in school, where Valentín protected Ricardo, but exacted in return absolute obedience—forcing the boy to participate in his all-too-numerous pranks. After Valentín left the city, he returned from time to time to force Ricardo into all manner of excesses, thus causing him to fail an examination while he was studying medicine. Then after a long interval, in which the two did not see each other and Ricardo had attained an excellent reputation as a doctor, Valentín appeared; although Ricardo struggled against the baneful influence which had induced epilepsy, he was powerless and in the end lost not only his reputation but his wife's love. Desperate in his desire to liberate himself from this influence, he imagined himself choking Valentín to death; instead, Ricardo was found dead, with the print on his throat of his own fingers.

Both the fantasy and poetic language of "Las Novias del Mendigo" ("The Beggar's Sweethearts") recall the stories of Valle-Inclán. Its main character is a queer individual who occupies himself with telling women weird, superstitious stories, in exchange for which he sought prayers. Among the women was one who pretended to be in love with him; but her jesting proved to be his undoing, for when he discovered her deception his mind was unable to withstand his grief. "Sol de Antaño" ("Autumn Sun") recalls the ruminations of a painter, who, on returning to Venezuela after some years, discovered in an inn near his old home a beautiful girl who proved to be his own child, a souvenir of an illicit love affair with the *mayordomo's* daughter.

"El Milagro del Año" ("The Miracle of the Year"), the last story in the collection, is, in regard to plot and character portrayal, one of the best. Especially commendable is the analysis of the character of El Chavato, a devout villain, whose behavior is consistently at variance with his religion. Although devoted especially to Our Lady, he murdered and robbed his employer—the owner of a fishing boat—killed one helper and mortally wounded another one day while they were at sea. Believing that the Virgin, whose help he had invoked, had aided in the acquisition of the boat bought with the stolen money, El Chavato placed on her altar, as evidence of his appreciation, a little silver boat. The survivor, whose silence the murderer bought, confessed the crime to the village priest, El Chavato's own brother, who tried in vain to make the criminal atone. Then came the day on which each year the villagers revered their patron saint, the Virgin, who, according to the priest, would then demonstrate her power through a miracle. That, he hoped, would be the confession by El Chavato of his crime; but when the latter remained obdurate, the priest explained that the Virgin, angered by a crime committed in her name, refused her favor. To appease her, the villagers, who already suspected El Chavato, slew him.

Between the publication of these short stories and his first novel—a seven-year period—the literary ideals of Gallegos materially changed. The stories emphasize form rather than content; but such is not the case in at least the first three novels he wrote—*Reinaldo Solar*, *La Trepadora*, and *Doña Bárbara*—

all of which, although not lacking in literary embellishment, contain a vital message. The first of these novels satirizes in the protagonist Reinaldo Solar a type generally accepted as characteristic of Spanish America in general. Reared in comfort and ease in Caracas, Reinaldo was the descendant of an old and honorable family whose male members down to Reinaldo's grandfather had been active men who had attained a place in the world. As the same energy, rare talent, personal charm, and great enthusiasm for whatever he undertook characterized Reinaldo, a brilliant future seemed in store for him. Why he did not attain it the author sets forth at length in the novel.

Very susceptible from childhood, Reinaldo fell so deeply under the influence of whatever philosophical work he read that he attempted to put its ideas into effect in his own life. At one time the advocate of chastity and continence, at another the devotee of all the carnal pleasures Caracas afforded, he became, even as a student, the plaything of the conflicting views of the authors he read. But Reinaldo was by no means ridiculous in his comrades' eyes, for his charming personality and brilliance as a speaker and conversationalist predicated fame from the outset, although he had done nothing to deserve it. Motivated by the desire to justify his reputation, and imbued with the idea that his own regeneration as well as that of the race lay in coming into close contact with nature, with becoming a man of action, Reinaldo left Caracas to assume charge of the family hacienda. He discharged the crafty manager; made himself master of the plantation; decided, in spite of advice to the contrary, to plant wheat instead of cane, for he was obsessed at that time with the idea that cereal-producing countries were the most civilized; and started a book, with himself—a man of action and vigor—as the protagonist. But Reinaldo's chief weakness soon showed itself, for he abandoned both his plans for the plantation and his book, to devote himself to a healthy country girl, with the purpose of producing vigorous offspring. Inconstant again, he yielded the girl to a friend who loved her, and, somewhat disillusioned, returned to Caracas.

There Reinaldo experienced the atmosphere of his youth. At home were his doting mother and his sister, both devout and wholly under the influence of the clergy, although for a time a cousin turned his sister's thoughts to worldly rather than heavenly love. Among his close associates were a pessimistic but earnest student of law, Antonio Menéndez; a talented youth with literary ambitions, Manuel Alcor; and two painters, Benítez and Rivero.

But soon Reinaldo, following a precedent set by others of his country when they felt their talent was not duly appreciated at home, determined to go to Europe. Whether he should go or not was a question hotly debated by both friends and relatives. While Antonio Menéndez opined that Venezuelan writers had greater possibilities for attaining success in their own country, Reinaldo's uncles, glad to relieve him of the management of the estate, encouraged his departure. With a tragedy as his literary baggage, Reinaldo took passage, first class and not third as he had at first decided, for Spain, where he hoped to win fame with his pen.

His first disillusionment came in Madrid when the Venezuelan consul told him that it would probably take years before he could succeed in having his play performed on the stage; that in Spain Venezuelans were regarded as Indians; and that it would be far easier for him to attract attention as a writer in his own country. Although he had barely arrived in Spain, Reinaldo decided at once to return home, moved to this decision less by the consul's advice than by a beautiful woman, Rosaura, of whom he had caught a glimpse in the consulate, where he learned she was on the point of returning with her husband, Luciano Mendeville, to Caracas.

Again in his native city, Reinaldo, in addition to devoting himself to Rosaura, organized a civic league that was to be entirely free from politics; but it quickly slipped out of his hands into those of selfish politicians. Only Rosaura was now left to Reinaldo, who took her in when her husband cast her off. Charmed with her and her playing—for she was an accomplished musician—he decided to study music. "But he would not resign himself to the tiresome monotony of scales and arpeggios; he wanted to play, quickly, without subjecting himself to the discipline of patient study." Finally, when Rosaura realized that she herself had begun to tire him, she left to give a series of concerts in Havana. Dejected over the break with her, Reinaldo failed to find, as he had done in the past, any justification for his conduct. Many factors contributed to his complete disillusionment. His sister was about to enter a convent; the only woman that ever loved him, Graciela Aranda, whom he never found time to notice, was betrothed to another; his favorite project, the civic league, was in the hands of professional politicians; his health was undermined; and, as he had lost his family fortune through bad management, he was faced with the necessity of earning a living. Quite desperate, he took part in a revolution which failed because its four generals fell to quarreling among themselves over the office of president. Reinaldo became captain of one of the wandering bands into which the army broke up; but when, dejected and sick with malaria, he ordered his men to attack a superior force, they refused to obey and, instead, clubbed him to death with their guns.

While the novel is not entirely pessimistic, there being other characters that, in contrast to Reinaldo, show determination accompanied by persistent effort, the general tone is one of despair, especially over Venezuela as a nation. In his musings over a revolution, Reinaldo analyzed the general weakness of his countrymen, without realizing that he himself shared it:

> This disease is incurable. It is in the blood. We are incapable of patient and silent effort, and for this reason we are lured by the violence that accompanies an armed revolution. That incurable impulse to right matters impels us to violent effort which, while it might lead to heroic deeds, is only passing and momentary. Afterwards we fall

asleep and forget everything. With us it is everything or nothing. We are a race of adventurers who do not hesitate to risk our lives but who are absolutely incapable of devoting them to an undertaking that requires persistence.

And again, as he walked dejectedly through a miserable district of Caracas, his conclusions in regard to his countrymen are hopeless:

> The fact is that we live a life filled with irritation, sorrow, apprehension, and endless disappointment. And these tragic masks cover faces that are expressionless, on all of which is stamped the ugliness of hybridism. We do not constitute a race. What faces! In no one of them is there any trace of strength that is not brutal; all of them reveal the same awful derangement of character. Such people cannot be relied upon for anything; they seem the foetus of an abortive nation.

The laboring classes, the peons, in the opinion of Reinaldo, who is again Gallegos's own mouthpiece, are little more than animals and far from possessing noble qualities.

> They [the peons] have no inner life. They never utter a word that reveals any disquietude within their minds; they have no feeling that is not purely animal. Their souls are buried, entirely obliterated. For this reason those that have attempted to create a national literature have failed miserably. For the first essential is lacking, the soul of the race. To supply it, our literary men have had to have recourse to imitation; this, then, is the source of that romantic *criollismo* which places in the hearts of these people exquisite delicacies and that has nothing of truth in it except the names, more or less picturesque, of a few tropical plants mixed in skillfully with a psychology that is entirely foreign to the people themselves. Trees and plants supply the lack of a national soul. For the rest, descriptions, more or less adulterated, of the external phase of popular life. Of the inner life, of that which is deep within, the only thing that is true, there is never a word

nor a vague indication of penetration into that buried soul.

It is in these words in his first novel that Gallegos comes nearest to expressing his creed as a novelist. And *Reinaldo Solar* is primarily a novel of character rather than of plot, for the latter is rather loose, consisting only of a series of incidents that demonstrate the weakness of will power in the protagonist. Likewise, it is the inner life of those that come in contact with Reinaldo that interests Gallegos, in some cases so extensively that sight is lost of the central figure. These minor characters in the novel afford a varied panorama of Venezuelan society: country and village folk, politicians, students, ambitious young writers and artists who have come to Caracas to make a name for themselves, and excellent specimens of those strong, brutal generals "who sink into the physiological weakness of the Venezuelan people like a wedge into soft wood." Perhaps it is Gallegos's conception of Venezuelan society as a whole that Reinaldo symbolizes—a society that has not decided what it wants; a capricious group, flitting from ideal to ideal, scattering its energy without accomplishing any worthy purpose. Next in importance to characterization is the background, both rural and urban. We turn from the Solar estate—where we hear in the early morning as the clouds lift, the lowing of the cows and the incessant creaking of the cane mill, and even sniff the cane juice impregnating the air— to the old, dilapidated, foul-smelling boarding house in Caracas, where struggling young writers and artists slept and ate.

In this work the tone throughout is pessimistic, but in his next novel, *La Trepadora*, even more thoroughly Venezuelan in both background and characters, Gallegos has assumed a more hopeful attitude. At least two-thirds of the action takes place in a rural upland district of Venezuela at Cantarrama, the coffee plantation of Don Jaime del Casal, who had spent his youth restoring the estate. When the story opens, in the closing years of the nineteenth century, Don Jaime was residing in Caracas, having just returned from a three-year stay in Europe for his health. Again the plantation was in a run-down condition—the result of the bad management of Jaimito, his eldest son—but the family spent Christmas there as usual. With them went two relatives: Carmelita, a widow of good blood, and her daughter, Adelaida, a beautiful girl of a romantic turn of mind, who was fond of playing Chopin and Liszt on the piano.

At Cantarrama at this time was the bastard son of Don Jaime, Hilario Guanipa, who had earlier been its manager but had lately returned with his pockets full of money from a three-year stay on the plains. Hilario's mother had been in her youth an exceptionally beautiful mulattress whom Don Jaime came to know when she and her mother gathered coffee on his plantation. Although her brothers, the Guanipas, a bad lot, once attempted to kill Don Jaime, they finally came to live with their sister on a piece of property he had given her, and for years terrorized the community with their thieving and brigandage. Hilario did not share the law-breaking proclivities of his uncles, whom on one occasion he daringly thwarted when they attempted to sack the town, but he was gay, amorous, and convivial. Not only did he snare the rustic beauties of the community but even the sensitive and refined Adelaida, who from the moment he lifted her in his arms to help her across a stream, fell completely under his spell. Equally attracted, Hilario at first planned to carry her off to the wild plains, but after hearing her play Chopin and Liszt, sent instead a note telling her he loved her and would some day make her his wife. He set himself to improving the property he had inherited from his mother, and, in time, by means none too honorable, came into possession of Cantarrama, which was put on the block by Jaimito's bad management. Owner now of the estate, Hilario went to Caracas and brought back Adelaida as his bride.

But their marriage brought entire happiness to neither for many years. He loved her, but the fact that she came of a superior family irked him; and to humiliate her he had only vulgar and unlettered folk about him and delighted in embarrassing her with his coarse jokes, his drinking, and his infidelities. When their only child, Victoria, was born, he showed plainly his disappointment, because he had hoped for a male heir; nevertheless, reconciled, he taught her, among other manly pursuits, to hunt, to swim, and to ride. Victoria was contented in Cantarrama until she was sixteen, when a young dandy of Caracas, a member of a deer-hunting party, awakened in her a desire to know and be a part in the high society of Caracas, of which the Alcoys, descendants of the Casals, were leaders.

An incident occurred shortly that caused Hilario to send her to her grandmother in Caracas, where her natural beauty and good taste in dressing attracted attention. Venturous by inheritance, she assumed the name of Casal and extended her acquaintances beyond her grandmother's circle of gossipy old men and women, dauntless in her determination to meet the aristocratic, Parisian-bred Alcoys, whose villa she would have entered had the old lady not strenuously objected. Later, in a fashionable modiste's shop she tried to attract their attention by giving her name as Casal, but all of her attempts to make their acquaintance met only with rebuffs.

Not of such haughty tendencies was a young kinsman she came to know at this time—Nicolás Casal, only son of Jaimito, who had committed suicide when a large part of the family estate was lost through his bad business ventures. Reared in Germany, Nicolás had returned to the land of his birth to make a place for himself and to repair the family losses caused by his father. With her heart set on Nicolás, who returned her love, Victoria ceased to think of breaking into the high society of Caracas and returned to Cantarrama, as Nicolás had acquired coffee lands nearby. Hilario transferred his hatred of Jaimito to his son and vowed he would kill him if he ever appeared at Cantarrama. But Nicolás dared to do that very thing, and when Hilario saw him he was completely disarmed, so struck was he by the extraordinary resemblance of Nicolás to Hilario's own father.

Such is the action of *La Trepadora*, which as a novel is praiseworthy in some respects and disappointing in others. Among its merits must be listed its various settings or backgrounds: a small village surrounded entirely by mountains covered with coffee trees, and the manners and customs of its inhabitants, particularly those relating to Christmas festivities, which are picturesquely portrayed; the coffee plantation, Cantarrama, and Venezuelan rural life, notably the festivities that followed the marriage of Hilario and Adelaida and the deer hunt Hilario staged for his friends from Caracas; and the capital itself with the various social strata Victoria came to know there—her grandmother's circle of devout, doddering old men and women; some rather questionable characters, free in their attitude toward life, that she met through one of her newly-made acquaintances; and the exclusive aristocratic set, to which some of her blood-relatives belonged, that would have nothing to do with her.

Most excellently done is the characterization of Hilario, the protagonist of the novel, a carefree, daring, and convivial youth whose many latent qualities develop with time. His love for Adelaida aroused an ambition for wealth, which he did acquire by means none too honorable. But his marriage brought him to realize that Adelaida was his superior both socially and educationally, and he tried to bring her down to his own level. When that failed, he accepted the situation; but later he learned to enjoy the feeling of equality. For, in spite of his dictatorial disposition, Adelaida at times asserted her own will, as when she refused to be sent with Victoria to Caracas. At this point in the development of the plot, just when the reader is expecting some solution of the Hilario-Adelaida situation, the author commits the error of beginning another story, that of Victoria and her experiences in Caracas. "In her veins the blood of an upstruggling race which stopped at nothing," his daughter was a strange mixture of rebellion and arrogance, tenderness and emotionalism, and in this part of the novel Hilario yields his place as the central figure to her, the general result being that in *La Trepadora* two stories have been indifferently joined together. Each of these, too, has a different theme or message: in the first, the disintegration of the old aristocracy through the loss of property and the rise of the less favored through its acquisition; and, in the second, the common-sense attitude of the poor but ambitious aristocrat Nicolás, who had no prejudice against marrying a person of inferior birth who attracted him. This lack of a single well-conceived plot and well-defined purpose constitutes the most serious defect of the novel.

Such defects certainly cannot be attributed to *Doña Bárbara*, Gallegos's third novel and universally acclaimed masterpiece. As in *Reinaldo Solar*, the author brings a message in *Doña Bárbara*, his spokesman being Santos Luzardo, the central figure. Although a man of refinement, Santos sprang from bold, rash stock of the plains district of the Arauca River, a tributary of the lower Orinoco, in the southern part of Venezuela. After his immediate family, aside from himself and his mother, had been wiped out by a family feud, she had taken him while very young to Caracas in order to educate him. Santos, when first presented, had just completed a very brilliant academic career and was planning to go to Europe. As sole heir of the estate in the Apure region, he determined to visit his property with the hope of selling it, for under the management of an administrator it had ceased to be profitable and besides he was threatened with a lawsuit in regard to the dividing line between his estate and that of a neighbor, Doña Bárbara, who had acquired extensive holdings in those parts. But as Santos passed through the wild region of the Arauca River en route to his estate, in a boat pushed by oarsmen, the spirit of his forbears, and their love for the region, rose within him and aroused a determination to hold on to his property, to fight the woman who was endeavoring to take it from him.

Doña Bárbara's career up to this time had been colorful to

the point of improbability. As a cook on a pirate boat on the Orinoco, she fell in love when very young with a man whom the pirates shortly killed; they then assaulted Bárbara and would have sold her into slavery had not an old Indian rescued her and taken her to a ranch near the Luzardo property. Sensual herself but, on account of the tragedy in her life, a hater of men, she used her charms to lead them to their doom. Her first victim was Lorenzo Barquero, a cousin of Santos Luzardo, a talented young man who abandoned prospects of a brilliant legal career in order to live on his ranch near her. Stultified with her drugs and drink, Lorenzo finally conveyed most of his property to Bárbara, who at once abandoned him and an infant daughter she had borne him. The two—he a wreck and his daughter entirely untaught—lived in a cabin in the neighborhood. Other victims followed Lorenzo, with the result that Bárbara became one of the wealthiest persons in the district. Unscrupulous, but with the officers of the law on her side, she had for some time been making encroachments on Santos's property, for his overseer had become one of her henchmen. With a personality that drew loyalty from desperate men, still attractive in spite of her forty years, she carried a pistol and could rope a steer as well as any of her men.

Shortly after his arrival Santos discharged his overseer, the rascally, boasting Balbino Paiba, who was hated by all on the ranch. This act together with the breaking of a beautiful black horse won for Santos the admiration and respect of his men, who at first were apprehensive lest the city-bred owner might lack the qualities necessary for the management of his property. When Doña Bárbara learned of the mettle of Santos, she ordered the disputed property line rightfully established. She was actuated not by any sense of justice but by a determination to conquer the handsome Santos by peaceful methods. Before Santos came face to face with Doña Bárbara, however, he became acquainted with others in the neighborhood: his cousin Lorenzo, a hopeless drunkard; his daughter Marisela, not ill-featured but totally uncivilized; and a North American hunter and trapper, Mr. Danger, who had his eye on Marisela and her father's remaining property. A clash occurred between Danger and Santos the first time they met, and when Santos fully understood what Danger sought he persuaded Lorenzo and Marisela, in whom he had already instilled some desire for cleanliness, to come and live with him.

While Marisela was being converted into a civilized being, Santos's relations with both Danger and Doña Bárbara became tense. The immediate cause of the increased hostility was his determination to fence his property and thereby break up the open range system by which unbranded cattle were part of the public domain. Through law, but quite fortuitously, Santos forced them both to conform to his demands. Then followed a great round-up of the wild cattle to be divided between Santos and Doña Bárbara; he displayed great skill in both riding and roping, while she appeared, contrary to her usual habit, decked out in strictly feminine apparel. But the wiles of this forty-year-old woman, either actually in love or piqued, were without effect on Santos. Varying her usual tactics, she showered him with favors and even offered to restore to him, under pretense of a sale, lands she had robbed him of. But when Santos proposed that she transfer to Marisela, her own daughter, the property she had tricked Lorenzo out of, she flew into a jealous rage and accused Santos of keeping Marisela as his mistress.

Even Marisela, who frankly let Santos know she loved him, was going through a storm-and-stress period, exasperated by his slowness in love-making. But he wanted to send her to Caracas to school; besides, the fact that Doña Bárbara was her mother, that her instincts were savage, that as a primitive being she was absolutely indifferent to the sufferings of her father, made him doubt seriously whether he should marry her. And her passions were truly as unbridled as those of a savage. For one day when she became aware that Bárbara, renowned in the neighborhood as a sorceress, was attempting to bewitch Santos, she rushed on horseback to her very house

and engaged her in a hand-to-hand fight, which was terminated only by the interference of Santos himself, who had
followed to protect her. But when Marisela realized fully
that the wicked Doña Bárbara was her own mother, she became moody, and finally deserted Santos's home and returned
with her father to their old cabin.

Other direful happenings excluded her for a time from
Santos's mind. Carmelito, one of his most trusted men, was
assassinated and robbed; the dispute over the property line
was revived; and Santos's property suffered depredations at
the hands of dangerous ruffians in the service of Doña Bárbara.
Frustrated by a venal political boss when he again attempted
by law to secure justice, Santos lost all patience and began to
employ the tactics of his enemies. Doña Bárbara planned to
have El Brujeador assassinate Santos, whom she induced to go
one night to a lonely spot she designated. Fearless, Santos
went, accompanied by one of his men, Pajarote; in the shooting that followed, El Brujeador was killed. With the latter's
body on his horse, Santos—desperate now, for he regarded
himself as a killer, quite beyond the pale of a law-abiding
man—went to Doña Bárbara's house and charged her with
responsibility for the crime. In her, there surged up again love
and admiration for Santos, although he treated her most contemptuously. The death of El Brujeador, who might one day
have proved dangerous, gave her almost as much satisfaction
as would that of Santos, for she was determined that if he
could not be conquered by love, to see him dead. Actuated
as much by the desire to placate Santos as by the determination to dispose of Balbino, her paramour, guilty of both the
murder and the robbery, she had two of her men kill him.

Meanwhile Marisela, after the death of her father during
all this turmoil, and with no one left to her but Santos, now as
lawless as any plainsman of the region, felt it her duty to bring
him back to his former ideas in regard to law and order. A
reconciliation between the two followed, and it was through
her perspicuity that Santos was convinced that it was not he

but Pajarote that fired the shot that killed El Brujeador. With Santos and Marisela about to be married, Doña Bárbara lost all interest in life. Attempting to atone in a measure for her many crimes, she transferred her property to Marisela, and then disappeared forever.

This dramatic struggle between Santos Luzardo and Doña Bárbara, who as individuals represent the struggle in the Venezuelan plains region between civilization and barbarity, is enacted against a background that is portrayed with a wealth of detail. And, more than either plot or characterization, it is the background that contributes to *Doña Bárbara's* worth as a novel. A vivid and kaleidoscopic composite of the physical aspects and the social life of the region, it passes like a cinema film before the eyes of the reader. The region itself, semi-arid half of the year and inundated by torrential rains the other half, far from cultural influences, and sparsely settled, has from the outset an exotic appeal. Singular, too, is Gallegos's artistic personification of it as a beautiful but terrible Circe that lures men to their death. While there are detailed, photographic descriptions, as of the old neglected ranch house of the Luzardos, imagery and imagination enter far more into the creation of the background, which is enlivened by the presence of both human and animal life and intensified by an appeal to other senses than sight.

Illustrative of Gallegos's artistry are the factors he chooses in his depiction, in the first chapter, of the Arauca River and its environs: the yellow water of the river itself, its wooded banks, from which stretch vast plains on one side and small prairies surrounded by trees on the other; the green grass of the plains, blackened occasionally by wandering cattle; the burning sun that beats down on all; the fetid odor that arises from the slimy mud of the river when the boatmen thrust their poles in it to push the boat along; the dull thud of alligators as they strike the muddy water; and the harsh cries of tropical birds in the trees along the banks. In other scenes, such as the depiction of the countryside on the Luzardo ranch

at twilight, life and movement take precedence over the landscape: night birds of various kinds fly about uttering shrill
cries; fleeting deer disappear in the distance; wild cattle assume
threatening attitudes or scatter away at the sight of a horse-
man; the gentle cows move slowly toward the corrals, guided
by the smoke from burning dung piles; herons disappear in
flight; and clouds of dust arise as herds of wild horses dash
away. Alive with animal life and movement is the same landscape at dawn when a morning breeze laden with the odor of
vegetation and cattle blows over the plain; chickens fly down
from their roosting places in the trees; a dozen species of birds
whistle, shriek, and sing; "and down beneath the savage confusion that the birds create while they are tingeing their wings
with gold in the tender light of the dawn—across the wide
expanse over which wild herds are scattering, over which
droves of unbroken mares that greet the day with bugle-like
neighing are galloping—in broad and powerful rhythm
breathes the free and vigorous life of the plains."

As much a part of the background as the birds and beasts
are the human dwellers on the plains, whose life colors and
animates the whole while they themselves contribute more or
less to the working out of the plot. In the vast panorama of
human life in the region are the boatmen on the Arauca River,
ignorant and superstitious but kindly and extremely devout;
venal and corrupt individuals empowered with the enforcement of the law but in fact in league with the criminal element; and the tenantry of the ranches themselves, both men
and women, some of whom, as those on Santos's estate, were
law-abiding, while others, for instance those that had gathered
about Doña Bárbara, were cutthroats and robbers. One of the
most interesting figures among the cowboys is Pajarote, versed
in every kind of ranch work and familiar, through taking
cattle to market, with all sections of the plains. Everywhere
he is welcome for his stories of ghosts, apparitions and the
like, some of which are reproduced in the novel. Graphically
described also are many phases of life on the ranches: the

animation about a ranch house that precedes a round-up; the rounding up of the cattle themselves, which are then roped and branded; the diversions—dancing, singing, and story-telling—that follow at night; the driving of the cattle, across the plains and over swollen rivers, to market; the capturing of wild horses; the stealing of cattle; and the hunting of certain birds, during the rainy season, for their valuable feathers. A rather unusual diversion described is the annual alligator hunt on Maundy Thursday,

> a day of abstinence from the flesh of animals...for he who eats meat on this day desecrates and injures the body of Our Lord; a day on which no one works, either on the prairie or in the corral, for this would be fatal for all one's life; a day on which no work is done in the dairy, for milk does not curdle on holy days but turns to blood; a day on which nothing is done except to catch turtles, to hunt alligators, and to rob beehives, the object in the first place being to obtain a food for Maundy Thursday and Good Friday that is highly prized by the dweller on the plains, and in the second place to take advantage of the leisure of those days to chase the alligators out of the canebrakes, not so much merely to run them out from those places as for another reason, and that is that the musk and long tusks of the alligators that are caught on these days have greater curative value and are more efficacious as amulets.

In the drama enacted against this background, Santos Luzardo and Doña Bárbara are the chief actors. Of the two, Santos, the author's mouthpiece, is the more easily comprehended. Although born on the plains of headstrong pioneer folk that were quick to kill, he was of the landed aristocracy and of pure Spanish blood; and while education had molded him into a law-abiding man, he was not lacking in either courage or determination. Only when his struggle against the lawlessness and barbarity of the community seemed entirely futile did he resort to violence and sink to the level of his enemies; and only when he believed he had killed a man, although in self-defense, did he regard the civilized man in him as completely lost. And so it would have been had not Marisela, whom he had taught in a measure to subdue her impulses, whom he had made into a civilized being, restored him to reason, by quoting him the very arguments he had at one time advanced to her.

Doña Bárbara as a character is enigmatical and perhaps for that reason more interesting than Santos. The puzzle in regard to her arises not only from the complexity of her personality but from the poetic and figurative treatment of her by the novelist. "She came from beyond the Cunaviche, from beyond the Cinaruco, from beyond the Mata.... From there came the dreadful mestiza." She was the offspring of a white adventurer and an Indian woman; although sensual, she had been driven to her hatred of men by the murder of her sweetheart and the violence done her person by the river pirates. Figuratively Gallegos describes her two conflicting passions:

> The Orinoco is a river with yellowish brown water; that of the Guainía is black. The waters of the first of these unite in the heart of the forest with those of the second, but they flow for a long time without mixing, each keeping its own particular color. So it was with the mestiza, for some years passed before her intense sensuality and her hatred for man fused within her heart.

Sensual and passionate, she lured men to her, not only for the gratification of her own desires, but to make use of them in some way or to rob and cheat them of what they had, becoming thus a destroyer of men, like the terrible region she personifies. She owed her wealth and power in the community to sex appeal and to fortuitous circumstances which "had aided her ... which when looked at superficially seemed to be the result of rare foresight, but it was not so, for Doña Bárbara was incapable of conceiving an actual plan." She exercised, however, a certain power over her ignorant henchmen through the supernatural powers they, as she herself, believed that she possessed. In her totality she was a succubus rather than a human being. Absolutely contemptuous of human life, she did not hesitate to put out of existence anyone that stood in her way; and not only was she a stranger to maternal love but, in a jealous fit, came near to killing her own daughter. Only when she realized that as a woman she had no appeal for Santos, that he had won in the struggle for supremacy in the community, did she feel herself completely defeated, did she feel any remorse for her many crimes. Then, after transferring to her daughter the property that was rightfully hers, without giving herself time to regret that small atonement, she disappeared; whether by casting herself to the crocodiles in the river or by wandering off to be swallowed by the forest, none will ever know. She and Santos symbolize the eternal struggle between good and evil; between culture and barbarity; between the city and the wilds.

The plains country is also the background of *Cantaclaro* (*The Ballad Singer*), Gallegos's fourth novel, which is truly a lyric of a desolate region:

> The plains begin at the foot of the Andine range; they extend widely, following in silence the course of the great solitary rivers that move slowly toward the Orinoco; they pass beyond this great river and, after languishing in level stretches strewn with loose rock, they surrender themselves to the forest.

On one of these tributaries of the Orinoco, the Cunaviche, which parallels to the south the Arauca—the background of *Doña Bárbara*—lived as ranchers the Coronado family, Doña Nicomedes and her two sons, José Luis and Florentino, nicknamed Cantaclaro. On José Luis fell the burden of the management of the ranch, for Florentino, a wastrel known for his amours, had for the greater part of his thirty years devoted himself to pleasure, which he sought for the most part at the convivial gatherings of the rough country folk of the region. A great favorite he was at such meetings, for he had possessed from childhood a remarkable facility in versifying, which enabled him to take a leading part in a very popular amusement of the region—a contest in which two rhymesters displayed their skill in making impromptu verses.

In an excursion to a neighboring district to compete with one whose reputation had come to his ears, Florentino came upon Hato Viejo, a ranch belonging to a certain Dr. Payara, the "Devil of the Cunaviche" as he was popularly known. Here Florentino's horse died and he himself fell ill. Payara treated the wanderer and invited him to remain in his house until fully recuperated, for he had heard that in one of Cantaclaro's ballads he himself was pictured as hanging a poor Indian caught stealing his cattle. Florentino accepted because he wanted to know the "Devil of the Cunaviche" personally; and Payara's men, among them a negro, Juan Parao, cared for him.

But the incidents in his ballad, Florentino learned from Juan Parao, were false. Payara had indeed hanged a man, but it was Carlos Jaramillo, the owner of a neighboring ranch and long an enemy of his, not for stealing cattle, but for refusing to marry Angela Rosa Luján, after deceiving her with the promise of marriage shortly before she was to have been married to Payara. Rosa Angela had confessed to Payara after he prevented her from taking her own life; furthermore, to save her honor, he had gone through with the marriage; and no one except Juan Parao knew that Jaramillo had wronged her or that Payara had hanged him. Later, after giving birth to a daughter, Rosángela, Angela Rosa took poison, purposely or otherwise, and died. Accepting the child as his own daughter, Payara sent her to relatives in Caracas to be educated, and he with Juan Parao took part in a revolution. As an army officer, he distinguished himself for his honesty and bravery. Rosángela followed his career with great enthusiasm, and years later when he retired to Hato Viejo, she, now a young lady, persuaded him to take her there to live.

She had not been long at Hato Viejo when Florentino arrived. Although at first she had been delighted with life on the plains, a decided contrast to that of Caracas, she had grown dissatisfied. Especially disquieting to her were queer acts on Payara's part, for in spite of the difference in their ages and their supposed relationship, he had fallen in love with her; but when he attempted to explain that he loved her, that he was not her father, a fact she already suspected, she became almost hysterical, and appealed to Florentino to take her away. At the same time Juan Parao left Payara, after years in his service, with the intention of arming a body of men to take part in a revolt against the government.

Without opposition from Payara, Florentino took Rosángela away with him. Although it was not at all unusual in Florentino's life that a woman should ask such a thing of him, Rosángela had done so through fear rather than love. Consequently, he respected her and took her to his own home, where she was welcomed by his mother and his brother José Luis. She was discontented at first, but nevertheless, she remained there, and both Florentino and his brother, a confirmed bachelor, fell in love with her. At this juncture Florentino, who had been living an exemplary life after his return from Hato Viejo, returned to his old ways, in order to leave José Luis free to marry Rosángela; and the band of revolutionists under Juan Parao made their appearance in the community. In a fray, the revolutionists were victorious, but later government troops forced them to flee. Although Florentino was not with the revolutionists at the time of the battle, he joined the few of them that were left. And here ends the novel, without the author's choosing to tell us what became of him, of Payara, of Rosángela, or of José Luis. Again, as in *Doña Bárbara*, the reader is left wondering.

The defects of *Cantaclaro* as a novel overbalance on the whole any merits it may have. Loose, diffuse, and disjointed, the story lacks a unifying purpose or motif. While Cantaclaro, who gives a certain unity to the various episodes, does undergo a change in that he gives up a pleasure-loving existence to fight against injustice, he remains after all a Venezuelan Santos Vega. The life story of that mixture of saint and madman, Dr. Payara, which occupies half of the book and contains material enough for a novel in itself, not only bulges out of proportion but overshadows Cantaclaro, who is presumably the protagonist. The last third of the book constitutes a novelette, in which there are various threads, no one of which seems to be of major importance in the mind of the novelist—the situation created by the two brothers falling in love with Rosángela; the financial difficulties of the Coronados; and the revolutionary flare-up that resulted in Cantaclaro's leaving the community—but the story terminates abruptly, without a disposition of any of the main characters except the very unsatisfactory one made of Cantaclaro, that the devil took him off.

But Gallegos, in this novel, was interested less in characters and plot than in the poetic treatment of the region itself, its vastness, its silence, and the awe it occasioned, and of its inhabitants, who "inspired distrust, who in that land moved about terribly alone, as if they were the last to linger under the final twilight of the world."

A book of the same type as *Cantaclaro*, diffuse, loose in plot structure, is *Canaima*. Again it is the background that predominates—the state of Bolívar, which lies to the south and east of the branches of the Orinoco, a region of arid, sandy plains in the north and of dense, tropical forests in the south. The central figure of the book is Marcos Vargas, a native of Ciudad Bolívar on the Orinoco, a city in the midst of vast low-lying stretches of marshland alive with alligators and tropical birds. Lured by the tales he had heard from childhood of those that had traveled that great waterway and its countless tributaries, he himself, after his school days in Trinidad, set out for the Yuruari, a region lying east of the Caroní River, a tributary of the Orinoco. He made the acquaintance of a friend of his father, Manuel Ladera, who controlled, in addition to extensive ranching interests, a freighting business

—there being no railroads in that remote region—of which he wished to dispose. Marcos purchased it on trust, but not without Ladera's telling him of the existence of a competitor, José Francisco Ardavín, a cowardly but exceedingly dangerous individual. "Tigers of the Yuruari," he and his brother Miguel were called, the latter being also the political boss of the region. Given to drinking, less astute, and more unscrupulous than Miguel, José Francisco had a personal grudge against the Laderas because Maigualida, a daughter, had refused his offer of marriage. The spurned suitor avenged himself by preventing anyone from paying suit to the girl, and already had killed a young man who dared to do so.

The Ladera family lived in Upata, headquarters for freighters, the first town of importance on the road running south from San Felix, a port of the Orinoco near the mouth of the Caroní, to El Callao, the site of a once famous gold mine. Marcos Vargas accompanied Ladera to Upata to take over the freighting equipment, and there was presented to his three daughters, among whom was the heartbroken Maigualida, and to a daughter of a rich merchant, the vivacious and talkative Arecelis Vellorini, who at once frankly let Marcos understand that she had taken a fancy to him. She attracted Marcos, too, but as he was in no position to marry, he gave her no encouragement. While in Upata Marcos dared to face José Francisco while he was losing at dice and drinking heavily, and even to gamble with him, winning not only his money but also his customers in the freighting business. Drunk and infuriated, José Francisco challenged Marcos to draw his gun, but the interference of bystanders prevented a shooting affray.

Other events that followed left a marked impress on the character of Marcos and directed his life into new channels. Manuel Ladera was assassinated, and Marcos accused José Francisco of the crime. In Tumeremo, south of El Callao and center of the balata industry, Marcos, in self-defense, killed Cholo Parima, one of the Tiger's henchmen. Next came news of the destruction of his freighting business—his wagons hav-

ing been burned, his animals killed, and his teamsters dispersed
—at the instigation, there was no doubt, of José Francisco.
Fate, it seemed, drove Marcos into the forests as overseer of
a large band of balata gatherers, a position given him by
Vellorini, who did not care for him as a prospective son-in-
law.

As overseer, Marcos came to know the balata gatherers and
to realize that they were little more than slaves who risked
a thousand dangers that others might live in comfort. The
tragedy of their existence they expressed in weird, pessimistic
songs. He associated, too, with bandits of the region; with certain individuals upon whom the forest had cast its spell and
was holding captive within its grasp; and with native Indians,
whose principal divinities were Canaima, the spirit of evil,
whence the book takes its name, and Cajuña, the spirit of
good. Awed by the spell of the forest, which brought upon
him a temporary madness, Marcos reverted to primeval instincts, becoming temporarily, if not an actual savage, at least
a madman.

But at last when the balata season closed and the gatherers
returned to the towns where they lived, happy because
Marcos's honesty had swelled their profits, he himself recovered from the madness he had suffered in the forest, but was
left a willful, fractious man. His old enemy, José Francisco,
now was demented through drink, and Maigualida had married Gabriel Ureña, manager of the Ladera estate. Aracelis
still loved Marcos, but her father, although he offered him the
management of a branch house, was unwilling to accept him
as a son-in-law. She would have gone into the forest with
Marcos, as he wanted her to do, but Gabriel made the impetuous Marcos see the error of such a course. Back into the
forest Marcos went again, thoroughly disgusted with civilization, and took an Indian bride, in accordance with the rites of
her tribe. While he himself remained there, reverting to primitive customs but accumulating at times gold along the Cuyuní
River, he finally sent his son, twelve years of age, to Gabriel

Ureña to be educated. He had not entirely shaken off the impress of civilization, for he still desired it for his son.

So, unlike Santos Luzardo in *Doña Bárbara,* who proved himself superior to the environment, Marcos Vargas succumbed to the forest, whose dire spell, poetically expressed, dominates the tonality of the work.

> Trees, trees, trees! The exasperating monotony of endless diversity; the multiplicity and oneness that oppresses to the point of stupefaction.
>
> At first he was deceived. It lacked grandeur; at least it was not as he had imagined it. There were no huge trees which a man's arms could not reach around; on the contrary, they were all spindling, weak, one might say, on account of the density of vegetation that disputed every inch of the soil. . . .
>
> But then he himself began to perceive that the grandeur lay in the illimitableness, in the obsessing repetition, as it seemed, of a single motive. Trees, trees, trees! A single green canopy over myriads of columns, with plush-like coverings of moss, lichen-stained, wrapped about with parasitic plants and climbing vines, choked by interlacing rattan as large as the trunks of the trees themselves. Parapets of trees, ramparts of trees, and solid walls of trees. Rising through endless centuries from the roots to the tops, a prodigious force, apparently in absolute immobility, a torrent of sap that flows in silence. . . . Rattan, a jungle. . . . Trees! Trees!
>
> This is the enchanting forest from whose influence Marcos Vargas would never free himself. . . . The merciless forest. As soon as one crosses its boundary, he begins to be something more or something less than a man.

Also stylistic in form, *Pobre Negro,* Gallegos's next novel, abandons both plains and forests as a background, for Venezuelan history. The novel begins on the eve of St. John's Day of 1830, on the Alcorta plantation, not far from Caracas. Among some negro slaves, chopping away rhythmically the rank tropical vegetation in a field of cacao trees, was a huge black, "Malo Negro," daring and sharp of tongue, working most zealously, for the overseer had led them to believe that they would take part that night in a festal celebration. Instead, when the time came, he ordered them to their quarters. But when the sound of the drums beaten in true African fashion began to come from the distance and the slaves to sway to their rhythm, "Malo Negro," still resentful, stole away to attend the festivities. Near the Alcorta home, he came upon Ana María, a young girl of neurotic tendencies, whose horror from childhood of everything black had caused her much suffering. When she saw "Malo Negro" she evidently fainted; and he, after violating her, escaped into the forest, for he realized the dire consequences of his act if discovered.

The infant, who survived Ana María, was entrusted by her brother Fermín to a mulatto couple, and was known as their son Pedro Miguel.

About a dozen years later, Cecilio Céspedes, a queer wandering scholar, returned home at the death of his sister, the wife of Fermín. Fermín was especially glad to see his brother-in-law, for he wished him to take charge of the education of his only son, also named Cecilio, who would inherit the family estate. Fermín's other children were three girls, of whom the youngest was Luisana. After visiting briefly with his kinsmen, Cecilio went to see Pedro Miguel, whose origin he knew, and gave further evidence of eccentricity by transferring to that individual certain lands. Both the younger Cecilio and Luisana showed, despite their wealth and position, sympathy for Pedro Miguel, who—timid, sullen, conscious of his inferior social position—was imbued very early, through his contact with the priest of the neighborhood, with the idea of educating the slaves and inciting them to revolt against their masters.

To the morose and evasive Pedro Miguel, Luisana was irresistibly drawn, and more than once she tried to soften his nature and to make him a more tractable human being. No such interest did she have in an aristocratic cousin, Antonio Céspedes, a cadet in the national military school, to whom she was tacitly engaged. Consequently, she was glad to break with him to care for her brother Cecilio when he returned home from Europe a victim of leprosy. This was in the early fifties, at the time that Monagas, then president of Venezuela, abolished slavery. Pedro Miguel, now a youth, was making his living as a trader, for he proudly refused to touch any of the income from his property; but with civil unrest increasing, and many of the former slaves at the point of starvation, he consented to manage the Alcorta estates, now held by Luisana and her brother Cecilio, for their father was dead and the two married sisters lived in Caracas. Loving Pedro Miguel, as she did, Luisana knew that he would never seek her hand on account of the social and financial barrier between them. In the long political struggle that followed, the leader of one of many marauding bands, "El Mapanare," for whom Pedro Miguel had a great contempt, cast his eyes toward Luisana; then Pedro Miguel realized that he loved her deeply. Her former betrothed, now a government commander in the neighborhood, offered troops for their protection and tried to take Luisana as his wife to her sisters in Caracas. But she, an aristocrat by birth, decided to cast her lot with the struggling liberals, and secured an officer's commission for Pedro Miguel in their forces and persuaded him to enter the struggle.

In the next four years of strife, whose horrors the novel reveals impressively, all the crimes and atrocities that hate engenders in a conflict between the poor and the rich were committed. On each side there were struggles between high-principled commanders like Pedro Miguel and vicious bandits such as "El Mapanare," with whom coöperation was sometimes necessary. Although "El Mapanare" hated Pedro Miguel, he continued with him, and in time their joint forces arrived in the neighborhood of the Alcorta property, which so far had escaped destruction. Pedro Miguel then suffered an attack of the desperation characteristic of Gallegos's heroes, in which they lose temporarily their usual reason and moderation. With all the hatred of the underdog, feeling keenly his lowly place in the scheme of things on account of his negro blood, he had determined to destroy the Alcorta property and to violate Luisana. But when he ascended the steps of the house, unsheathed sword in hand, to carry out his purpose, the friendly attitude of Cecilio the elder disarmed him, and he was even moved when told that the young Cecilio was dead and that love awaited him. Meanwhile "El Mapanare" made himself leader of the band, and was victorious in a fray. Luisana and her uncle, taking Pedro Miguel with them, for he had been wounded in the fighting, then fled toward the seacoast bound for Trinidad, to which most of the property-holding class had gone. When Cecilio saw Luisana and Pedro Miguel on board together, their destinies at last united, he disappeared.

Poetic in style like *Lanzas Coloradas* by Uslar Pietri, *Pobre Negro* is similar also in subject matter. Both novels depict life on a country estate while slavery still existed as an institution; but in this particular *Pobre Negro* is the richer of the two, for, as is characteristic of all of Gallegos's novels, it contains interpolated essays on manners and customs that are complete within themselves, such as those descriptive of the corn-husking parties and the celebration of Corpus Christi and other religious festivals. Especially effective is the rhythmic and onomatopoetic prose which conveys the sounds of the distant drums on St. John's Eve when spirits ride. The novels are alike, too, in the panorama that each presents, although of different periods in the nineteenth century, of the marauding bands of negroes and mulattoes that plundered, raped, and murdered in the many revolutions that the country suffered. The psychological motive that actuated such wholesale destruction is keenly analyzed in the chapter entitled "La Furia" in *Pobre Negro:*

> War was on in Venezuela. Superficially ... it was the political struggle of the liberals against the oligarchy ... but inwardly and truly ... it was a duel to death between genuine barbarity, in which the great mass of the people remained steeped, with their hunger, their rancor, and

their ambitions, and a transplanted civilization, with codes and constitutions that, while admirable in appearance, protected in fact the interests of the ruling class. . . . It was a war against the people with property, who were all included under the loathsome name of "white" or of "mantuana"—to crush them and to destroy the property that made them strong. First, the towns were sacked in order to ruin the merchants and then they were burned in order that not a single white person might have a roof over his head.

But Gallegos's sympathies are unmistakably with the underprivileged, and young Cecilio, no doubt, expresses Gallegos's own views when he says:

Our negroes are a race in a state of progress, and they are not in the country merely temporarily; if those that brought them did wrong in transplanting them from their native soil, we do worse if we do not cultivate them as a plant that is already ours. . . . It is necessary to incorporate them into our national life. Besides, do not we whites owe much to the blacks? The men cultivate the land and work in the mines; the women cook our food and from their own breasts they give us milk when our own mothers do not have it; they serve us and care for us lovingly, and they lull us to sleep with those ingenuous stories with which the formation of our minds begins.

If there is any one theme or purpose that characterizes Gallegos's novels, it is the advocacy of the amalgamation of the various races—Indian, white, and negro—that compose the population of Venezuela. *La Trepadora* concludes with the union of the aristocratic Nicolás and Victoria, who on her father's side inherited both negro and Indian blood; in *Doña Bárbara* Santos Luzardo married Marisela, who through her mother was partly Indian; in *Canaima*, Santos Vargas took a wife from the wild Indian tribes of southern Venezuela; and in *Pobre Negro* a young white woman of an aristocratic family preferred as a consort the mulatto Pedro Miguel to one of her own social rank.

Viewed as a whole and in perspective, the fictional output of Gallegos is uneven. Opinions and theses, while not absent from his novels, are not dominantly characteristic of them. On the whole, too, it might be said that Gallegos, like Azuela, lacks the first essential of a great novelist—the art of telling a story. Only a few of his short stories and his first two novels tell stories that interest for their own sake; best of all is *Doña Bárbara*, in which the various fictional elements are most completely harmonized; on the other hand, *Cantaclaro, Canaima*, and *Pobre Negro* are almost absolutely formless in regard to plot.

Nor can it be said that Gallegos is a master of the first class in creating flesh and blood individuals, for most of his characters are personifications or idealizations. Reinaldo Solar personifies Venezuela—inconstant in purpose, impatient for results; Santos Luzardo and Dr. Payara personify the civilizing influence in the plains; Doña Bárbara, the barbarous and unpitying aspects of that region. Cantaclaro, a sort of Santos Vega, typifies the wandering ballad-singer of the Venezuelan plains; but Luisana and Cecilio are clearly idealizations. His best characters are Hilario Guanipa (*La Trepadora*) and Reinaldo Solar, although the latter as an individual is almost a caricature.

More impressive than either story or characters is Gallegos's treatment of background. In *Reinaldo Solar* he essayed largely urban life, with mediocre results; in *La Trepadora*, with greater success, village and rural life; then, in *Doña Bárbara*, he found a setting that responded to his genius and that he was to use in both *Cantaclaro* and *Canaima*—the vast region drained by the Orinoco and its numberless tributaries, which, in one or more of its various aspects, dominates more than any character in these three books. Unforgettable are the canvases that they present: the low-lying swamp lands around the slowly-moving waters of the Orinoco; the limitless plains, bone-dry in summer and rain-soaked in winter; and the trackless forests of the Guayana. In *Pobre Negro* are the coastal plains of the Caribbean, but depiction of this background is secondary to another feature—wholesale murder and destruction by guerrilla bands. A writer of fiction who depends for his effects on background rather than on plot or characters, who is, as Gallegos, more of the poet than the novelist, would also be a stylist. Such is Gallegos, under the influence of the "modernistas" in his first stories, many of which have nothing to commend them except their imagery and the rhythm and harmony of their sentences. While such criticism is certainly not applicable to his first three novels, in those that followed, style returns again to be almost an end in itself.

Gallegos's novels have all won considerable commendation in both Spanish America and Spain, but *Doña Bárbara* has achieved a spectacular success and carried his name into a wider world. First printed in February, 1929, it was at once hailed as the outstanding contemporary Spanish-American novel. In the same year it was chosen as the best book of the month in Madrid and its author recognized as "the first great novelist of South America." For the second edition, Gallegos rewrote the work in part. In the next decade more than twenty editions were printed. Before two years had passed an English translation brought the author added praise from a new group of critics. It has so far proved his masterpiece.

CHAPTER X

JORGE ICAZA, DEFENDER OF THE ECUADORIAN INDIAN

❄

SINCE 1930 the novelists and short-story writers of Ecuador, through the vigor and originality of their work, have attracted wide attention. Having much in common, both in technique and in sociological principles, these writers, too, come nearer to forming a school than any other group in Spanish America today. The thoroughly autochthonous work of all is characterized by forceful portrayal of social injustice, unidealized characters, extensive use of dialectical and obscene language, and utter disregard of the usual novelistic patterns.

This literary movement had its origin in Guayaquil, principal seaport of Ecuador, where a collection of short stories—*Los que se Van: Cuentos del Cholo i del Montuvio* (*The Passers-By: Tales of the Cholo and the Montuvio*), by Aguilera Malta, Gil Gilbert, and Gallegos Lara—was published in 1930. These writers undertook, as the subtitle of their work indicates, to portray the Indian and the "Montuvio"—a creature of Indian, negro, and white blood—of their own tropical coastal region. This was followed three years later by Aguilera Malta's *Don Goyo* and Gil Gilbert's *Yunga* (*The Tropics*) and *Nuestro Pan* (*Our Daily Bread*)—all in the same vein. In connection with these writers, two of their fellow townsmen who share their literary inclinations deserve high praise. One is the recently deceased José de la Cuadra, author of various works on the "Montuvio": *El Montuvio ecuatoriano* (*The Ecuadorian Montuvio*), 1937, which is of a sociological nature; short stories, notably the collection *Guasitón* (1938); and *Los Sangurimas* (1939), a novelette. The other is Alfredo Pareja Diez-Canseco, a full-fledged novelist, who in some six or more novels has taken as his principal setting the river and port life of his native Guayaquil.

Differing ethnologically and climatically from that tropical city, the capital of Ecuador, Quito, high up in the sierras, has also its group of young writers who have concerned themselves with the exposition in fictional form of its social problems. Smaller in number but greater in renown, the three main writers of this group are: Humberto Salvador, who in *Camarada* (*Comrade*), 1933, *Los Trabajadores* (*The Workers*), 1935, and *Noviembre* (*November*), 1939, has given an insight into the life of its submerged classes; Jorge Fernández, whose novel *Agua* (*Water*), 1936, deals with Indian life in the arid Ecuadorian sierras; and Jorge Icaza, whose works dealing with the social injustices toward the Indian of the region have already brought him an international reputation.

Icaza was born in Quito in 1902. He is still a young man in appearance, of affable and gracious manner, and an excellent conversationalist. His secondary education was received in a Jesuit school in that city; he then began the study of medicine in the University of Ecuador, but the death of his father shortly forced him to abandon his studies in order to gain a livelihood. He secured various types of distasteful employment, but eventually worked in the national theater. There, he undertook to translate French plays for the local stage; then, encouraged by his success, he turned his hand to original productions. *El Intruso* (*The Intruder*), *La Comedia sin Nombre* (*A Play Without a Title*), *Por el Viejo* (*In Behalf of the Old Man*), *¿Cuál Es?* (*Which Is It?*), *Como Ellos Quieren* (*As They Wish*), and *Sin Sentido* (*Without Meaning*) are all works of this period. One of his plays, Icaza told the writer, raised such a furor that the authorities closed the theater. Although Icaza did not succeed in having the ban removed from the play, the affair ended with his appointment as censor of the national theater—a post he declined, but with the realization that his playwriting in Quito had ended. While not altogether abandoning the drama, Icaza turned more to fiction after 1933, the year in which he published a volume of short stories, *Barro de la Sierra* (*Mountain Soil*). In the main these stories tell of injustices committed by the church and the landed aristocracy against the laboring class—the Indians, the country's indigenous population. These injustices, which Icaza had observed at first hand on some of the great estates in the region of Quito, furnish the thematic material for his three novels—*Huasipungo*, 1934, *En las Calles* (*In the Streets*), 1936, *Cholos* (*Half-Breeds*), 1938, and a play, *Flagelo* (*Flogging*), 1936.

Of the six stories in *Barro de la Sierra*, three—"Cachorros" ("Whelps"), "Sed" ("Thirst"), and "Exodo" ("Exodus")—have a rural background. The first of these is based on the jealousy of a small child, Manuelito, eldest son of Nati, a young Indian woman. As Manuelito was a blond, his father was evidently not José, Nati's Indian husband, but the owner of the estate on which they lived. Soon a second child, a pureblooded Indian, was born to Nati; on him she and José centered more and more their attention. Jealous and conscious of an innate superiority, Manuelito began, when the two were alone, to torment his little brother, by pinching and other devilish means. Finally, one day while the two were imitating in play an incident in which a landed proprietor had soundly kicked an Indian laborer caught stealing potatoes during the harvest, Manuelito purposely kicked his younger brother over the side of a steep cliff—to his death.

Such is the brief plot of *Cachorros*, but in the story there is much which is interesting, even if extraneous or overdone from the standpoint of artistic short-story writing. For it brings home to the reader the filth, the servility, and the abject plight of the Indian at the mercy of a beastly and unscrupulous landlord; and describes with grim details the horrors of child-birth endured by Nati when her second child was born, and the treatment of the sick child a few years later by a quack woman doctor.

Icaza's style, in this story as in the entire volume, is striking for its originality. The language of the Indians is expressed in their own way of speaking Spanish; the sentences are often short but rhythmical; and there is, too, figurative language, which, as in the following, often disturbs by its individuality.

> The morning has dawned with a cold, and it wraps itself under a gray sky which suggests a circus tent; in the pastures the wet grass bites the callous feet of the Indians but it bites with less fury than the lice under their rough blankets. The Indians, trembling under their ponchos, harvest with the sickle of their imagination cups brimming with rum. . . .

The utter disregard of the landowning class for even the life of an Indian peasant is the theme of both "Sed" and "Exodo." Told in the first person, "Sed" is based evidently on a definite, concrete experience of Icaza himself. It is an account of a short visit to an Indian village where as a child he had frequently spent his vacations; then the citizens of the prosperous town were contented; now they are in a state of great despair. This situation—one not at all uncommon in the sierra —had developed when the owner of a great estate in the district dammed up the stream that passed through the village and appropriated nearly all the water to his own use, thereby not only preventing the Indians of the village from irrigating their gardens but also cutting them off from drinking water. The sick and starving natives, the author discovered as he wandered about the town, also suffered other injustices, for they were fleeced both by dissolute priests and by rascally civil authorities.

Through his account in "Sed" of the mistreatment of human

beings, Icaza succeeds in arousing the indignation of the reader but, from a literary standpoint, it is merely a personal account, with no plot and very little character portrayal. "Exodo," on the other hand, is more effective as a story. It reveals incidentally another of Ecuador's evils, the collusion between priest and landowner to keep the Indian in a state of perpetual servitude. The story concerns, for the most part, José Quishpe, a young Indian peasant, who was about to leave the estate where he had lived, because he found that the girl he had planned to marry had recently been violated by the son of his master. As his labor was needed, the landowner enlisted the influence of the priest, through whose intimidation José finally married the girl. To enable him to celebrate his wedding in proper style, his master generously lent him a small sum of money; this debt bound him to the estate for life since he would never be able to pay it. Then one day, after some years of service, he was dragged to death by a wild bull, which his master dictatorially ordered him to rope. Before he died, however, José begged his eldest son to go elsewhere, and so he did, taking with him his mother and the younger children. Then began a veritable odyssey: they wandered over the sierras; they were for some time in Quito; and finally they reached the tropical lowlands of the coast. Their wandering was, after all, in vain. The scenery changed; the masters remained ever the same.

But sometimes, it seems, an Indian accomplished the impossible by becoming rich and forcing his way into the Caucasian-blooded circle, which, nevertheless, retained all its aversion to him. "Interpretación" ("Interpretation"), another story in *Barro de la Sierra*, presents such a situation in the family of the well-to-do Don Enrique Carchi, whose wife, of Caucasian blood but poor, had married him solely for his money; she, however, as well as their daughter, despised him on account of his Indian origin. Practically a member of this household was a friend, who in fact was the wife's lover. Needless to say these three individuals earnestly desired the death of Don

Enrique, as he well realized. He bore their hatred without reproach, and outwardly they were always courteous to him. Of quite a different tenor, however, were their inner thoughts, which Icaza succeeds in making known. Finally Don Enrique died; only then, his wife admitted, did she find him acceptable to her.

Intolerance, but of another type, is also the theme of "Mala Pata" ("Faux Pas"), in the same collection; like "Interpretación," it deals with middle-class urban society. The subject of the story is Carlos Aparicio, a violinist and minor government employee, who admitted one day in an interview that he was a communist and was trying to organize the musicians of the city into a trade-union in order to better their economic status. As soon as this became known a storm of protest against him arose from the conservative elements throughout the city. He was immediately discharged from his position; a marked man, he was unable to secure another; and ultimately he was saddled with a murder he had not committed. For, reasoned the authorities, no one but a communist would have committed such a crime.

"Desorientación" ("Disorientation"), the only remaining story in *Barro de la Sierra*, is a protest against the opposition to birth control on the part of the conservative forces in Ecuador. A poor porter in a railway station in Quito, Juan Taco was struggling under the burden of maintaining a wife and six children. His earnings were scant, and since he and his family were already living most wretchedly, on the barest subsistence level, he determined to curb his sexual desires in order to prevent a still further increase in children. In desperate straits when his earnings decreased, he sought aid of a well-to-do family that had reared him according to the precepts of the Catholic Church, but they would do nothing for him; then he realized that it was to the interest of the conservative forces—the State, the Church, and the rich—for the population of the proletarian classes to increase so that there might be more human beings to enslave. The downfall of Juan's family was swift. His daughters, in order to help meet the needs of the family, took up prostitution and thieving; and he himself, desperate, seeking forgetfulness in alcohol, died in a drunken stupor.

A more magisterial as well as aesthetic treatment of the same general themes in *Barro de la Sierra* is to be found in Icaza's novels, especially *Huasipungo*, which is by general acclaim his masterpiece. The most earnest proletarian novel of Spanish-American literature, it has much in common with *The Grapes of Wrath* by John Steinbeck. Both the North American and the Ecuadorian have espoused in their respective works the cause of the unorganized underprivileged, who have to make their living by the sweat of their brow, and against whom have joined, seemingly with the purpose of exterminating them, both law-maker and capitalist. Each writer has undertaken to present, through individual circumstances and characters, a problem that actually confronts great bodies of peoples. Although there are vast differences between the protagonists themselves of *Huasipungo* and of *The Grapes of Wrath*—the mistreated Indians as represented by the family of Andrés Chiliquinga, and the Joads of pure Anglo-Saxon stock—they are confronted by a very similar situation, that of being ejected from land to which they had no legal right but which they considered as their own.

Huasipungo consists of a series of scenes that exhibit the relations in Ecuador between the poverty-stricken Indian peasantry and the more favored Caucasian property-holding class. Representative of the latter is Alfonso Pereira of Quito, one of the principal characters. Finding himself in debt, Pereira decided to build a road through a great tract of land that he owned in the sierra to facilitate communication between his estate and the capital, confident that thereby he could sell his property more advantageously to North-American capitalists. With great difficulty he and his family moved from Quito to his country property. On it was an Indian village in which the workers on the estate lived, under conditions—according to Icaza's description—not much above those of the hogs that rooted about their tumble-down huts.

An Indian couple, Andrés Chiliquinga and his young wife Cunshi, typify the oppressed Indians of this miserable village. Shortly after the arrival of the Pereiras, Andrés was sent with other Indians to a distant part of the estate to cut wood, and Cunshi was ordered to give up her baby and betake herself to the Pereira household to serve as wet nurse for the master's young child. The treatment of the Indians at the wood-cutting camp to which Andrés was sent was inhuman; longing for Cunshi, he stole away one night and returned to his cabin, but found her gone. He went back to the camp but, in desperation, determined to do something that would enable him to return home. Next day, while he was cutting off the limbs of a tree he had felled, he cut a great gash in his own foot with his axe. After being treated by the "curandero," or quack doctor, as he was useless in the camp, he was finally permitted to return home where he could do light work. Some time later when Cunshi was permitted to return to him, she was with child, by Pereira himself.

The wood-cutting over and his family back in Quito, Pereira determined to organize a "minga" in order to effect the real purpose of his visit to his property, the construction of the road. The "minga," which dates from the Inca period, consisted originally of a great body of citizens that came to-gether to do, more or less gratuitously, the actual physical labor involved in some project of general interest to the state or community. The same custom, of which the Spaniards made use to construct roads and public buildings, has survived. As social intercourse and the free distribution of alcoholic drinks are features of the "minga," the institution is by no means entirely unpopular with the Indians; and although they are paid little or nothing for their work, it is not difficult for one who understands their psychology to persuade them to take part.

As the village priest could be an effective aid in organizing a "minga," Pereira at once set about convincing the cleric that it would be to his interest to coöperate. One more libidinous and avaricious than Icaza portrays here it would be difficult indeed to encounter. Each day after mass he would tell the Indians of Pereira's ambitions for the community and argue that it was their religious and patriotic duty to help him realize them. Finally he and Pereira, with an engineer, overseers, and a great horde of Indians—among them Cunshi and Andrés—set out for the locality where the road was to be built.

Work on the road, which was begun at once in order to take advantage of the enthusiasm of the Indians, was extremely perilous. Many of them perished, both in the quagmires of the swamps to be drained and in loose sand that caved in and swallowed them up. The engineer would have followed a more time-consuming plan endangering fewer lives, but Pereira refused. Many of the Indians became sick, for they were utterly without protection, even at night, from the rain and cold. The treatment, too, that the sick received from the "curanderos" and overseers was barbaric. As an inducement to remain, all of the Indians were regaled with cheap alcohol and diverted by cock-fights.

When the road was at last finished, after great sacrifice of life, Pereira turned to harvesting and storing his abundant grain crop with the hope of getting a good price later; but he refused to let the Indians have even the small amount of inferior grain that was customarily conceded them. The road, instead of contributing to their prosperity, had increased their poverty, for those who had formerly transported the grain to market on pack animals now had to give way to trucks. Pinched by hunger, the Indians resorted to stealing; they also demanded corn of Pereira, but he refused to give it to them, and to prevent their taking it by force, he secured police from the government in Quito.

At this point the author resumes the story of Andrés, Cunshi, and their child—now, like the other Indians, starving.

So desperate was their condition that Andrés stole some of the meat of a half-decayed ox of Pereira that had died of disease. It made the three of them violently ill; and Cunshi died. In order to obtain a select spot in the cemetery—another bit of graft the priest enjoyed—Andrés stole a cow; and when his crime was discovered he was severely flogged.

Not long after this, some North-American capitalists came to look over the Pereira property. In holiday attire, but apprehensive, the Indians received them, for they sensed that the coming of the foreigners would bring them no good; and they were right, for the capitalists offered to buy the land provided the Indians were forced to vacate. But when Pereira's overseers attempted to drive them away and burn their huts—for which the Ecuadorian Indian has a profound attachment—the poor serfs, led by Andrés, resisted and killed them. Their victory was of short duration, for troops rushed to the scene at Pereira's request and mowed down the revolters—among them Andrés and his son—with machine-gun fire.

And so ends *Huasipungo*, which is greater as a social document than as a work of fiction. Its plot is very slight; on the other hand, presenting as it does, in a dramatic, tense, and satiric style, wrongs to a people that are inconceivably barbaric, it is very rich in emotional content. Also, of permanent value, is its abundant description of the social life of present-day Ecuador. As a novel its greatest weakness is in its characters, which are entirely types and not individuals; in this respect *Huasipungo* falls far below *The Grapes of Wrath*. Pale, indeed, are Pereira, the priest, Andrés, and Cunshi in comparison with the Joads. Icaza, it is apparent, selects his characters merely to exhibit social injustice, not because he is interested in them as individuals.

Defiance to constituted authority, which appears at the very end of *Huasipungo*, is the dominant note in *En las Calles*. This opens with an account, in the excellent dialogue that characterizes Icaza, of an interview between the president of Ecuador and a delegation of Indians from the town of Chaguarpata.

They had come to Quito to complain of wrongs they had suffered at the hands of Luis Antonio Urrestas, owner of a large tract of adjoining land, for he had deprived them of water by damming up a stream that ran through the town, and was endeavoring to eject some of them from his estate because, with tractors, he no longer needed their services. But as the president was a friend of Don Luis, he did nothing more than threaten the leader of the delegation, who intimated that they intended to get their rights by force. Tension between Don Luis and the Indians increased, until troops were sent to intimidate them by arresting their leaders. The latter escaped, some of them taking refuge eventually in Quito. Other inhabitants of Chaguarpata sought work in the same city, among them the shoemaker Yáñez, who took with his own children, Francisco, son of the leader who had defied the president, for the boy's mother had been killed when the soldiers entered the town.

In Quito the shoemaker found it difficult to compete with the more modern shops. He was a drunkard and the family was often in want. In the course of time he drove out not only Francisco, now grown, but his own daughter Dolores. As Francisco earned a meager subsistence as a policeman, the two cast their lots together. Meanwhile, a certain Landeta, who had resisted Don Luis very tenaciously in Chaguarpata, continued in Quito to annoy him, by attempting to unionize the workmen. In a demonstration of these laborers against injustices, many were beaten or shot outright by the police, among whom was Francisco. Landeta escaped and returned to Chaguarpata, where he undertook to organize the workers engaged in the preparation of material used in hat-making. Upon learning of his activities, Don Luis had him arrested. Sick with influenza, he was, through the machinations of the capitalists, nevertheless pronounced a leper. The guards bound the sick man on top of a boxcar, where he died before reaching the leper colony.

There is much in the book about Don Luis, who always

contrived to make his trickery for his own self-interest seem to the interest of civilization and the state. At last, as a climax to his career, the landowning faction chose him as their candidate for the presidency. The Indians from his estate, against their will, were brought by truck into the capital to celebrate his honor. Then it occurred to him that if they were fired upon while parading it would furnish grounds for declaring the existence of an emergency which called for a dictatorship. The police did fire upon the Indians, many of whom were killed; and the soldiers answered with a volley which struck the police as well. In the fray, Francisco fell mortally wounded; in his dying words, begging soldiers and police to cease fighting each other, to cease being the tools of their oppressors, is to be found the real message of this attack upon the vicious practices of those in power in Ecuador.

The quality that distinguishes *En las Calles* as well as *Huasipungo*—the author's indignation which burns flamingly in every page of these two books over injustice to a defenseless people—is less felt in Icaza's third novel, *Cholos*. While this book gains in many respects for its more sober and dispassionate tone, it is diffuse and lacks, if not a definite purpose, at least a harmonious coördination of its varied subject matter. For some two-thirds of the work the author is concerned mainly in tracing, for about a score of years, the careers of two types in Ecuadorian society, that of Braulio Peñafiel and of Alberto Montoya, both of whom had property in the neighborhood of San Isidro, a village composed largely of Indians, not far from Quito.

Braulio, a devout Catholic and broken-down aristocrat of Spanish blood who was wont to taunt his young wife with the taint of negro blood, was forced by financial straits to leave his ancestral home in Quito for his estate, where he hoped to mend his fortune; but he was weak, given to drink, and lacking in courage to carry out his bold determinations. After his Indians were attracted away by the better pay of his neighbor, Montoya, he lost even the estate, on which Montoya held a mortgage. After his return to Quito, he lived in shame, for his wife resorted to very questionable means of maintaining herself and the family.

In contrast with the downfall of Braulio Peñafiel, which symbolizes the disintegration of Ecuadorian society based on Spanish blood, is the rise of the half-breed Alberto Montoya, which in turn exemplifies the ascendancy of a new aristocracy based on wealth. Because of the complexity of his character, Montoya, energetic and resolute, is one of the most interesting figures that Icaza has created. At the beginning of his career the half-breed had a fellow-feeling for the Indians that worked for him and he treated them with a certain amount of consideration; he was anticlerical, and he had no pride of family; instead of marrying, he kept a mistress in San Isidro. With an innate sense of justice and of honor, he was nevertheless on occasions both unjust and dishonest. Despite his material wealth, he was never able to overcome a sense of inferiority, particularly in the presence of Don Braulio. As he grew in wealth, he became more conservative; and eventually he married his mistress, who was devout, and moved with her and their daughter to Quito to live, leaving the estate to be managed by overseers.

From this point in the story, the interest centers on another character, Guagcho, whom Montoya left in charge. Also a half-breed, the natural son of Don Braulio and a lowly Indian, Guagcho was a strange, impetuous youth in whom the two strains seemed to contend for supremacy. Like other overseers, he also took to fleecing the Indians and he falsely accused a certain one of them, José Chango, of a murder that he himself had committed. José was convicted of the crime and imprisoned. Then, strangely enough, Gaugcho became conscious of the wrong that he had done and began to suffer qualms. A remark by a legitimate son of Don Braulio, now a school-teacher in San Isidro, to the effect that an Indian was a human being brought about Guagcho's whole-hearted conversion. Determined to make amends regardless of risk to himself or his interests, he liberated José in a melodramatic manner and placed him, seriously wounded, in safety.

So when Icaza takes up here, in the last third of *Cholos*, the rank injustice to which the Indians of Ecuador are subjected, he returns to the fundamental theme that absorbs almost his entire attention. And, all in all, he will be remembered as a reformer and not as a novelist. His success as a writer lies not at all in plot or characterization but in his vigorous, cryptic, Quevedo-like style in which he reveals abuses that cry out to Heaven to be righted, and that arouse in his readers his own spirit of boiling indignation. The outstanding characteristics of that style are a brutal frankness, an almost total lack of idealism, and a use of words that are almost universally regarded as taboo. Purely from the standpoint of technique, what strikes one most in his novels is his disregard for form. Almost plotless, consisting only of a series of scenes rich in details of various phases of social life but very loosely connected, his novels move along somewhat artlessly, like life itself. Icaza's greatest personal deficiency as a novelist lies in his lack of interest in people as individuals; his characters represent the psychology of their class, but with the possible exception of Montoya they are not flesh and blood humans. Of the two classes they symbolize, the exploited and the exploiter, the latter stands out in bolder relief. For his Indian characters, who only now and then dare to assert themselves, are so tame and servile that they seem as hopeless a lot as their masters through the ages ever have found them.

That Icaza's work has had a strong appeal outside of Ecuador is shown by the seven editions of *Huasipungo* in Spanish and by its translation into English, French, Italian, Russian, and German. Particularly did it move the Russians, who have known similar conditions in the not long-distant past.

CHAPTER XI

CIRO ALEGRIA, *CRIOLLISTA* OF PERU

❊

I N PERU, fiction had a place of honor before the twentieth century. The chronicler Garcilaso de la Vega was a pioneer in achieving fame in the sixteenth century; and in the nineteenth Ricardo Palma earned for himself distinction in bringing the *tradición* to its highest artistic perfection. The *tradición*, which originated in Spanish America and was of particular significance there among the various manifestations of Romanticism, was a short prose work treating in an imaginative manner and with literary embellishment an incident generally of an historical nature. In six volumes of *tradiciones*, Palma covered some five centuries of his country's history in such a spicy and humorous anecdotal form that his influence on the *tradición* extended to all of Spanish America. The major portion of his work relates to his native city, Lima, the capital of Peru and consequently the center of its culture, which is in the main European.

In the twentieth century, metropolitan Lima continued to absorb the attention of a number of prose writers; but others have shown a marked tendency to turn to less known regions of the country where life is more primitive. Continuing in the present century the literary tradition of Ricardo Palma and the interest in Lima, José Gálvez has written *Una Lima que se va* (*A Lima That Is Passing*), 1921, and *Estampas Limeñas* (*Sketches of Lima*), 1935; Pedro Benvenutto Murrieta, *Quince Plazuelas, una Alameda y un Callejón* (*Fifteen Little Plazas, an Alaméda, and a Narrow Street*); and Clemente Palma, son of Ricardo, *Crónicas político-domésticas taurinas de Juan Apapucio Corrales* (*Tauromachian Chronicles of Juan Apapucio Corrales*), 1938. Also of Lima and eminently cosmopolitan is Ventura García Calderón, poet, critic, and short-story writer. A thorough-going novelist, however, is to be found in José Diez Canseco, who has undertaken in his novel *El Duque* (*The Duke*), 1934, to satirize the idle rich of Lima.

Those writers who have sought background outside of the capital have found it in one of the three distinct regions that traverse the country from north to south: the low-lying, semi-arid, narrow strip along the Pacific coast; the high, cold sierras of the Andes; and, to the east of these, the forest-covered slopes and valleys of the Amazon and its tributaries. Treating the latter region, Fernando Romero has written *12 Novelas de la Selva* (*Twelve Stories of the Forest*), 1934, which deal particularly with the district of Loreto and with Iquitos, on the Marañón River. Pedro Barrantes Castro and Enrique López Albújar have exploited the sierras, where Indian life predominates—the former, the region around Cajamarca, in *Cumbreras del Mundo* (*Lofty Crests*), 1935, and the latter, in *Cuentos andinos* (1920) and *Nuevos Cuentos andinos* (1937), the region around the Andean city of Huánuco, in more or less the central part of the country. The coast, the home of the "zambo," or mixture of Indian and negro, has had, too, its partisans: Abraham Valdelomar, in a collection of stories entitled *El Caballero Carmelo* (*Gentleman Carmelo*), 1918; José Mejía Baca, in *Aspectos criollos* (*Creole Side-Lights*), 1937; Diez-Canseco, in *Estampas mulatas* (*Mulatto Sketches*), 1938; and Fernando Romero, in *Mar y Playa* (*Sea and Shore*), 1940.

Of all the regional writers of Peru, however, Ciro Alegría has won greatest acclaim. Although he was born (1909) and reared in Trujillo near the seacoast, he has been accorded great praise for his interpretation of sierra and forest life. While still a student in his native city, he became a leader in the "Aprista" movement, which was organized in 1930 by an altruistic group of intellectuals headed by Haya de la Torre, with greater social justice for the Indians and other less favored classes as one of its aims. The government undertook at once to stamp out this organization, and in December, 1931, Alegría was imprisoned. He was liberated by his friends in July of the following year through an armed revolt of the "Apristas." After much bloodshed, the uprising was suppressed, and Alegría, again a political prisoner, was sent to the penitentiary in Lima for safekeeping. Here he remained, with great detriment to his health, until August of 1933, when he was granted his freedom by the conciliatory government of President Benavides that had recently come into power. With the resumption of his "Aprista" activities, he was very soon in trouble again and in 1934, with other Peruvian intellectuals, was forced to take refuge in Chile.

As a writer, Alegría attracted attention in the early thirties with his verse and short stories, which were published in various periodicals of Peru. His international fame, however, rests on three prize-winning novels which he published after his arrival in Santiago: *La Serpiente de Oro* (*The Golden Serpent*), 1935, probably begun during his imprisonment in Lima and winner of the first prize in a contest fostered by the Nascimento publishing house of Santiago; *Los Perros hambrientos* (*Hungry Dogs*), 1939, written in a sanatorium while he was recuperating from his prison experiences and winner of a second prize offered by the Zig-Zig company; and *El Mundo es Ancho y Ajeno* (*Broad and Alien is The World*), 1941, which was awarded the first prize as the best novel submitted from all Latin America in a contest sponsored by the Farrar and Rinehart Company of New York.

As a novelist Alegría has many features in common with other Spanish-American writers of fiction of the present century. Like Quiroga, Güiraldes, and Gallegos, he is strongly attracted by the physical aspects of certain regions of his native country; particularly like Icaza and Rivera, he is interested in certain groups of people who, generally on account of social injustice, are in a tragic situation; and, despite the interest in the sociological he shares with Icaza, Azuela, and other outstanding Spanish-American novelists of today, he is, particularly in the matter of style, a literary artist.

The chief concern of Alegría as a novelist is the indigenous race of his country, the Indians, whom he represents as engaged in a constant struggle—with Nature, with man, or with both. In *La Serpiente de Oro* he pictures Calemar, a primitive community of civilized Indians in a valley that slopes from the eastern side of the sierra down to the Marañón River—a tropical district alive with dangers. There are deadly snakes and insects whose bites cause loathsome and fatal skin diseases; in the rainy season the Indians live in danger of landslides that sweep away their houses and fill their valley with debris; and the Marañón itself, with its floods and whirlpools, is another dangerous enemy.

On this river, many in the community make their living as raftsmen. They are virile, fearless men who match their skill against the rocks, the sand bars, and the whirlpools; they are daring in love; and they are hard-drinking when off duty. Representative of these Calemar raftsmen are old Matías and his two sons, Arturo and Rogelio. Matías is an expert hunter and fisherman; well versed in the lore and tales of the region, he is also the story-teller of the community. The sons are worthy followers of their sire. Both are married to buxom, prolific women: Arturo, to Lucinda; and Rogelio, to Florinda. One of the most interesting chapters tells how Arturo fell passionately in love with Lucinda at a fiesta in a neighboring village and carried her off, against the will of her mother, on his spirited horse. Another lively account tells of a trip the brothers made in their raft to Shicún on the Marañón. After the usual drinking at their destination, they disagreed on the time to depart for home. Rogelio wished to leave at once; but

Arturo, the soberer of the two, advised delay so that they would pass a certain dangerous spot in the river by daylight. Rogelio had his way; as a result, their boat ran aground as Arturo had feared. Unable to get it afloat, they were desperate; finally, in an effort to reach the shore, Rogelio plunged into the river and was sucked down to his death by a whirlpool. Arturo remained with the boat; but not until days afterward, when a flood came, was he able to get it afloat. He reached home, sick and utterly exhausted.

In the vibrant picture of Calemar, there are besides Matías and his family other social types that impress themselves on the imagination. Among them are the widow Mariana Chiguala, at whose inn travelers tarried longer than they had intended; Lucas—the supposed teller of the tale, about whom the reader would like to know more than he chooses to disclose—who fell in love with Lucinda, Rogelio's widow, when he saw her one day bathing in the river, and eventually married her; and Don Juan Plaza, an educated landowner of the district, who tells various tales of men who had come there to seek a fortune. One such, indeed, is Don Osvaldo Martínez, a young engineer from Lima, who plays an important rôle in the novel. After exploring the sierras in the neighborhood, he discovered that gold had been washed down into the Marañón and planned to return to Lima to form a company that would exploit his findings. Despite his dream of wealth and a luxurious life in Lima, he tarried in Calemar, for the place had laid its hold upon him. He had come to love the people there; from them he had learned to chew coca leaves; and he had become interested in a girl in the village. But the stress of deciding between returning to Lima and remaining in Calemar was not of long duration; for, while making a trip on the river in company with some of the village raftsmen, he was bitten by a small but deadly snake, and died.

The study of the social environment of the people of Calemar, as well as their attitude toward life and certain civil institutions, constitutes another excellent feature of the novel.

There are chapters that in themselves are essays on manners and customs. One such describes the fiesta, vibrant with drinking, dancing and singing, that Arturo and Rogelio attended in Sartún; and another tells of the festivities in Calemar that accompanied the yearly visitation of the priest when he came to perform, among various rites, baptismal and marriage ceremonies, and to say masses for the dead. While fights often occurred at these fiestas, the people on the whole were peaceful and good at heart. They had, however, a general contempt for all charged with the enforcement of law and order. Not only did they shield their own people when officers of the law came to arrest them, but they gave aid and shelter to strangers pursued by the law. Their chief characteristic in the face of danger was their stoical and philosophic attitude.

And their greatest danger was the Marañón, "the yellow serpent," from which the book derives its title. For months it flowed along in harmless unconcern; then the floods came, and lucky indeed were the villagers of Calemar if only their rafts were washed away. It was at the same time the greatest influence in their lives. It provided many with a livelihood; time was reckoned by its floods; and, in the case of Arturo and Lucinda, it served as an intermediary, for they met at Sartún when he was returning on his raft from Shicún.

The grimness of certain aspects of nature also plays an important part in *Los Perros hambrientos*. Here the scene again is in northern Peru, but shifted from a tropical region to the lofty cordilleran highlands where droughts often bring dire distress to both man and beast. In this book Alegría pictures again a rural community composed largely of indigenous people who make their living by raising sheep and growing grain, on which they largely subsist.

As in *La Serpiente de Oro*, a family serves to typify the community—that of Simón Robles, consisting of his wife Juana; Antuca, a girl of twelve, herder of the sheep; a grown girl, Vicenta; and a son, Timoteo. Important, too, in this household are the dogs: Wanka, Güeso, Zambo, and Pellejo,

accustomed from birth to being with the sheep and aiding
Antuca in her task of herding; and Shapra, another dog, who
guarded the house.

For his excellent breed of dogs, Simón Robles was known
throughout the surrounding country; and since Wanka was
a prolific bitch, he always had pups to sell or give away to his
friends. He gave one to a son-in-law, Mateo Tampu, whose
small son, Damián, named the pup Mañu. Even Cipriano
Ramírez, wealthy owner of a large estate in the neighborhood,
secured one of Robles's pups for his young son. Indeed, so
esteemed were Robles's dogs that two bandits, Juan Celedón
and his brother Blas, lassoed Güeso when they came upon him
one day helping Antuca with the sheep and dragged him off
by force.

These recipients of Robles's dogs play more or less important rôles in the community. Officers, appearing suddenly
one day at the home of Mateo Tampu, accused him of avoiding military service, knocked his wife down when she pro-
tested, and carried Mateo off. Don Cipriano, a well-to-do
landowner, does not appear, as the type he represents frequently does in novels of this kind, particularly oppressive. To
the Celedón brothers considerable space is given in the book.
They had become bandits when Julián killed the proprietor of
the estate on which he lived for mistreating him. On account of
their depredations, they were hotly pursued by the officers
of the law, who, unable to capture them, devised a means of
poisoning them and thus got them out of the way.

But by far the most impressive feature of this book is the
account of a prolonged drought that brought great suffering
to the community. Wheat that was planted either failed to
sprout or, if it did, withered in the fields. Hungry, for there
was no food for them, Simón Robles's dogs broke into an
irrigated field of young corn, and one of them was killed. At
this critical time a band of Indians under their leader Mashe,
who had been expelled from their lands through the legal
trickery of a neighboring landowner, appeared before Don

Cipriano and begged him to let them settle on his estate. He did so, for he saw that they would increase his labor supply, but he let them understand that he would not furnish them food, which was daily becoming scarcer.

Desperate, the Indians of the district decided to seek the intervention of Our Lady of Carmen, whose image was enshrined in the parish church.

And Simón Robles went, with the exception of the girl that cared for the sheep, with all his family, in the same way as all the rest of the peasants in the region. Every year the Virgin, who was the patron saint of the district, had her fête and procession; but it was customary also to take her out when there was a drought. Then she always brought rain. Indeed she had always done so! Simón, who was old, recalled only one bad famine, which came when he was small and was herding the sheep.

At night there was praying in the church; on the altar the wax candles burned with a yellowish glow; a black mass of human beings that were crowded closely together in the narrow limits of the church cried, "Blessed Mother, help us"; there was a smell of tallow and of wool; the eyes of the faithful looked imploringly at the image; everywhere—in the church, in the houses of the town, and in the fields—there were human beings asleep, dreaming of bounteous crops.

The following morning at daybreak the procession began. In a sky in which there were a few thin clouds the sun was shining brightly. Then, Indians and more Indians, *cholos* and more *cholos*, gayly bedecked but troubled at heart, came trotting along the roads that, twisting over the hills and down the slopes, converged finally in the plaza of the town. Ding, ding, ding, sounded the bell, calling the faithful. Finally the Virgin came out, white and rosy cheeked, dressed in purple satin, bordered with spangles, on a small litter, which those present vied with each other in carrying. She stood erect; her mien was sacred; and her eyes gazed off in the distance upon the cultivated patches where the grain withered. *Cholos* and Indians crowded about the litter, and a great long line of them stretched out behind it. Among them there were both combed and tousled heads. Their faces were dark with a devout and serious mien. There were black shawls, purple ponchos, and striped *habanos;* and red, yellow, and green skirts and black and gray trousers. In one hand each held a candle whose smoky flame paled in the splendid sunshine, and in the other a white or yellow hat. "Blessed Lady, help us," was the lament that was heard above all the noise. The procession left behind the sorry street of the town and advanced along a country path until it came to the top of the hill where the most famous cross of all the surrounding country spread its great arms over a rustic stone pedestal. Here they stopped and knelt to pray. "Blessed Lady, help us; send us rain, send us rain," they cried. Then they started back slowly, very slowly. A pack of dogs closing the procession, among them Pellejo, looked upon the sight with disgust. The slowness with which they moved was tiresome, and, besides, hunger takes away good humor. Timoteo was there in the thick of the crowd, and with him was Jacinta. O, if the times were only different! He would have sunk the plow to the beam and afterwards he would have said to the girl: "Now there is something to eat. Come along with me."

But Timoteo did not realize his dream, for our Lady of Carmen failed to send rain. Both man and beast slowly starved. Simón's dogs did an unheard-of thing; they began to kill the sheep they had always guarded so carefully and had to be driven away from home. Martina, who had anxiously awaited Mateo's return, finally set out for her father's home in search of food; in her absence Damián, her son, perished by the side of his faithful dog Mañu. Then the starving Indians of the community went in a body to Don Cipriano, whose barns were full; and although they pled with piteous voices that he save them from starvation, he was obdurate. They attempted to storm the place and take the food by force, but armed men who were concealed about the granaries fired upon them and drove them off.

When their plight seemed completely hopeless, the rain finally came, and abundantly too. Its effect on the countryside was miraculous. All put aside their present want and began to plan for the future. Listening to the steady fall of the rain as if it were sweet music, Simón Robles suddenly spied Wanda.

> She was standing at the extreme end of the hall, awaiting his voice. Dirty, her hair clinging close to her skin and dripping with water, she was a pitiful sight; and Simón felt as his own the suffering of the poor abandoned animal, and it moved him as he considered that she, too, comprehended that the rain had put an end to her expulsion and that she could now return to her former life; and it moved him, too, when he realized that Wanda had returned to occupy her place as guard over the sheep, of which there were only several pairs in the fold.

The expulsion, on the part of an influential landowner, of a community of Indians from lands they had worked in common and according to socialistic principles is a minor incident in *Los Perros hambrientos*. A similar case becomes the main issue, however, in Alegría's third book, *El Mundo es Ancho y Ajeno*. For, here, the principal concern is the socialistic community of Rumi, situated in the highlands of northern Peru, in the same region as the city of Cajamarca. This community, which had held to the socialistic principles it had inherited from the period antedating the Spanish conquest, was as late as 1912, when the story begins, a veritable Arcadia. Particularly devoted to San Isidro, their patron saint, the people of Rumi were on the whole a happy and contented lot, making their living through the raising of livestock and the cultivation of wheat and other grains. They had had their troubles, to be sure. Revolutionary bands had plundered the region from time to time, and plagues of smallpox and typhus had frequently decimated their numbers; but, as their women were most prolific, such losses were soon restored. The prosperity of Rumi in recent times was attributable to the wise counsel of their alcalde, Rosendo Maqui, who had governed them for many years.

Still mayor of the village despite his age, Rosendo not only brought material benefit to the community, but he had attempted to establish a school in Rumi so that his people might enjoy the benefits of education, and had failed only because of obstacles that had been placed in his path. Although he was wise, he was unlettered and not altogether free from superstition. For one day as he was descending one of the many peaks surrounding Rumi he failed to kill a snake that happened to cross his path—an incident he took as a bad omen. On arriving home he found his aged wife had died; and a few days later Don Alvaro Amenábar, the owner of an adjoining estate, appeared in Rumi and laid claims to the communal lands on which the village stood.

A long lawsuit followed, which was eventually decided in Amenábar's favor, for the judge was predisposed in his behalf and Bismark Ruiz, a rascally lawyer the people of Rumi had employed to defend their cause, deceived them mercilessly. As Amenábar had proceeded against the community not on account of the value of the land involved but in order to secure the people themselves as laborers in a mine he proposed to work, he agreed to let them remain in their houses. But they refused his offer, for Rosendo argued that it would bring about their enslavement; and on the day set by the court for their evacuation they, with all of their effects, left Rumi and established themselves in Yanañahui, a far less favored spot. Although the villagers were sullen as they abandoned their homes, there was only one instance of violence. Mardoqueo, a certain villager who some days previously had been severely whipped by Amenábar's order when caught on the latter's property, concealed himself on a high cliff which overlooked the road leading into the village, and just when Amenábar and his party left after formally taking possession of Rumi,

Mardoqueo let a huge stone fall upon them; it crushed to death a lawyer whose chicanery had helped win his suit. Mardoqueo's revenge, however, cost him his life, for the gendarmes soon spotted him and sprayed him with machine-gun bullets.

Angered because he was not able to enslave the villagers, Amenábar proceeded to make life miserable for them. He drove off or appropriated their livestock; he trumped up a charge of theft against Rosendo and had him imprisoned; and when the villagers, with the help of an idealistically minded lawyer, Correa Zavala, attempted to recover their property, Amenábar's men waylaid the messengers and seized the documents that had been prepared to appeal the case to a higher court. Even in the face of such oppression, Rosendo Maqui, still in jail, continued to advise his people against acts of violence. A few of them, however, joined a bandit band commanded by a certain Fiero Vázquez and not only raided Amenábar's property but avenged most drastically acts of treachery on the part of others who had pretended to be their friends.

Fiero was imprisoned, but succeeded in escaping; Rosendo, however, suspected of complicity, was severely beaten and died. Then Amenábar went to Lima to aid in his son's election to the national congress, and the villagers were left somewhat in peace; but the barrenness of the land around Yanañahui made existence so difficult that many had to seek a living elsewhere.

The fortunes of many of these dispossessed are recounted, too, in great detail. Some, as has been seen, became bandits. Amadeo Illas sought work in the coca fields in the tropics, where he was treated horribly and, having contracted a debt, became virtually a slave. Calixto Páucar met death in a conflict between police and strikers in the mining town of Navilca, where he had gone to work. Augusto Maqui, Rosendo's grandson, also went to the low country to labor in the rubber fields, and his experiences there equal in oppression and cruelty any that are told in *La Vorágine*. Juan Medrano and his family found a home in the highlands, where they built their house, cleared ground for a field, and planted wheat; but at harvest time the landlord came and took almost all they had raised.

The widest and most varied experiences of all those who left Rumi to seek a living out in the world were those of Benito Castro. He worked on ranches as a cowboy; he helped to harvest grain on the haciendas; and he cut cane on the plantations on the coast. He worked in Lima, and later in its port city, Callao, where he acquired a lighter; but misfortune overtook him and he made his way up the coast to Salaverry and then to Trujillo, where he enlisted as a soldier. Everywhere he witnessed injustice in one form or another to the natives. Despite new scenes, he always longed for Rumi, whose misfortune had not yet reached his ears; and after an absence of some fifteen years, around 1925 he returned there and thence to Yanañahui, which chose him as alcalde. Serious trouble soon loomed. Amenábar had returned from Lima, and, still stubborn in his purpose, was preparing to do to Yanañahui what he had done to Rumi. Calling his people together, Benito addressed them in this vein:

The law has been hostile to us and by a judgment it seeks to push us into slavery, into death itself. Our neighbor, the cacique Alvaro Amenábar, tried first to take us to his mine. . . . Now, he desires a few more thousands of pesos and is going to plant coca in the valleys of the Ocros River. That's what he needs us for—to make us work from morning till night although we die of fever. He doesn't want land; he wants slaves. What has he done with the land he took away from us? There it is unworked, overgrown with brush, untouched by the loving hand of a farmer. The houses are falling down and the one our beloved Rosendo lived in is a pig pen. He doesn't want the lands around Yanañahui either. He persecutes us in order to break us to his will. When the law gives lands, it forgets what is going to be the fate of the men that live on those lands. The law doesn't protect them as men. Those that command will justify themselves by saying: "Go somewhere else; the world is wide." To be sure, it is wide. But, my fellow men, I know the wide world in which we poor are accustomed to live. And I tell you in all truth that as far as we, the poor, are concerned the world is wide, but it belongs to somebody else. You know it, too. Those of you who have gone out have seen it with your own eyes. Some dream and believe that what they haven't seen is better; and they go away—to make a living. Who of them has returned? Only Pedro Mayta was able to come back. The rest of them haven't returned, and I tell you that you can grieve for them as either dead or slaves. . . . In that wide world, we move from place to place, trying to make a living. But the world belongs to someone else and it gives us nothing, not even good wages. . . . Let's defend, then, our land, our place in the world, for thus we will defend our liberty and our lives. The fate of the poor is ever the same, and we beseech all of them to join us. Thus we will win.

And the people of Yanañahui did resist, but with dire results; for the superior arms and numbers of the government forces that came to Amenábar's aid wiped them out almost completely, including their alcalde, Benito Castro.

Such in the main is the story, or rather are the many stories, of *El Mundo es Ancho y Ajeno.* The plot is extremely loose in structure, carelessly planned and organized; the book would have gained much by more careful revision and much pruning. The characters are multitudinous, including people from many walks of life: the indigenous peasantry of both the socialistic community of Rumi and of the haciendas; the owners of large estates, such as the Amenábars and the Córdovas; bandits, itinerant peddlers, and petty revolutionary leaders who visited Rumi; and public officials, lawyers, and loose women in the small town near Rumi that served as the seat of the local government. On the whole, it might be said that the characters are overdrawn, either idealistically, as Rosendo and others of the Rumi community, or inhumanly cruel and base, such as Amenábar, Bismark Ruiz, and others. In regard to the medium in which these numerous and varied characters move, there is a great store of information, treating not only their physical background, but their beliefs, their lore, their way of life, and their amusements and diversions. In fact, it is very doubtful whether there exists in all Peruvian literature any other one book so rich in this respect. Of particular interest is Alegría's interpretation of the people of Rumi. He shows how their democratic political organization functioned, reveals their religious customs and beliefs, and writes with understanding and feeling of their domestic animals, as in *Perros hambrientos*, and of their means of earning a livelihood—such as the shearing of their sheep, the rounding up and branding of their cattle, and of the harvesting and primitive threshing of their wheat, which was also a sort of mating season for the villagers. Marked, indeed, is the contrast between this Arcadian life and the mistreatment of the Indian laborers on the coca plantations, in the mines, and on the ranches. There are, too, in connection with the wanderings of Benito Castro, full descriptions of queer festivities that he witnessed on certain haciendas, of conditions among the workmen of Lima and Callao, and of life in the army. Among the various aspects of life of the upper classes that are bared, are the corruption and immorality of the lawyers and public officials in the small town near Rumi, and the ambitions of such feudal barons as the Amenábars and Córdovas, who not only oppressed the Indians but fought each other for supremacy. While passages of poetic prose characterize *La Serpiente de Oro* and *Perros hambrientos*, the style of *El Mundo es Ancho y Ajeno* is on the whole long-winded. Avoiding largely the colloquial language that colors the pages of other contemporary writers, since he quotes little direct speech, Alegría has instead adopted the prolixity and incoherence that so often characterize the thoughts and utterances of his unlettered characters.

El Mundo es Ancho y Ajeno lacks certainly the artistic perfection of either *La Serpiente de Oro* or *Perros hambrientos;* it is, nevertheless, the most powerful of the three; and the strength of its power lies principally in the high quality of the mental and moral fiber of the author himself, who, in his defense of the downtrodden, has set forth a fundamental and vital problem of the people of Peru and treated it both energetically and fearlessly.

CHAPTER XII

TRENDS IN
SPANISH-AMERICAN FICTION

❋

Thoughtful consideration of the many aspects of life presented by each of these ten authors emphasizes the importance of their joint contribution and reveals the many implications of their concepts, the great variety and scope of their emotional life, and the full richness of their Spanish-American coloring. For, contrary to the general belief that Spanish Americans are pure idealists, these writers have shown themselves to a surprising degree realistic in their presentation of human emotions. Not that they are entirely without idealism; but it takes a different and more subtle form; it is to be found in their applications of irony, of satire, of tragedy. Foreign completely to their forms of expression is comedy; and only one of them has the quality of humor. But taken as a whole they present vivid and colorful pictures of human nature, often at its worst, in situations of great emotional conflict.

With the exception of Gálvez, Azuela, and Gallegos, none of the writers has so far produced more than five novels; and the works of those now dead and of Barrios, who gives no promise of future fiction, are exceedingly limited in extent. Rivera wrote only one and Loveira five novels; Güiraldes two novels, a novelette, and twenty prose sketches; Barrios two novels, two novelettes, and eight stories; and Quiroga less than a hundred stories. Each of them, however, has succeeded in giving to his work an individual stamp, a peculiar personal quality which distinguishes it. And in that quality, the writer as a man stands revealed. Gálvez has subjected Argentine life to the clear, searching analysis of a restrained, minutiae-minded, nationalistic historian; and points out, in direct and measured style and in the tone of a traditionalist, the flaws in the social fabric, without implication that time will rectify them. Azuela caught at close range successive impressions of Mexican society reacting to existent conditions, but he colored his films with his own deep pessimism and even bitterness. Loveira's is the argumentative tone of the nineteenth-century socialist who, like the first Spanish-American novelist, Fernández de Lizardi, resorts to realistic fiction only as a means toward attainment of the reforms he sees as drastically necessary. Delicately tinged by recollections of the pampas is the lyricism of Güiraldes, which gives to his every line a peculiarly poetic touch. The righteous wrath of Icaza over injustice to the "underdogs" of Ecuador finds adequate expression only in a stark realism, forcefully colored by biting satire and obscenity. Barrios is the greater artist in resorting instead to pathos and tragedy; the deep personal feeling of his autobiographic works is succeeded, in his masterpiece, by the calm reflection of the philosopher who can smile at the frailties of humanity and inject a touch of gentle, whimsical humor into his jottings. Quiroga is romantic always; brightly imaginative at times; at others, Poe-like in fantastic visions. Rivera's genius is free and impetuous, charged now and then with a high degree of nervous intensity. Alegría is folkloristic; his is a lyric realism ranging from the idyllic to the terrifying. Gallegos is more vigorous and more balanced, more dynamic and more masterly, more grandiose in conception, more awe-inspiring in sweep, more symbolistic in intent, and more hopeful in outlook.

In spite of this individual quality of each writer, as a group they have in common certain characteristics in conception, technique, and purpose. They all portray, in the main, the life of the last half-century—their own lifetime. For these writers are not concerned with reconstructing a bygone age, but with recording life as they have seen and lived it. Only in *Pobre Negro* has Gallegos departed from this pattern; and only in their biographies and historical novels have Azuela and Gálvez interested themselves in a period of the nineteenth century before their own day. In place of documents, each used as basic material either himself, his environment, or the reaction of the one on the other. Though differences in viewpoint do exist, even in writing of the same period—Gálvez looks backward and is interested in analyzing the past, while Azuela is concerned with the past only as it affects the present—all restrict their interest largely to their own day.

Three of them, indeed, cover the contemporary scene rather completely: Loveira pictures Cuba from the close of the colonial period until the late twenties; Azuela records his impressions of Mexico from the palmy days of Díaz to 1939; and Gálvez places the action of his novels either in the pre-World-War decade or in that which followed its close. Barrios, whose interest is less in the times and more in himself, lays his scenes around the opening years of the century; and Alegría raises the curtain on an idyllic Rumi in 1912 and transforms it rapidly into a site of tragedy. The twenties is the era of the four novelists who stress background, although some of the interwoven incidents of *La Vorágine* extend back to the early years of the century and the second part of Quiroga's "El Salvaje" to the prehistoric period. Before the decade closed, the work of three of the group had been ended by death; Barrios had ceased fictional production; Gálvez and Gallegos had turned to history; and Quiroga, to imaginative incidents in which the time element was quite immaterial. But the third decade had another portrayer in Icaza, who was deeply concerned with its events and conditions.

Each of the ten writers employs in the main only his own

native country as background; and background is, on the whole, the most distinctive of the novelistic elements that enter into their total work. But the treatment of that background is not conventional. In general there is little physical description except of the wild, uninhabited regions; and to these is given a character apart from the photographic picture. Even Gálvez, who began his novel-writing by portraying the provincial city with the greatest detail and accuracy in *La Maestra normal* and *La Sombra del Convento*, later shows little interest in background, although touches of his descriptive artistry light up his historical novels as he sketches the Corrientes and Asunción of the late sixties.

The extent of the background presented by the ten as a whole is vast, but few, individually, treat more than a very limited geographical area. Three restrict themselves to exceedingly small fields: Quiroga to Misiones; Güiraldes to the province of Buenos Aires; and Icaza to the sierras about Quito. The others employ more extensive and contrasting backgrounds: Azuela, Jalisco and the Mexican capital; Barrios, the Chilean coastal towns and Santiago; Alegría, the coastal, Andine, and forest regions of Peru; Rivera, the plains and forests of Colombia; Gallegos, the capital and various regions of Venezuela; Gálvez, Buenos Aires and the provincial cities of northwest Argentina; and Loveira, Cuba mainly, but Panama, Yucatan, and the United States incidentally.

But though their pages have revealed something of the fast-changing character of Buenos Aires, Mexico City, and Havana; of change-resistant Quito, Caracas, and Santiago, Cuba; of provincial La Rioja, Córdoba, Guadalajara, and Matanzas; of petty Alamos, Cieneguilla, and Placeres; of communistic and landlord-ruled Indian villages in Ecuador and Peru—we have few photographic pictures. Instead, each writer to a large extent succeeds in the attempt to give to his readers the atmosphere of the place; the spirit with which it is imbued; the quality that pervades the life he describes. We never know from Azuela that Mexico City lies in a valley enclosed by mountains and overlooked by two great snow-clad volcanoes; but we do know the spirit prevailing there at certain definite times: when revolutionists swept in and Indian hordes became masters; when the wealthy sought bread while wily chieftains held the governmental reins; when pseudo-politicians ruled and union leaders controlled the masses; when wealth had changed hands and a new aristocracy, born of the Revolution, had come into power; and when the poor folk from the provinces had immersed themselves in the life of the capital, only to find it wanting in spiritual invigoration. So with Gálvez in his treatment of Buenos Aires: it is not the city in the physical sense that is his background, but the life that is lived there—of students, writers, ecclesiastics, government officials, high society, or the wretchedly poor and criminal. Not so with naturalistic Loveira, who gives us such detailed pictures of Havana and other Cuban towns as leave no shadow of doubt about the appearance of any of them. But he, too, does more. For, while he omits no detail of the filth, his emphasis is on the personal degradation, the economic misery, the political corruption and their causes. In a seemingly unending stream, he pours it all out, seasoning it, as does Icaza later, with hot indignation and biting indictments of those in power.

Away from the cities we have seen the sugar, coffee, and cocoa plantations of Cuba and Venezuela, before and after the first World War, peopled by two conflicting social groups—the owners and the laborers. But the most impressive pictures of all—the ones that linger in our minds—are those of the vast immensities of the plains, with their myriad shifting cattle, horses, and plainsmen; of the dense humid jungle regions in process of surrendering to cultivation; and of the damp, almost impenetrable virgin forests, resolutely opposing with all the forces at their command the encroachment of mankind. In these pictures we see the pioneers of Spanish America in process of pushing the still-existent frontier forward.

Colorful details are nowhere lacking. Before our eyes course the waters of the flooded Paraná, the swift Uruguay, which join to form the muddy La Plata; the yellow Arauca, the blue Caroní, the black Guainía, the green Ventuari, the reddish Atabajo, which yield their waters and their coloring to the brown Orinoco; and the treacherous Marañón and the sullen Negro, as they flow eastward to form the mighty Amazon. Stormy Atlantic and quiet Pacific, the languorous Caribbean Sea and the Gulf of Mexico bathe the tropical and semi-tropical shores we have reviewed; and on the highlands of Chile, Peru, Ecuador, and Mexico the shadows of the mighty Andes and the Sierra Madres fall athwart both white and Indian. But it is everywhere the spirit, the character with which these writers invest each region that gives their portrayals value.

As varied as the background are the great number of figures presented, but few rise far above the general level of the multitude. Racial variety ranges from the white of either European or North American extraction to the negro and Indian of pure blood; besides, such varied strains as the mulatto, the *cholo*, and the mestizo appear. And it is clear from a glance at any of the red or black—whether of pure or mixed blood— that racial equality, either economic or social, has not been achieved. A further survey of the characters en masse brings out the striking preponderance of men, both in number and importance. And this is a characteristic of Spanish America as contrasted with the United States; in the main, Spanish America is still a man's world. Women enter into the various pictures, it is true, but mainly as foils; only in the last group of Gálvez' novels have they usurped the center of the scene.

Many social levels appear, but the proportion of characters from each level increases as the scale descends. Those represented by the men are wide in range, for they include the idle rich; cosmopolitan travelers; land barons; government officials and clerical and technical employees; priests and lawyers; doctors and *curanderos;* teachers, writers, painters, sculptors; army officers of high and low rank, soldiers, revolutionists, and bandits; engineers, mechanics, artisans, and jockeys; village *caciques*, small farmers, agrarians and their leaders; lowly tillers of the soil; cowboys of the plains; rubber workers of the forests; jungle clearers; and river raftsmen. The occupational variation of the women is much more limited. First in importance are wives, rich and poor; greater in number are the mistresses, among them innocent victims of lustful overlords; and still more numerous are the prostitutes. Small advance of women into the professional or business world is suggested; for here figure only a very few teachers, artists, clerical or factory workers, traders or venders, while boarding-house keepers and servants are numerous.

The threads of narrative by which the figures are woven into the background are frequently uneven and sometimes very thin, resulting in a fabric whose texture is of variable quality. In general the element of plot has received the least attention, and in none of the purely fictional works does a highly involved plot enter. This is not true of the historical novels of Gálvez, in which subplots of some complexity are ingeniously combined. Nor is this lack of interest in or mastery of narrative technique surprising, for seldom has the Spanish genius produced skillfully compressed plots as the basis for fiction. Few of these writers are primarily excellent as story-tellers, although Loveira has much natural facility for narrative and Quiroga can hold his own at times with the best —especially does he grip the attention of his readers with his analysis of animal psychology, of the morbid mind, and of streams of consciousness. Güiraldes, in a slender way, shows ability in *Rosaura* to handle a plot admirably; while Barrios in his recording of episodes—many of them personally experienced—depends upon subtlety of interpretation rather than upon ingenuity of plot. In *Doña Bárbara*, which has from every standpoint the best plot of all these novels, the narrative, while simple, is direct and of absorbing interest.

Aside from these exceptions, the tendency, increasing with the years, has been toward utter formlessness; these writers, like those of the United States, have cast aside all established rules and models of construction and set forth on uncharted courses in fictional production. Indeed, it is more than probable that the North American novelists who first had this inspiration pointed the way. The trend is very evident if the first of these contemporary novels is compared with the last. *La Maestra normal* is the most carefully and the most skillfully constructed of the many we have discussed, but not the best from the standpoint of interest: *El Mundo es Ancho y Ajeno* —showing little evidence of good planning, symmetry, or proportion—and the works of Icaza, the extreme of plotlessness, yet hold the attention. A device employed with good effect by Rivera and Gallegos is to leave the end of the story to the imagination of the reader. We can only wonder what finally became of Cova, of Doña Bárbara, of Cantaclaro, and of Dr. Payara. But the tendency—slight in Gálvez, stronger in Gallegos, and pronounced in Loveira, Azuela, Rivera, Icaza, and Alegría—is to consider the story itself as of minor consideration in comparison with its social significance; and this is a tendency they share with the best contemporary writers of the United States.

In contrast, the age-old love theme, which has largely disappeared from the more significant North-American fiction of today, is still present, if not dominant, in Spanish-American, especially in the works of Loveira, Quiroga, Barrios, and Gálvez, although some shifting of interest from the wooing period to that of marital adjustment is discernible. Even Güiraldes, in general little concerned with love, has left us, in the pages of *Xaimaca*, a matchless picture of the unfolding of passion, and a few of his stories are strikingly salacious. Another voluble exponent of romantic love, frequently at the wooing stage, is Quiroga, in so far as he treats the subject at all. Barrios shows the vital influence love exerts on the boy and the man, from the effects of the fondling of a mother to that absorbing passion for a woman which can wreck a man (*Un Perdido*). On the other hand, Loveira is the most absorbed of all of these writers with love as a motivating force in life and is in open defiance against the restraints imposed on it by church and state (*Los Inmorales*) and by social conventions (*Los Ciegos*). Azuela, not primarily interested in love, feels with Loveira its import to marriage: in *Sin Amor* and *El Desquite* he points out the disastrous spiritual effects of loveless unions. Rivera utilizes the love theme as the thread by which to join the various episodes of his disjointed narrative, but this function the reader cannot fail to sense, for the impress of genuine passion is lacking.

It is Gálvez, after all more closely related both in technique and spirit to the nineteenth than to the twentieth century, who has made love his basic theme. With characteristic thoroughness he has detailed the storm and stress of the wooing stage (*La Sombra del Convento* and *El Mal Metafísico*) and then presented four types of love: the spiritual (*El Cántico espíritual*); the marital (*La Pampa, Cautiverio, Un Hombre fuerte, Una Mujer moderna*, and *Hombres en Soledad*); free love, as exemplified by the many seductions (Solís, Padre Solanas, Claudio Vidamors) and mistresses introduced in all his novels; and that of the prostitute (*Nacha Regules* and *Historia de Arrabal*). All his main female characters of the post-World War group are better-class married women, largely promiscuous; under such circumstances, the tables have turned—the women select their lovers. Gallegos handles the love element more masterfully by presenting it in conjunction with others: in Doña Bárbara love is in conflict with pride and hatred simultaneously; in Reinaldo, with other interests that successively catch his attention; in Hilario and Luisana, with the problem of race (*La Trepadora; Pobre Negro*); and in Marcos Vargas, with the fascination of the forest (*Canaima*).

Of the varied conflicts within the individual, Barrios has given the most intimate and detailed pictures in the jottings of an adolescent boy (*El Niño que enloqueció de Amor*), the struggles of a weakling (*Un Perdido*), and the thoughts that course through the mind of a monk (*El Hermano asno*). Of such inner conflicts, Gálvez, too, has given excellent accounts:

Raselda, struggling against her love for Solís and yet yielding; Nacha and Rosalinda, resolving over and over to abandon prostitution, but forced to it by economic conditions; Carlos Riga in hot rebellion against the sacrifice of his love to wealth and social position; and Padre Solanas steeling himself against the calls of the flesh. Especially does Gálvez excel in the delineation of the struggles of religious convictions for dominance (*La Sombra del Convento, La Noche toca a su Fin, Cautiverio*). In Juan Cabrera, too, the material urge was in active opposition to the spiritual, for he had vowed to better the condition of the unfortunates about him and could not entirely forget them; and yet he yielded to easy money and a comfortable life for himself (*Juan Criollo*). In less serious tone, Loveira details the dilemma of Dr. Aguirre upon finding himself about to marry a woman of an entirely different social background (*La Última Lección*).

Through the conflicts presented, the character of the individual emerges. Some are clearly drawn—others but vaguely. The majority of the individuals here presented are the weak —those unable to cope with or escape from conditions prevailing about them. Yet a few, for various reasons, are unforgettable. Some are more genuinely human; others are purely idealizations; many are of interest because they typify Spanish-American society; and a very few—and they are the greatest—because they symbolize something greater than themselves.

Loveira had the rare art of making his characters human; perhaps because he injected into them much of himself. No one will forget the lovable Ignacio García (*Generales y Doctores*), the wily Juan or the aristocratic Nena (*Juan Criollo*). In spite of Gálvez's predilection for weaklings, he created the adamant Ignacio Belderrain, a Catholic to the marrow, willing to sacrifice country, family, or friends on the altar of the Church (*La Sombra del Convento*). In few of Azuela's characters is the human element predominant: among his best are Demetrio, fighting persistently against a power he could not understand, and yet only a plaything of Fate (*Los de Abajo*); Procopio and Agustinita, facing the adversities of life with attitudes entirely different (*Tribulaciones de una Familia decente*); and the four eminently selfish Llanos and their victim Juan Viñas (*Los Caciques*). All the main characters of Barrios are human but tragic: like those of Loveira, each is largely the author himself. Like them, too, Quiroga was interested mainly in characters in which he himself lived; but he produced a few whom we shall not soon forget, among them the patient and long-enduring Kassim, driven to desperation by a vain, dissatisfied wife. Three of Rivera's are very lifelike: Cova, fighter to the end against the forces of Nature; Zoraida, strange mixture of lust and avarice; and Barrera, cruel master of enslaved people. In contrast, how delicately human are the figures Güiraldes molded! Rosaura, the dainty small-town girl, victim of unrequited love; Raucho, product of the pampa, returning thereto to find the only real peace; and Don Segundo's worshipful ward, boylike, eager, and adventurous. Among the Venezuelans, the most genuine is the mulatto Hilario, proud, ambitious, and determined.

Of the idealizations, we have Nacha, the romanticized prostitute, battered by fate again and again, but winning her way triumphantly to a noble and respected end; Luisana, overstepping racial barriers in giving herself to Pedro Miguel (*Pobre Negro*); Don Segundo, in whom are united all the virtues of the man of the plains; and a group of idealistic internationalists—Monsalvat (*Nacha Regules*), Reséndez (*Los Fracasados*), Antonio Reyes (*Andrés Pérez, Maderista*), Rodríguez (*Los Caciques*), Regina Landa, and Rosendo Maqui, all of whom learned the price—whether of position, fortune, or life itself—that is paid by those who resist oppression or seek to bring about reforms of any kind.

Azuela is the master painter of types, for his pages abound in victims of lust, disease, drink, and avarice; in unprincipled figurehead politicians; in government employees willing to sacrifice anything for a job; in labor leaders who supplant both *hacendado* and priest in mass control; and in those who have taken on city airs in the last decade. Gálvez excels in typical figures of weak men and frivolous women of the better class; Quiroga, of laborers and immigrants; Rivera, of rubber exploiters. All Icaza's characters are types; none attain the distinction of individuals, for he is not interested in them as such.

Of the characters presented, those that make the most lasting impression are the symbolic. Reinaldo Solar is far more impressive as a representative of Venezuelan society than as an individual; so, too, is Don Segundo, as the personification of the pampas; and Santos, Marcos Vargas, and Cova, as contenders in a struggle between civilization and barbarity, between man and the forces of Nature. Even Icaza's and Alegría's Indian characters assume new interest and importance if regarded as symbolizing the century-long struggle of the red man against the usurping white, or of man against Nature as personified in the river or the drought. Doña Bárbara is the only woman whose character is drawn on a massive scale; in her, hatred, determination, and cunning all play their rôle. And so, Gallegos envisages the *llanos*—wild and resistant to civilization, and employing all the arts of Nature in the struggle. Even as the *llanos* yield to the inevitable, so is she transformed—from a young girl untouched by tragedy she becomes the victim of lust; from an untutored woman actuated by hatred she becomes the ruling power of the plains; torn between love and hatred, she weakens until faced by ultimate defeat; then, with one last gesture of atonement, she passes from the scene, whither we shall never know. No other character created by a Spanish American can stand beside her in strength, breadth, or final tragedy.

While the development of individual character interests some of these writers, all but Quiroga and Rivera turn to families or larger groups as representative of certain ideas or reactions. These groups all necessarily figure in some type of conflict; either they themselves defend power and authority or they are in rebellion against it. The Andrades (*Mala Yerba*), the Llanos (*Los Caciques*), the Rodríguez (*Los Fracasados*), the Belderrains (*La Sombra del convento*), and the Ruiz y Fontanills (*Juan Criollo*) dominate all about them; on the other hand, the family of Matías the raftsman (*El Serpiente de Oro*), of Robles the dog-breeder (*Perros hambrientos*), and of Andrés Chiliquinga (*Huasipungo*) share in the struggle against Nature, overlord, or class distinctions. The groups figure in similar conflicts, sometimes of wider scope, against such institutions as government, church, economic conditions, slavery, and social conventions of sex, class, or race; or against Nature on a larger scale. Thus we see the revolutionists in revolt against established government and the church (*Los de Abajo*); the laborers in conflict with their employers (*Los Inmorales, Los Ciegos, Huasipungo, En las Calles*); agrarians and laborers clashing with their leaders (*Avanzada, San Gabriel de Valvidias*); women as a group in revolt against social conventions (*La Tragedia de un Hombre fuerte, Hombres en Soledad*); communal landowning Indians engaged in struggles with overlords (*El Mundo es Ancho y Ajeno, Perros hambrientos*); the peons in rebellion against their masters (all of Icaza's); and the rubber workers resisting as best they can their exploiters (*La Vorágine*). These slaves are also engaged, as are the jungle people and the balata gatherers, in the more desperate contest for supremacy over Nature.

While all ten authors have as their chief interest the social significance of the emotional reactions of the characters and groups they present, nearly all of them have some vision of a fundamental equality among all people and all classes; and the attainment of this equality is, in a sense, their objective. And early in their work can be found the inclination to make clear the obstacles thereto—the causes and conditions productive of distress. Moral and mental attitudes are deliberately traced back by seven of these writers to environmental conditions, especially the economic; and these in turn are in some cases laid squarely at the door of society and government.

Against the forms of government operative in their respective countries are arrayed Loveira, Azuela, Icaza, and Alegría; against racial prejudice and injustice especially pronounced are Gallegos and Icaza; against economic conditions that reduce human beings to slaves of one type or another are allied all of these and Rivera.

Half of these writers picture Spanish America as a land ruled over by members of a decadent aristocracy lacking a social conscience. Cursed with the pride and prejudice of their forbears, with ingrained stubbornness and an exceedingly narrow outlook, these people refuse to face the fact that even for slaves, whether black or red, there comes an end to endurance and that an aroused mass can trample underfoot all that stands in its way. Instead, relying upon the power of the church, general ignorance, and dire poverty to hold the people in check, the large landowners of Ecuador, Peru, and Cuba are pictured as cloaking their secret fears under a false show of security. For Mexico has served to some extent as a warning; what has happened there might be repeated elsewhere.

Gálvez is interested, too, in the submerged classes; but he does not need to drive his lessons home as some of the others do, for Argentina has no such racial problem to solve. She is instead a melting-pot for European bloods and creeds, and her level of literacy is high. But, strangely enough, of this decemvirate of writers, Gálvez is the lone champion of Catholicism, in spite of the fact that Spanish America is nominally solidly Catholic. But against the church are arrayed Azuela (especially in his early works), Loveira, and Icaza, for to them the Roman hierarchy is a power linked hand-in-hand with corrupt government. Broad, too, in social significance do they regard the struggle of mankind with Nature; this is the theme of Alegría and all the writers of background; it is the conflict supreme—of greatest scope and vastest implication. For this struggle is the struggle of life as it is going on in many parts of Spanish America today.

What does life offer these people as satisfaction or relief from the miseries, the antagonisms, the conflicts, the ugliness they face, materially and spiritually? On the basis of these eighty-odd novels, the greatest avenues of escape are sexual pleasures and drink. Sports, except horse racing and cock fighting, have relatively little appeal. The masters of the Spanish-American "Old South" find their satisfactions either in perverted religion, sexual relationships with members of the submerged race, or through inhuman cruelty. Religion of a higher type offers solace to others: Raselda, Claudio, Belderrain, María Elena and her husband. Some find their highest joy in the creation or appreciation of beauty: Riga dies faithful to his poetic ideals and Mauricio Sandoval experiences the greatest degree of passion in the conception of a work of art. Another type—like Raucho, as he lies alone by the quiet lake listening to the call of the birds—finds that only communion with Nature on the pampas brings that "peace which passeth all understanding"; Santos, too, becomes a changed man under the spell of the Arauca, away from the haunts of men. Mastery of Nature brings the thrill of success to those who cope with jungle and river; and the joy is none the less because the task must be over and over repeated. Rest for the weary, leisure for the busy, social intercourse for the dweller in the woods—these are the simple joys to be found in such grim surroundings.

The few stories of material success which figure here differ pointedly from the average North American "success" story, for these authors never regard the attainment of wealth or social position as an end; they prefer to call attention to the inevitable bitterness of the cup of success. Hilario, rich and wedded to the woman he loved, discovered to his sorrow that something more was necessary to a mulatto's happiness. Indians and half-breeds who achieved financial success also learned its shortcomings, for Enrique Carchi could not command the respect of his family ("Interpretación"); Alberto Montoyo could never lose his sense of inferiority; and Guagcho, his Indian *mayordomo*, found that a conscience at ease was a priceless jewel (*Cholos*). In this indirect fashion, these writers suggest some of the intangible spiritual values—far-reaching in their influence—to which many of the characters they portray are strangers.

If the plots of the novels are in general structurally poor and few of their characters outstanding, their stylistic effects are distinctive. And, as a group, these writers are more concerned with effects than form. Their poetic and colorful diction, their unusual figures, and the musical quality of their prose are all reminiscent of the Modernists. In certain of them, the change from nineteenth-century directness of style to twentieth-century impressionism is marked. Azuela's early work is clear and simple; but his later works are frequently enveloped in baffling obscurity. So, too, at one time, did simplicity and directness characterize Gallegos, but in *Canaima* and *Cantaclaro* he cultivates obscurities in style. Güiraldes's is a carefully studied style colored by daring figures; Barrios's lines offer splendid examples of the rhythmic possibilities of modern prose. Into the descriptions of Nature of both Rivera and Gallegos imagination enters to such a degree as to invest each region with distinctive characteristics.

The personal note, too, contributes insistently to individuality. The autobiographers—Barrios, Quiroga, Loveira—are scarcely ever able to leave themselves out of the picture; Rivera in his works is laying bare a page from his own life; and Icaza and at times Alegría pour out their innermost feelings without reserve. Güiraldes expresses no views outright, but his background is colored by his own feelings. Less personal, Gálvez and Gallegos are invariably present in the offing, and Azuela betrays himself through his irony.

Their language is on the whole well chosen with reference to time, place, and character. All except Quiroga and Barrios make free use of Americanisms and localisms, and so extensive does the use of such terms become with Gallegos that he attaches a list to the later editions of *Doña Bárbara* and *Pobre Negro*. The exaggeration of figures so striking in Güiraldes is also employed by Azuela in some of his later works, by Barrios in *El Hermano asno,* by Rivera, and by Alegría in his first books. Yet in many passages the figures are simple; they charm not by their strangeness but by their inherent beauty.

As creative artists all ten writers are serious in tone, persistent in effort, eager and impetuous, and to a great degree beauty-loving. Although theirs is the Spanish tendency to place too great faith in inspiration and often too little effort on the details of organization and thematic development, in them all will be found great sincerity of purpose, an honest effort to give the stamp of truth to their work, and a great desire to create genuine literature. Of the ten, only Loveira and Icaza are insensible to the beauty of polish; and for this they compensate with unvarnished truth.

As a group these writers have worked toward an important objective. For they have presented in the form of fiction the Latin American as they see him in action, and the conditions and influences that formed him; they have pointed out the flaws in the social fabric and the frequent lack of appreciation of spiritual values; and they have made comprehensible to their readers the psychology of the "underdog" and his resort to ruthless cruelty and destruction as vengeance for wrongs long endured. This study has attempted to contribute to the same ends through a synthesis in English of the ideas of the ten. The inherent value of their work, both in content and in manner of presentation, has already been pointed out, and its appeal shown to have transcended national and continental boundaries.

For among the novels here discussed are some which will surely stand the test of time and sustain their international reputations. It was once thought that Spanish-American fiction might well rest on a triangular foundation, *La Maestra normal* supporting one corner in Argentina; *Los de Abajo,* another in Mexico; and *La Vorágine,* the third in Colombia. But this triangular base became diamond-shaped when *Doña Bárbara* brought Venezuela for the first time into international fiction.

Now, it might better rest on a base in the form of a five-pointed star, which would join all these countries and Chile; for *El Hermano asno* should also figure among the distinctive Spanish-American novels destined to hold a permanent place in literature.

A BIBLIOGRAPHY OF THE NOVELS AND COLLEC-
TIONS OF SHORT STORIES DISCUSSED, WITH
EXISTENT ENGLISH TRANSLATIONS AND
SOME PERTINENT REVIEWS

ALEGRÍA, CIRO.
  El Mundo es Ancho y Ajeno. Santiago, Chile, 1941. Trans-
  lated by Harriet Onís as *Broad and Alien is the World*.
  New York, Farrar and Rinehart, 1941.
    Reviewed in *Books* (*New York Herald-Tribune*), Nov.
    9; the *New York Times Book Review*, Nov. 16; and
    the *Nation*, Nov. 29, 1941.
  Los Perros hambrientos (*Hungry Dogs*). Santiago, Chile,
  1939.
  La Serpiente de Oro (*The Golden Serpent*). Santiago,
  Chile, 1935. Translated by Harriet de Onís. New York,
  Farrar and Rinehart, 1943.
AZUELA, MARIANO.
  Andrés Pérez, Maderista (*Andrés Pérez, a Madero Parti-
  san*). Mexico, 1911.
  Avanzada (*The Advance Guard*). Mexico, 1940.
    Reviewed by A. B. Franklin in the *Inter-American Quar-
    terly*, III (April, 1940), 115-117.
  Los Caciques (*The Caciques*). Mexico, 1917.
    Discussed by L. B. Simpson in *Hispania*, XIV (Nov.,
    1931).
  El Camarada Pantoja (*Comrade Pantoja*). Mexico, 1937.
  El Desquite (*Tit for Tat*). Mexico, 1925.

Los de Abajo. El Paso, Texas, 1915. Translated into English as *The Under-Dogs* by E. Munguía, Jr. New York, Brentano's, 1929.

   Reviewed by E. K. James, *New York Herald-Tribune*, Oct. 19; by E. Montenegro, *New York Times Book Review*, Oct. 28, 1928; L. Gannett, *Books* (*New York Herald-Tribune*), Aug. 25, 1929; A. Brenner, *Evening Post*, New York, Aug. 31; F. Blom, *Saturday Review of Literature*, Sept. 28; W. Frank, *New Republic*, Oct. 23; E. Gruening, *Nation*, Dec. 4, 1929; and I. Goldberg, *The New World Monthly*, I (1929), 66-68.

Los Fracasados (*The Disillusioned*). Mexico, 1908.

La Luciérnaga (*Firefly*). Madrid, 1932.

   Discussed by L. B. Simpson in *Hispania*, XV (1932), 415-417.

Mala Yerba (*Bad Blood*). Guadalajara, Mexico, 1909. Translated into English by Anita Brenner as *Marcela*. New York, Farrar and Rinehart, 1932.

   Reviewed in the *Saturday Review of Literature*, Sept. 24; the *New York Times*, Sept. 25; the *Nation*, Nov. 30; and the *New Republic*, Dec. 14, 1932.

La Malhora (*Ill-Fated*). Mexico, 1923.

María Luisa. Lagos, Mexico, 1907. The 2nd edition, Botas, Mexico, 1938, contains the following short stories: "Víctimas de la Opulencia" ("Victims of Wealth"), "De mi Tierra" ("Of My Homeland"), "En Derrota" ("In Flight"), "Avichuelos negros" ("Black Vultures"), and "Lo que se Esfuma" ("In Passing").

Las Moscas (*Hangers-on*). Mexico, 1918.

La nueva Burguesía (*The New Bourgeoisie*). Buenos Aires, 1941.

Pedro Moreno, el Insurgente (*Pedro Moreno, the Insurgent*). Mexico, 1933. Fictionalized biography.

Precursores (*Forerunners*). Santiago, Chile, 1935. Fictionized biography.

   Reviewed in the *New York Times Book Review*, May 10, 1936.

Regina Landa. Mexico, 1939.

San Gabriel de Valdivias. Santiago, Chile, 1938.

Sin Amor (*Without Love*). Mexico, 1912.

Las Tribulaciones de una Familia decente (*The Trials of a Genteel Family*). Mexico, 1918.

BARRIOS, EDUARDO.

Del Natural (*In the Naturalistic Style*). Santiago, Chile, 1907. This includes "Amistad de Solteras" ("The Friendship of Maidens"), "Lo que Ellos Creen y lo que Ellos Son" ("What They Believe and Are"), "Celos bienhechores" ("When Jealousy Works to the Good"), and "Tirana Ley"("Tyrant Law").

El Hermano asno (*Brother Brute*). Santiago, Chile, 1922. Translated as *Brother Ass*, in *Fiesta in November*.* Boston, Houghton Mifflin, 1942. Edited by Angel Flores and Dudley Poore.

El Niño que enloqueció de Amor (*The Love-Crazed Boy*). Santiago, Chile, 1915. Included are two stories: "Pobre feo" ("Poor Ugly Man") and "Papá y Mamá."

Páginas de un pobre Diablo (*Pages from a Poor Devil's Diary*). Santiago, Chile, 1923. Includes the stories "Canción" ("An Idyl") and "Antipatía" ("Antipathy").

Un Perdido (*A Down-and-Outer*). Santiago, 1917.

GALLEGOS, RÓMULO.

Los Aventureros (*Adventurers*). Caracas, 1913. Includes also "El Apoyo" ("The Prop"), "Estrellas sobre el Barranco" ("Stars over the Gorge"), "Las novias del Mendigo" ("The Beggar's Sweethearts"), "La Liberación" ("Escape"), "Sol de Antaño" ("Autumn Sun"), and "El Milagro del Año" ("The Miracle of the Year").

Canaima. Barcelona, 1935. John T. Reed's "Spanish-American Jungle Fiction," *Inter-American Quarterly* (Jan., 1940) includes a review of *Canaima*.

Cantaclaro (*The Ballad Singer*). Barcelona, 1931.

Doña Bárbara. Barcelona, 1929. Translated by R. Malloy. New York, Cape and Smith, 1931.

* Reviewed as a whole by C. Fadiman in *The New Yorker*, Aug. 1; by N. L. Rothman, *Saturday Review of Literature*, Aug. 15; D. Trilling, *Nation*, Sept. 5, 1942; and E. L. Tinker, *New York Times*, Jan. 10, 1943.

Reviewed in *Books* (*New York Herald-Tribune*), Aug.
9; *New York Times*, Aug. 9; *Boston Transcript*, Aug.
22; *New Republic*, Oct. 28; *Spectator* (London), Nov.
21; *Times* (London) *Literary Supplement*, Dec. 3,
1931.

Los Inmigrantes (*Immigrants*). Caracas, 1922.

Pobre Negro (*Poor Negro*). Caracas, 1937.

La Trepadora (*The Climber*). Caracas, 1925.

El Ultimo Solar (*The Last of the Solars*). Caracas, 1920.
Published in subsequent editions under the title of
Reinaldo Solar.

For a discussion of Gallegos's works, see E. Montenegro,
"The Literary Scene in South America," *New York
Times Book Review*, March 30, 1941.

GÁLVEZ, MANUEL.

Los Caminos de la Muerte (*Paths of Death*). Buenos Aires,
1928.

El Cántico espiritual (*Hymn to the Spiritual*). Buenos Aires,
1923.

Cautiverio (*In Captivity*). Buenos Aires, 1935.

El Gaucho de "Los Cerrillos" (*The Gaucho of "Los Cerrillos" Ranch*). Buenos Aires, 1931.

El General Quiroga. Buenos Aires, 1932.

Historia de Arrabal (*A Den of Vice*). Buenos Aires, 1922.

Hombres en Soledad (*Lonely Men*). Buenos Aires, 1939.

Humaitá. Buenos Aires, 1929.

Jornadas de Agonía (*Agony-fraught Marches*). Buenos
Aires, 1929.

Luna de Miel y otras Narraciones ("*Honeymoon*" *and
Other Stories*). Buenos Aires, 1920. For list of stories included, see pp. 43-44.

La Maestra normal (*The Normal-School Teacher*). Buenos
Aires, 1914.

El Mal metafísico (*Idealism—An Ill*). Buenos Aires, 1916.

Miércoles Santo (*Holy Wednesday*). Buenos Aires, 1930.
Translated by W. P. Wells. New York, Appleton-Cen-
tury, 1934.
Reviewed in the *Spectator* (London), Feb. 16; *Times*
(London) *Literary Supplement*, March 15; *New York*

Times, July 22; *Boston Transcript,* Aug. 4; *Books (New York Herald-Tribune),* Aug. 19; and *Saturday Review of Literature,* Sept. 29, 1934.

Una Mujer muy Moderna (A Very Modern Woman). Buenos Aires, 1927. For list of stories included, see p. 45.

Nacha Regules. Buenos Aires, 1919. Translated into English by L. Ongley. New York, Dutton, 1922.

Reviewed in the *New York Times,* April 1; *Boston Transcript,* May 5; *Nation,* May 23; *New York Tribune,* June 10; *Bookman,* Sept. 23; and *Times (London) Literary Supplement,* Dec. 20, 1923.

La Noche Toca a su Fin (The End of Night draws Near). Buenos Aires, 1935.

La Pampa y su Pasión (The Pampa and Its Craze). Buenos Aires, 1926.

La Sombra del Convento (The Shadow of the Convent). Buenos Aires, 1917.

La Tragedia de un Hombre Fuerte (The Tragedy of a Superior Man). Buenos Aires, 1922.

Vida de Fray Mamerto Esquiú (Life of Fray Mamerto Esquiú). Buenos Aires, 1933. Novelized biography.

Vida de Hipólito Yrigoyen (Life of Hipólito Yrigoyen). Buenos Aires, 1939. Novelized biography.

GÜIRALDES, RICARDO.

Cuentos de Muerte y de Sangre (Stories of Death and Blood). Buenos Aires, 1915. Among the stories included in the title group are "Al rescoldo" ("Embers") and "Trenzador" ("A Leather Worker"). In the same volume are three other groups: "Antítesis" ("Antithesis") to which "La estancia vieja" ("The Old Ranch") belongs; "Aventuras grotescas" ("Curious Adventures"), which includes "Arrabalera" ("Suburban"), "Máscaras" ("Masks"), "Ferroviaria" ("A Train Trip"), and "Sexto" ("The Sixth"); and "Trilogía Christiana" ("Christian Trilogy"), which is made up of "El Juicio de Dios" ("Divine Judgment"), "Güele," and "San Antonio."

Don Segundo Sombra (Shadows on the Pampas). Buenos Aires, 1926. Translated as *Shadows on the Pampas* by Harriet Onis. New York, Farrar and Rinehart, 1935.

Reviewed in *New York Times Book Review*, June 10, 1928, and Jan. 6, 1935; in *New York Herald-Tribune*, Jan. 16; *Saturday Review of Literature*, Jan. 19; *Books* (*New York Herald-Tribune*), Jan. 20; *Boston Transcript* and the *Nation*, Jan. 30; and the *New Republic*, March 20, 1935.

Raucho. Buenos Aires, 1917.

Rosaura. Buenos Aires, 1922. Translated by Anita Brenner in *Tales from the Argentine*, pp. 181-235. New York, Farrar and Rinehart, 1930.

Tales from the Argentine is reviewed as a whole in *Books* and the *New York Times*, Sept. 7; the *New York Evening Post*, Sept. 13; the *Nation*, Oct. 15; and the *Saturday Review of Literature*, on Oct. 18, 1930.

Seis Relatos (*Six Tales*). Buenos Aires, 1929. Includes "Diálogo y Palabras" ("A Dialogue and Words"), "Esta Noche, Noche Buena" ("This Christmas Eve"), "Politiquería" ("The Knack of Politics"), and "Telesforo Altamira."

Xaimaca (*Jamaica*). Buenos Aires, 1923.

ICAZA, JORGE.

Barro de la Sierra (*Mountain Soil*). Quito, 1933. Includes "Cachorros" ("Whelps"), "Sed" ("Thirst"), "Exodo" ("Exodus"), "Interpretación" ("Interpretation"), "Mala pata" ("Faux pas"), and "Desorientación" ("Disorientation").

Cholos (*Half-Breeds*). Quito, 1938.

Reviewed by A. B. Franklin, *Quarterly Journal of Inter-American Relations*, April, 1939, pp. 131-133.

En las Calles (*In the Streets*). Buenos Aires, 1936.

Huasipungo. Quito, 1934. Translated into English in *International Literature* (Moscow), February, 1936.

LOVEIRA, CARLOS.

Los Ciegos (*Those who Will not See*). Havana, 1922.

Generales y Doctores (*Generals and Doctors*). Havana, 1920.

Juan Criollo (*Juan, the Creole*). Havana, 1929.

Los Inmorales (*Who are the Immoral?*). Havana, 1919.

La Ultima Lección (*The Last Lesson*). Havana, 1924.

QUIROGA, HORACIO.

Anaconda. Buenos Aires, 1923. Includes "Anaconda," "El Simún" ("The Simoon"), "Gloria Tropical" ("Tropical Glory"), "El Yaciyateré" ("The Sinister Call"), "Los Fabricantes de Carbón" ("Charcoal Burners"), "El Monte Negro" ("Black Mountain"), "En la Noche" ("In the Night"), "Polea Loca" ("Off Balance"), "Dieta de Amor" ("A Diet of Love"), and "Miss Dorothy Phillips, mi Esposa" ("Miss Dorothy Phillips, My Wife").

Los Arrecifes de Coral (*Coral Reefs*). Montevideo, 1901.

El Crimen del Otro (*Another's Crime*). Buenos Aires, 1904. Includes, among others, "La Princesa Bizantina" ("The Byzantine Princess"), "La Muerte del Canario" ("Death of the Canary"), "Idilio" ("An Idyl"), "Historia de Estilicón" ("History of Estilicón") "El Hashish," "La justa Proporción de las Cosas" ("Things in Exact Proportion"), "El triple Robo de Bellamore" ("The Triple Robbery by Bellamore"), and "El Crimen del Otro" ("Another's Crime").

Cuentos de Amor, de Locura y de Muerte (*Stories of Love, Madness and Death*). Buenos Aires, 1917. Includes "Una Estación de Amor" ("A Season of Love"), "El Solitario" ("The Solitaire"), "La Muerte de Isolda" ("The Death of Isolde"), "La Gallina Degollada" ("The Beheaded Hen"), "Los Buques Suicidantes" ("Barks that Lure to Death"), "El Almohadón de Pluma" ("The Feather Pillow"), "A la Deriva", ("Down Stream"), "La Insolación" ("Sunstroke"), "El Alambre de Púa" ("Barbed Wire"), "Los Mensú," "Yaguaí," "Los Pescadores de Vigas" ("River Thieves"), "La Miel Silvestre" ("Wild Honey"), "Nuestro primer Cigarro" ("Our First Cigar"), and "La Meningitis y su Sombra" ("Meningitis and Its Delusion").

"Los Mensú" ("Hired Hands") is translated as "The Fugitives" in *Fiesta in November*. New York, Houghton Mifflin, 1942.

Cuentos de la Selva [para Chicos] (*Tales of the Jungle [for Children]*). Buenos Aires, 1921. Translated as *South American Jungle Tales* by A. Livingston. New York,

Duffield, 1922. Reprinted by Dodd, Mead and Co., 1940.

El Desierto (The Wilderness). Buenos Aires, 1924. Includes "El Desierto" ("The Wilderness"), "El Peón," "Una Conquista" ("A Conquest"), "Silvina y Montt," "El Espectro" ("The Specter"), "El Síncope blanco" ("In another World"), "Los tres Besos" ("Three Kisses"), "El Potro Salvaje" ("The Wild Colt"), "El León" ("The Lion"), "La Patria" ("The Homeland"), and "Juan Darién."

Los Desterrados (Exiles). Buenos Aires, 1926. Includes "El Regreso de Anaconda" ("The Return of Anaconda"), "Los Desterrados" ("Exiles"), "Van Houten," "Tacuara-Mansion," "El Hombre Muerto" ("The Dead Man"), "El Techo de Incienso" ("The Roof of Incense Wood"), "La Cámara Oscura" ("The Dark Room"), and "Los Destiladores de Naranja" ("The Distillers of Oranges"). "El Regreso de Anaconda" is translated by Anita Brenner in *Tales from the Argentine*, pp. 237-268. New York, Farrar and Rinehart, 1930.

Historia de un Amor turbio (An Ill-Fated Love). Buenos Aires, 1908.

Más Allá (The Great Beyond). Buenos Aires, 1934. Includes "Mas Allá" ("The Great Beyond"), "El Vampiro" ("The Vampire"), "Las Moscas" ("Flies"), "El Conductor del Rápido" ("The Conductor on the Flyer"), "El Hijo" ("The Son"), "El Llamado" ("Voices"), "La Señorita Leona" ("The Young Lioness"), "El Puritano" ("The Puritan"), "La Ausencia" ("A Case of Amnesia"), "La Bella y la Bestia" ("Beauty and the Beast"), and "El Ocaso" ("Sunset").

Pasado Amor (Bygone Love). Buenos Aires, 1929.

Los Perseguidos (The Haunted Ones). Buenos Aires, 1905.

Las Sacrificadas (The Sacrificed). Buenos Aires, 1920.

El Salvaje (The Savage). Buenos Aires, 1920. Includes "El Sereno" ("The Watchman"), "La Realidad" ("Reality"), "Una Bofetada" ("A Slap"), "Los Cazadores de Ratas" ("Rat Hunters"), "Los Inmigrantes" ("The Immigrants"), "Los Cementerios belgas" ("Belgian Ceme-

teries"), "La Reina Italiana" ("The Italian Queen"),
"La Voluntad" ("Will Power"), "Navidad" ("Christmas"), "Reyes" ("Kings"), "La Pasión" ("The Passion
of Jesus"), "Corpus" ("Corpus Christi"), "Tres Cartas...
y un Pie" ("Three Letters...and a Foot"), "Cuento
para Novios" ("A Story for the Betrothed"), "Estefanía,"
"La Llama" ("The Flame"), "Fanny," "Lucila Strinberg," and "Un Idilio" ("An Idyl").

RIVERA, JOSÉ EUSTACIO.

La Vorágine. Bogota, 1924. Translated into English as *The
Vortex* by E. K. James. London, Putnam, 1935.

Reviewed in the *New York Times Book Review*, Jan.
23, 1927; *Books* (*New York Herald Tribune*), April
21; *New York Times*, April 28; *Saturday Review of
Literature*, May 11; *Boston Transcript*, May 18; *New
Republic*, June 19; and the *Nation*, June 26, 1935.

INDEX

Cambacèrés, Eugenio, 9, 15
Los Caminos de la Muerte, 51-55;
 picture of Buenos Aires, 53-54;
 listed, 290
Campo, Estanislao del, 191
Campo, 154n
Canaima, descriptive power, 208;
 story, 229-32; setting, 237;
 theme, 277; style, 284; mentioned, 206; listed, 289
Canalejas, Francisco, 58
"Canción," 150, 289
Cané, Miguel, 20
Cantaclaro, descriptive power,
 208; minstrelsy, 226-27; story,
 226-28; estimate, 228-29; background, 229; style, 284; mentioned, 206; listed, 289
El Cántico espiritual, psychological study, 38; Platonic love
 theme, 38, 277; mentioned, 31;
 listed, 290
Capdevila, Arturo, 21
Capitalism, 34, 119-20, 281-82
Caracas, Gallegos in, 205, 206; as
 fictional background, 210-11,
 214-15, 218, 272; prostitution,
 210; society, 213, 217, 228
Caras y Caretas, 158, 160, 178
Cárdenas, José María, 6
Cárdenas, Lázaro, 98
Carranza, Venustiano, struggles
 with Villa, 68, 79, 80; Huerta's
 downfall, 79; corruption of his
 régime, 82; favored by revolu-
 tionary faction, 84
Carrasquilla, Tomás, 9, 179
"La Casa colonial," 43n
Casa grande, 10
El Casamiento de Laucha, 10, 21,
 191
"A Case of Amnesia," 177, 294
"The Cask of Amontillado," 163
Castelar, Emilio, 58
Catamarca, 56
Catholicism, as agency of social

justice, 16; antagonism toward,
 94-95; of Loveira, 106, 111-12;
 influence in Córdoba, 27-28; in
 Mexico, 80; in Venezuela, 211;
 in Ecuador, 243-44, 246-47; influence on individual, 30, 39-40,
 46, 90, 118; defense of by
 Azuela, 96
Cautiverio, 40, 46, 47, 290
"Los Cazadores de Ratas," 170,
 294
Cecilia Valdés, 6, 7
"Celos bienhechores," 138, 289
"Los Cementerios Belgas," 174,
 294
El Cencerro de Cristal, 192
Censorship in Mexico, 4
Character types, romantic, 6, 7,
 41, 279; exaggerated, 7; human,
 7, 278-79; weak, 23, 30, 33, 45,
 278; adamant, 30; idealistic, 33-
 35, 72, 78, 96-97; villainous, 35,
 78; debauched, 36; historical,
 49-50; noble, 55-61; social, 70;
 unprincipled, 79-80; idealized,
 279; symbolic, 280
"Charcoal Burners," 167, 293
Chateaubriand, François-René, 5
Children, illegitimate, in fiction,
 22, 34, 44; attitude toward
 mother of, 26; in Mexico, 71,
 89; in Chile, 139, 142; in Colombia, 186; in Venezuela, 209,
 215, 219-21, 225, 227, 233-35; in
 Ecuador, 241, 243, 246, 251
Chile, costumbrista sketches, 6;
 first novels, 6; social life, 7,
 145-146; aristocracy, 10; economic conditions, 137, 155;
 collections of *cuentos*, 154,
 154n; unorganized labor, 155;
 manners and customs, 198;
 refuge of Alegría, 255; description, 274
Cholos, estimate, 250; plot, 250-
 52; theme, 284; listed, 292

typifies community, 258, 281; story, 259-62; listed, 287

Los Perseguidos, published, 158; influence of Poe on, 163; autobiographical elements, 164

Peru, Barrios in, 136; injustice to Indians in, 9, 155; characteristics of Indians in, 155; fiction in, 253-68; background of Alegría's fiction, 13, 262; description of, 274

Pesado, José Joaquín, 5

"Los Pescadores de Vigas," 168, 293

Pessimism, of Azuela, 73, 79, 92; of Gallegos, 212-14

Physicians. *See* Medical profession

Pi y Margall, Francisco, 58

Picaresque elements, 4-5

Picón-Febres, Gonzalo, 206

The Pilgrim Girl, 207

"The Pin," 153, 154

Placeres, as fictional background, 108-10, 118, 272; school in, 113; description of, 115-16

Plantation life, in Cuba, 119-21, 127-28; in Venezuelan fiction, 210-11, 215-217, 232-35

"A Platonic Banquet," 45n

A Play Without a Title, 240

Plot, fantastic, 7; plausible, 7; absence of, 10, 276; of Gálvez, 27, 48; of Azuela, 69; in general, 275; of Gallegos, 275

"Pobre feo," 142, 289

Pobre Negro, breaking-down of class distinctions, 206; historical background, 232, 271; story, 232-35; style, 235; religious celebrations, 235; setting, 238; race problems, 277; idealized characters, 279; language, 284; listed, 290

Pocaterra, Rafael, 206

Poe, Edgar Allan, as short story model, 154, 270; influence on Quiroga, 156, 163, 178; mentioned, 194

Poemas místicos, 192

Poemas solitarios, 192

Poems of Solitude, 192

"Polea loca," 167, 293

"Politiquería," 193, 292

Poor Negro, 206, 232-38, 277, 279, 284, 290

"Poor Ugly Man," 142, 289

Por el Decoro, 137

Por el Viejo, 240

Pot-pourri, 15

"El Potro Salvaje," 173, 294

Precursores, 69; brigandage in Mexico, 92-93; style of, 93; listed, 288

La Prensa, 160

Prieto, Guillermo, 6

"La Princesa bizantina," 163; listed, 293

Proa, 192

El Proconsulado, 66n

The Proconsulate, 66n

El Progreso, 6

Promiscuity, of women, 41, 46-48, 122-25; attitude toward, 43; of men, 118

The Promised Land, 180

"The Prop," 207-208, 289

Propaganda novels. *See* Thesis novels

Prostitutes, 32-34, 70, 145, 245, 251

Prostitution, in Buenos Aires, 16, 33-36; causes of, 35-36; in Mexico, 9; houses of, 75; in Merida, 129-30; in Havana, 132; in Chile, 137, 145-47; in Spanish America, 275

Psychological novels, of Gálvez, 38-40, 46-47; of Barrios, 143-52, 277

Psychology, individual, 13, 73, 76; abnormal, 140-41, 275; ani-

mal, 170-74, 275; child, 142-43, 241
"The Puritan," 176, 294
"El Puritano," 176, 294

La Quijotita y su Prima, 4, 5
Quince Plazuelas, una Alameda y un Callejón, 254
Quiroga, writer of cuentos, 12, 13, 21, 154, 154n, 155; interest in background, 155, 255, 272; life of, 155-61; character, 161-62; attitude toward religion, 162; work autobiographic, 162, 164, 175-76; morbid subjects, 162, 165-66; technique, 163-64, 176; stories of Misiones, 166-72; fables, 172; apologues, 172-73; stories related to Christianity, 173-74; miscellaneous tales, 174-75; content of last collection, 176-78; best stories, 178; individual quality of, 270; bibliography, 293-95
Quiroga, Facundo, fictional treatment of, 49; in Catamarca, 56
Quito, writers of, 240; Icaza in, 240-41, 272; as fictional background, 243-45, 249-52, 272

Rabasa, Emilio, 9
The Race of Cain, 11
Race, problems of, 11; Latin, 19; white in Argentina, 64; mestizo in Venezuela, 225; amalgamation, 236-37; equality, 274. See also Indians, Montuvios, Mulatto, Zambo, and Cholos
The Railroader, 103
Ranch life. See Gauchos; Haciendas
Raselda, 22-23
"Rat Hunters," 170, 294
Raucho, Argentine characters,

196; story, 196-98; episodic narrative, 200; mentioned, 192; listed, 292
La Raza de Caín, 11
"La Realidad," 170, 294
Realism, 2, 4; without art, 5; in romantic fiction, 7; of Blest Gana, 7; hostility to, 10; of Alegría, 270
"Reality," 170, 294
The Recurrence of Madness, 154n
Regina Landa, social problems, 69; story, 96-97; listed, 288
Registro Yucateco, 6
"El Regreso de Anaconda," imaginative snake story, 168, 171-72; estimate of, 178; listed, 294
"La Reina Italiana," 174, 295
Reinaldo Solar, publication, 206; style, 206, 210; theme, 209; story, 210-12; characteristics, 212; laboring classes in, 213; estimate of, 214; background, 237; listed, 290
Religion, as basis of conflict, 27-31, 38-40; scorn for, 45
El Renacimiento, 8
Renan, Joseph Ernest, 32
Repisas, 154n
Restrepo, Juan de Dios, 6
"The Return of Anaconda," 168, 171-72, 178, 294
La Revista, 156
La Revista de Buenos Aires, 53
Revolution, interpreted, 65, 66n, 88, 100; in Mexico (1910-20), 65-67, 77-88; foreshadowed in fiction, 70-73, 75-76; society produced by, 88-100; ideals of, frustrated, 93-98; in Venezuelan fiction, 212, 227, 229, 234-35; in Peru, 266
"Reyes," 173, 295
Reyles, Carlos, 11, 191
The Rich Relations, 9